Black Orpheus, *Transition*, and Modern Cultural Awakening in Africa

Black Orpheus,
Transition, and
Modern Cultural
Awakening in Africa

Peter Benson

UNIVERSITY OF CALIFORNIA PRESS
Berkeley · Los Angeles · London

University of California Press
Berkeley and Los Angeles, California

University of California Press, Ltd.
London, England

© 1986 by
The Regents of the University of California

Library of Congress Cataloging in Publication Data
Benson, Peter.
  Black Orpheus, Transition, and modern cultural awakening
in Africa.

    Includes index.
    1. Black Orpheus.   2. Transition (Kampala,
Uganda)   3. African literature—Periodicals—His-
tory.   4. Africa—Intellectual life.   I. Title.
PL8000.B63B4   1986   820′.8   85–2534
ISBN 0–520–05418–0

Printed in the United States of America

1 2 3 4 5 6 7 8 9

For My Parents
ANN AND PETER E. BENSON

Contents

Preface

This book is the product of four years of research, reflection, writing, and revision. It was completed with the help of two successive visiting research fellowships in the humanities at the Rockefeller Foundation. I began the first draft at the foundation's offices in New York and completed it and revised successive drafts during a two-year teaching stint at Fourah Bay College of the University of Sierra Leone. I thank my colleagues and associates at the Rockefeller Foundation, especially Joel Colton, for their practical assistance and encouragement, and my students and faculty colleagues at Fourah Bay for providing an invaluable foil for testing the underlying notions of intellectual and cultural development.

Begun at the Rockefeller Foundation as a cross-cultural investigation of "the relationship of literary magazines to intellectual and cultural movements," this study both broadened in its intellectual scope and narrowed in its focus. I saw the currents of thought and creativity that had begun with the African independence movements as an interesting special case in literary and intellectual history. A few people, some of them cultural insiders, some cultural outsiders, had inspired, molded, and, it was subsequently charged, distorted the progress of a generation of writers, artists, intellectuals, and scholars.

To those familiar with *Black Orpheus* and *Transition*, it will perhaps be unnecessary to explain why I have limited this study to two magazines. For good or ill, these two magazines were at the center of much that happened intellectually and culturally in anglophone black Africa during the period from the late fifties to the late seventies. The small group of expatriate and indigenous editors who directed them had extraordinary power to open and close doors when theirs were almost the only doors. That they used their power with skill, openness, and goodwill did not prevent a succeeding generation from criticizing them for having misappropriated or abused it, and neither does later criticism invalidate what Ulli Beier, Rajat Neogy, and their successors accomplished.

Other cultural and intellectual magazines also commented on and published the works of the new African cultural and intellectual movements. The first, Alioune Diop's Parisian cultural review *Présence Africaine*, had been publishing the work of the *négritude* writers since its founding in 1947. *Présence Africaine* spoke for a movement whose effect upon anglophone Africa remained limited, however, even after Ulli Beier began a campaign in the early *Black Orpheus* to build bridges across that cultural border. Moreover, Diop's expatriate journal predates the period under discussion here and, like the *négritude* movement itself, was tied at least as closely to the black diaspora in Europe, North America, and the Caribbean as it was to Africa itself.

The only significant feature magazine on the African continent to rival the early *Black Orpheus* and the early *Transition* was the delightful, witty, and unrepentantly lowbrow *Drum* of Johannesburg, South Africa. Though run by a succession of British editors (among them Anthony Sampson and Tom Hopkinson), *Drum* was nevertheless a breeding ground for young black writers in white-ruled, and increasingly white-repressed, South Africa. However, although it was widely read in East, Central, and West Africa as well (for a time maintaining special East and West African editions), and in spite of its success in sponsoring literary apprenticeships, *Drum* does not fit the purposes of the present study. It merits a separate study (which Sampson and Hopkinson have themselves partially provided), but it too much resembled an African *Look* or *Life* (and too little resembled an African *Criterion* or *Encounter*) to qualify for inclusion in a study of intellectual and cultural magazines.

Once *Black Orpheus* and *Transition* had charted the routes of cultural commerce, a small galaxy of local little magazines (more limited in their contents, shorter-lived, and geographically parochial) sprang up in imitation throughout anglophone Africa. In Johannesburg, for example, two *Drum* alumni, Nat Nakasa and Lewis Nkosi, founded South Africa's first black-written, black-edited, black-run literary and artistic review, *The Classic*, using funds from the Congress for Cultural Freedom and the Farfield Foundation. While it lasted, *The Classic* rivaled *Black Orpheus* in the quality of its literary "discoveries," and *Transition* in the toughness of its political awareness. Its scope and influence elsewhere in Africa, however, in no way compared with *Transition*'s or *Black Orpheus*'s.

In independent black Africa, the little magazines centered themselves, as had *Black Orpheus* and *Transition*, on one or another of the new universities. In Nairobi, for instance, James Ngugi (Ngugi wa Thiong'o) brought out a few erratic issues of a stimulating review, *Zuka*. At Legon, the Ghana Society of Writers brought out, equally irregularly, a review called *Okyeame*, whose purpose was to publish younger Ghanaian writers. One of the magazine's founders, Kofi Awoonor, explained to me in a 1980 interview that the idea was to establish "a forum" for "the writers who were then emerging" and "to create a readership for Ghanaian literature." Neither goal could be fostered in "a widely circulated journal like *Black Orpheus*" alone.

Perhaps the most important parochial intellectual magazine was *Nigeria Magazine*. Subsidized by first the colonial and then the independent government of Nigeria, it had been founded privately by an expatriate school teacher and remained, through Michael Crowder's editorship in the mid-sixties, independent of government editorial control. Although basically an old-fashioned regional magazine, *Nigeria Magazine* ran exceptionally intelligent features and took a pioneering interest in African art and traditional society. It predated *Black Orpheus*, but its scope was limited to Nigeria and its career in many ways paralleled that of its better-known compatriot. The story of *Nigeria Magazine* is therefore also reluctantly reserved for another place.

Both in Africa and elsewhere, *Black Orpheus* and *Transition* have become hard to find. (When I taught at Fourah Bay College only a handful of copies of either magazine remained on the library shelves. A few weeks before my arrival, as a housecleaning measure, the bookstore had sold off a stack of old issues of *Black Orpheus* for five cents a copy.) Full runs of the magazines are often not available even in major research libraries. (For example, the New York Public Library's file of *Transition* is incomplete, though catalogued as complete through *Transition* no. 50/*Ch'indaba* no. 1; Rajat Neogy's haphazard methods of numbering volumes camouflaged gaps.) Since much of what appeared in them is not in print elsewhere, it has been necessary in the course of this study to focus in greater detail on the contents of individual issues of the magazines than might otherwise be called for.

Another reason for surveying the magazines' contents is their uniqueness. In a way rather rare in magazine history, *Black Orpheus* and *Transition* possessed distinctive personalities, as identifiable and individual as any single author's. Both succeeded in developing, refining, and adapting a tone, style, and perspective independent of individual contributions or contributors. This is not to say that the periodicals were more important than those who wrote for them, but only that a special kind of cross-fertilization of intellect had taken place (and cultural community, after all, has special meaning in Africa). In its analysis of their contents, therefore, this book seeks to define the development of each magazine's special personality, tone, and style.

That development, as the magazines' principals recall, was in some ways deliberate, in some ways fortuitous, and nearly always reciprocal. Though he perhaps "never really thought of the business of editing in such purposive terms," *Transition*'s second editor, Wole Soyinka, nevertheless reflected in a 1984 letter to me, "one damned well has an idea what one wants to do with a magazine." Kenyan political scientist and *Transition* associate editor Ali Mazrui adds, "It is not often realized that writers can sometimes be profoundly changed by the very media they use. I as a writer have used *Transition* as a medium over the years. I may have influenced *Transition*; what is certain is that *Transition* influenced me. I regard *Transition* as an important factor in my own personal intellectual history" (*Transition* no. 44, p. 12).

My research has been greatly aided by the reference staffs of the Schomburg Center for Research in Black Culture and the central library on 42nd Street of the New York Public Library, as well as by the staffs of the University of Nairobi Library, the Kenya National Archives, and the Rockefeller Foundation Library. I am also much indebted to the pioneering efforts of Dennis Duerden's Transcription Centre in London, whose audiotapes of interviews with African writers and intellectuals proved an invaluable primary source of information.

I would also like to thank the following for their suggestions, criticisms, encouragement, information, corrections, and help: Kofi Awoonor, Ulli Beier, Michael Crowder, Abiola Irele, Robert July, Bernth Lindfors (who made available his manuscript "Ngugi wa Thiong'o's Early Journalism"), Abu Mayanja, Ali Mazrui, Rajat Neogy, Demas Nwoko, Davis Sebukima, Wole Soyinka, John Thompson, and Theo Vincent. Finally, I must mention Vera Benson, without whose inspiration I would certainly never have written this.

Introduction

Other cultural and intellectual journals appeared (often rather briefly) in Africa during the period between 1957 and 1978, but Nigeria's *Black Orpheus* and Uganda's (later Ghana's) *Transition* were the most important to the intellectual history of that time and place. *Black Orpheus* was founded in 1957 in Ibadan, Nigeria, by an expatriate extramural lecturer at Ibadan University (then University College, Nigeria) named Ulli Beier, whose keen interest in Nigerian art and oral literature had led him to a variety of cultural activities there, including a magazine of Yoruba studies, a cultural center, a performing arts program, and (with Suzanne Wenger) a series of art workshops. His "Mbari Clubs" at Ibadan and Oshogbo were art centers and intellectual gathering places that stimulated or sponsored a variety of activities in the plastic and performing arts.

Black Orpheus, Ulli Beier's best-known project, was inspired, at least initially, by the black world's pioneer cultural magazine in exile, Paris-based *Présence Africaine*. It did not take the new magazine long to depart significantly from its model, however, and by 1961 it in turn had inspired the emergence of Rajat Neogy's Kampala-based *Transition*. Both of these new reviews soon redefined their editorial goals.[1] *Black Orpheus* became an experimental workshop and gallery for new artists and writers, and *Transition* became something quite unique—a mettlesome and irrepressible vehicle for cultural redefinition and social and political comment in a style at once imaginative and forensic.

Neither periodical enjoyed an entirely peaceful or secure tenure.

1

Black Orpheus at one point faced a rebellion of its new guard against its old. Its second editorial series, under Abiola Irele and J. P. Clark, deliberately defined itself in repudiation of the first. *Transition* was virtually suppressed in 1968 with the arrest of its editor and founder, Rajat Neogy, for alleged sedition against the government of Ugandan Prime Minister Milton Obote. A remarkable international campaign of protest was then mobilized to win Neogy's release from Kampala's Luzira Prison. Transplanted thereafter to Accra, Ghana, *Transition* resumed publication, first under Neogy and then under one of the best known of the *Black Orpheus* school of writers, Wole Soyinka.

At a certain stage in their editorial lifespans, both magazines faced a growing disaffection among some readers, correspondents, and contributors; and both, at roughly that moment, passed on to the control of a second generation of editors who were African both by citizenship and descent (Neogy was a Ugandan of Indian descent, Beier an expatriated European). Like *Transition*'s second editor, Wole Soyinka, *Black Orpheus*'s second generation of editors had been central figures in the cultural movement that the magazine had helped found ten years earlier. Under both the founding editors and their successors, both magazines also faced the difficult task of transforming their editorial philosophies in response to the radically changing circumstances of independent Africa.

So much indeed has changed in Africa since *Black Orpheus* and *Transition* were founded that one must deliberately remind oneself of the worlds into which they were born. Both magazines, after all, were launched in the rigidly circumscribed world of colonial Africa; yet both ultimately lasted long enough to endure the economic stagnation, coups, countercoups, and military violence of contemporary Africa. When Rajat Neogy founded *Transition* in Kampala in 1961, there were Baganda patriarchs old enough to have been feudal subjects of the first Mutesa—the *kabaka* (king) whose imperturbable sovereignty had so aggravated and impressed the first British explorer to reach his centuries-old kingdom, John Hanning Speke. Speke's description of nineteenth-century Buganda testifies to its orderliness and relative technical advancement. He found broad, well-maintained avenues; neat, well-ordered, and attractive dwellings; and a "magnificent sight, a whole hill covered with gigantic huts, such as I had never seen in Africa before"—the *kabaka*'s palace compound. He found a sophisticated culture whose energetic young king possessed both a power medieval in its absoluteness and a driving curiosity to see his first white man. Speke's *Journal of the Discovery of the Source of the Nile* suggests both the cold authority of Mutesa I and its author's credulity. Speke did witness harsh summary punishments. He also swallowed whole an envoy's report that the *kabaka* had "caused 'fifty big men and four hundred small ones' to be executed" in his impatience to see the white explorer.[2]

In Rajat Neogy's Uganda, the ancient hereditary monarchy of the *kabakas* persevered in the person of Edward Mutesa II, whose own conception of sovereignty was to provoke two successive political crises in modern Uganda, thereby nearly destroying Neogy's brainchild, *Transition*. When that inveterate "insider" John Gunther visited Uganda a few years before *Transition*'s first publication, he thought he had found one of the most peaceful and picturesque backwaters of British colonialism. Gunther, whose observations combine the vividness of good journalism with the fathomless curiosity of an intellectual tourist, provides an interesting perspective on that now distant time. He reminds one, first, of how readily even the most open-minded and constructive people accepted the prejudices of the times. He is full of stories about the "colorful" eccentricities of backward villagers. He is a gullible consumer, and retailer, of stories about cannibalism; and he is willing, on that basis, once he has described the barbarities of slavery, to see them as a lesser evil.

Nevertheless, one is grateful for Gunther's keen eye and well-worn notebook. And of all the places he visited on his research tour for *Inside Africa*, Gunther was perhaps most struck by Uganda and Nigeria. Arriving in Uganda from Kenya in 1952, the year of the first major outbreak of the Mau Mau rebellion and of Jomo Kenyatta's detention and trial, Gunther wrote, "One felt an almost physical sense of a weight being lifted, of emotional as well as intellectual relief."[3]

Built like Rome on seven hills, Uganda's commercial capital was a comfortable, easygoing place of fewer than forty thousand inhabitants (in Nigeria it would only have qualified as a fair-sized market town). Occupying one of the seven hills, East Africa's sole university college, Makerere College, whose students and faculty were drawn from throughout the region, lent Kampala a special air of tolerance. This, together with an equally characteristic somnolence, stuck in the mind as distinguishing Uganda from its neighbors to the south and east, Kenya and Tanganyika (later Tanzania).

In such an atmosphere, familiarity bred complacence. Gunther reports that he met one young nationalist who had organized a student strike at Makerere but was nevertheless viewed by the colonial administration only as "a demon, a scamp." To Gunther's astonishment, this "irritating and insurrectionary" young student turned out to be the recipient of a government scholarship to Cambridge University! A British official explained, "We really *like* that young man! He will be good human material some day, useful to the country" (p. 441). Asked by Gunther what would remain of the British heritage in Uganda after independence, one district commissioner singled out "group photographs, the visitors' book, bicycles, and football" (p. 430).

Gunther's sense of relief in this drowsy place was, of course, partly a reaction to Kenyan violence. He did not meet another young Ugandan who would one day be seen in some quarters as an important nationalist leader, and whose rise in the King's African Rifles during the 1950s and early 1960s was, like the young nationalist student's, due to friendly colonial preferment. Though nearly illiterate, this young solider, Idi Amin, who was for nine years to be Uganda's heavyweight boxing champion, would be promoted through the ranks by his British superiors—first to corporal, then to sergeant, and, finally, just before independence, to one of the first two African lieutenancies. If visitors' books and football survived independence, so did Idi Amin, who years later would give a demonstration to horrified fellow heads of state at the Organization of African Unity (OAU) summit in Rabat of how to choke a bound prisoner to death by forcing a handkerchief down his throat. He had learned that trick questioning Mau Mau suspects in Kenya.

If Gunther didn't hear of Corporal Amin, another guidebook author (and reporter, broadcaster, political theorist, and editor), Colin Legum, did. Years later, in Wole Soyinka's Accra *Transition*, he would recall:

> The first time I heard Amin's name was when he was still only Corporal Amin in the British colonial army fighting in Kenya against Mau Mau. In those days the Kikuyu spoke in fear of "Corporal Amin."
>
> (*Transition* no. 50/*Ch'indaba* no. 1, p. 88)

Even in 1962, as the British were preparing to leave Uganda and Rajat Neogy was struggling to resuscitate his new cultural magazine, *Transition*, there was another unhappy portent of Uganda's future suffering (though not widely remarked at the time). Sent by his superiors to quell cattle raiders in Karamoja, Lieutenant Amin led his troops in a massacre of villagers. He had been trying to force them to reveal caches of hidden arms. Amin was let off the hook, however, by the departing British and the new, Ugandan, prime minister, Milton Obote.[4]

The more obvious threat to Uganda's serenity at the time of Gunther's visit centered around the young *kabaka*, a man as different from Corporal Amin as it was possible to be, yet one who would also play a crucial role in the nation's future. In 1952 Buganda remained a stubbornly autonomous, semifeudal kingdom, although its young sovereign, Edward Mutesa II (called "King Freddie" by the British) had been educated at Cambridge (where he had "almost, but not quite, won a blue in soccer"). His brother, the Bugandan prime minister, was held in especially high regard by the British, "if only because he is a redoubtable cricketer" (p. 439). Mutesa, Gunther was surprised to discover, spoke "faultless English" (one wonders how the *kabaka* would have characterized Gunther's English), his conversation "larded with such phrases as 'My prime minister is a most dashing chap,' or, while mingling with guests at a reception, 'I say, a bit of a squash'" (p. 438).

Gunther was also surprised to discover that this affable young man, unchallenged potentate of one of the world's ancient feudal monarchies, was regarded by the British overlords of this "model colony" as a serious threat to colonial hegemony. To Governor Sir Andrew Cohen, indeed, Mutesa was Uganda's most dangerous nationalist. Faced with contemplated British colonial reforms, including most notably centralization and unification with Kenya and Tanganyika, the young *kabaka* demanded nothing less than a reaffirmation of the independence of his inherited kingdom. Buganda, he pointed out, had voluntarily joined the British empire by negotiated treaty; it had a right, therefore, to secede. Boycotts and strikes followed, and Governor Cohen declared a state of emergency. Soon thereafter he forced Mutesa's deposition and exile. Though Mutesa and the nationalistic Ugandan National Congress (UNC) had until then been somewhat restless bedfellows, the *kabaka* was suddenly a nationalist martyr and hero.

To a casual visitor such as Gunther in 1952, Uganda may have seemed British Africa's most peaceful colony, "a kind of lotus land," prosperous and tolerant, with no home-based armed forces, no permanent white settlement, and neither Kenya's ubiquitous color bar, its racial animosity (though Uganda, too, had a large Asian population), nor its strident factionalism. Nevertheless, it had within it the germs of disaffection, alienation, even violence. The *kabaka*'s brief insurrection in 1953 hinted of wider conflicts to come. When that seed bore fruit, nearly fifteen years later, *Transition*'s young editor, who had grown up in Kampala's deceptive air of calm and tolerance (and whose great-aunt, he later recalled, had once wound the *kabaka*'s wife into a sari),[5] would be among the first victims, along with the deposed Edward Mutesa.

Mutesa's second deposition and exile in 1967 under Milton Obote almost exactly paralleled the first in 1953 under Cohen. The officer who drove the *kabaka* and his followers from the palace was General Idi Amin (whose advancement, once the British left, had been owing to his usefulness to Obote). Among those who worked to bridge the gap between Obote's nationalist coalition and the *ka-*

baka's supporters was a young Baganda lawyer, Abu Mayanja, who ultimately also played a role in the more private drama of Rajat Neogy and *Transition*. His engagement in the political drama that began with the *kabaka*'s second deposition placed Mayanja and Neogy's magazine in a fierce confrontation that tested the validity in independent Africa of the borrowed concepts of free speech and debate.

Gunther's tour of Nigeria for *Inside Africa* in 1952 followed Ulli Beier's arrival there by two years and preceded by four years Beier's decision (taken at the World Congress of Black Writers in Paris) to found anglophone black Africa's first literary and artistic review, *Black Orpheus*. Gunther found in Nigeria, in contrast to sleepy Uganda, precisely what galvanized the creative energies of the young expatriate lecturer Beier—a world on the twitch, in a fever of growth, social change, nationalistic ferment, and internecine rivalry. Gunther wrote:

> Nigeria is, in some respects, the most exciting country I have ever visited in my life. Its politics are incandescent, and flicker violently. To say that it is more fully evolved toward self-government than any British colony except the Gold Coast [Ghana] is to make it sound far too tame and simple. (p. 765)

With Legon (Achimota) in Ghana and Fourah Bay in Sierra Leone, Beier's home base, Ibadan University, was one of only three rivals in all of the vast territory of anglophone black Africa to Uganda's Makerere, and one of only five in all of sub-Saharan Africa (excluding South Africa). But Kampala's air of patience and forbearance was missing from Lagos and Ibadan. Gunther soon found out how strident Nigeria's partisan, and independent, press could be. The *West African Pilot* greeted his arrival with the following notice:

> Mr. John Gunther, an American with a country as young as our great great great grandparents, is in Africa whose written and unwritten histories date back much further than the first Caucasian ape men.
>
> And what does this American want in this ancient land, shrouded in mystery, enveloped in enigma, and replete with as yet insoluble conundrums? He wants to write a book not on America, but on Africa.
>
> Has Mr. Gunther ever visited this part of Africa before? No. Has

he ever lived in Africa? No. Are his ancestors African? No. Yet . . .
Mr. Gunther of America is here . . . to tell us all about the inside
of Africa.   (pp. 750–51)

In the next edition, the *Pilot* was after Gunther again, this time
for neglecting the hospitality of African homes and accepting that of
Governor Sir John McPherson instead. Gunther's new book, the editorial writer suggested, probably ought to be called *Inside Government House*. Mindful of the "American taste" for "a nauseatingly re-
fractory sensationalism" in its literature, the writer proceeded to offer
advice about the mood of Nigeria:

> Out of our own kindness, we wish to inform Mr. Gunther that Africa is
> aflame and blazingly indignant against alien rule. For Nigeria freedom
> comes in 1956 with or without outside consent or assent. Let Mr.
> Gunther mark that down.   (p. 751)

Nigeria was at that moment caught in a fascinating tug-of-war between its two inspiring nationalist leaders, each striving to outdo
the other in nationalistic zeal—Obafemi Awolowo in the western,
Yoruba region and Dr. Nnamdi Azikiwe in the eastern, Ibo region.
March of 1953, in fact, witnessed a rare moment of accord between
"Zik" and Awolowo, who combined in their support of a dramatic
resolution in that month's session of the Central House of Representatives for complete independence from Britain by 1956 at the latest.
The representatives of the Muslim north had balked at this first introduction of an absolute deadline, and the emotional common cause
between "Zik" and Awolowo had been part of an effort to head off a
Muslim campaign to amend the resolution.

There were, and are, other striking differences between Nigeria
and Uganda as well. For one thing, there was Nigeria's massive scale
(now approaching 100 million people, in an area larger than any European country except Russia); for another, its extremely complex
ethnicity (literally thousands of ethnic and cultural subgroups, many
with their own distinct languages); for a third, the differences in the
two countries' fortunes. Their contrasting fates, indeed, are an instance of how much has changed in Africa in the twenty years since

John Gunther's visit, Rajat Neogy's return from college abroad, and Ulli Beier's arrival. There has, that is, been a complete reversal in the two countries' circumstances. In the aftermath of Amin's rule, Uganda's broken economy barely functioned on any level. Starvation and brigandage threatened to complete the work of Amin's reign of terror. In 1952, however, Uganda was one of the richest and most promising of Britain's African colonies—the Commonwealth's biggest producer of cotton and coffee and one of Africa's most advanced countries in terms of Africanization and development. Nigeria, which oil revenues have made independent black Africa's one heavily capitalized economy (though still an economy under the severe stress of a massive and disparate population), then depended for its export earnings on the unstable markets for agricultural products such as groundnuts and industrial raw materials such as tin. Burdened by its enormous population, Nigeria's economic future then seemed to demand a massive organization of national effort, an exercise in bootstrapping using simple, labor-intensive resources.

The other event that radically affected the course of independent Nigeria, its 1967–70 civil war, would have seemed equally incredible then, in spite of the obvious stresses on national unity. Although Gunther, for instance, described Nigeria as a "geographical monstrosity," cursed by sectionalism (p. 747), he was caught up, as everyone else seemed to be (including Ulli Beier), in the confident excitement of the time. Nigeria was in no danger, he predicted, "as some other African countries might be, of 'going back to the tribes'":

> The people are committed enough to education and modernization to keep anything like that from happening. Nor is Nigeria likely to become a tyrant state under a ruthless or unscrupulous dictator. Citizens are too diversified and individualistic, too conscious of their own growing stake in the community. (p. 775)

For all its stridency, nationalistic "impatience," and discord, however, Nigeria also had much in common with Uganda. It too, for instance, had a small, favored elite, led by two pyrotechnic nationalists who each seemed contradictorily anglicized and anglophobe. Azikiwe had once predicted that "by the year 2944 Black Africa will have destroyed Europe and brought the United States to the verge of extinction."[6] But he was also a former college athlete whom one Britisher admired because he "watches football like an Englishman" (p. 772). Like the second Mutesa, Awolowo was an intellectual in the English mold—precise and punctilious. His *Path to Nigerian Freedom* had been critically well received in England. Nevertheless, in his interview with Gunther, Awolowo mordantly charged that the British had saddled Nigeria with third-rate officials, adding, "In fourteen months, under the present [semi-autonomous African] government, we have done more for Nigeria than the British did in 120 years" (p. 775).

Even more so than in Uganda, Gunther felt the exhilaration of an "easy flowing mixture of black and white" in Nigeria (p. 758). He also felt something in the air—an eagerness to move ahead, a confidence in the future that was symbolized in the modern facilities of Ibadan's new university. Like Khartoum's Gordon College and Kampala's Makerere, Gunther predicted, Ibadan University would "produce an intellectual *élite* that in time will dominate the new society" (p. 762).

Gunther's observations were certainly accurate. Anglophone black Africa's two most distinguished intellectual magazines sprang up precisely there, in Ibadan and Kampala. Indeed, *Transition*'s last editor, Wole Soyinka, would later stand accused by three young Nigerian writers, Chinweizu, Ihechukwu Madubuike, and Onwuchekwa Jemie, of a deliberate effort to reserve domination of the new African literature for the group of writers that had arisen around Ibadan University and *Black Orpheus*.[7]

In one sense at least the charge was well founded—anglophone black Africa's contemporary cultural movements were created by very small, very influential, and tightly knit intellectual elites at moments of radical discontinuity in societies (especially in Nigeria) at the edge of an unknown and exciting abyss. In a way really exceptional in the history of letters, *Black Orpheus* and *Transition* concentrated the energies, the aspirations, and later, unfortunately, the disagreements of a whole literary and intellectual generation. These two magazines, suddenly founded so near to hand, were for a time its chief vehicles for interchange, self-definition, communication, and dispute.

Among the key artistic and intellectual questions argued out or exemplified in *Black Orpheus* and *Transition* were pan-Africanism, African socialism, the status of ethnic and racial minorities, tribalism, the need for an "African artistic aesthetic," the use of indigenous vs. Western languages, artistic primitivism and cultural condescension, the role of Western critics and Western standards of critical judgment, popular vs. elite audiences for literature, the role of Western publishers and publicists, the "black mystique" (black awareness) vs. artistic internationalism, political "partisanship" vs. free speech and literary "universalism," and the relevance of Euro-centered literary themes—for example, the place of the radical individualism of Euro-modernism in a traditionally communalist society.

Were one an Edmund Wilson or a Lionel Trilling, one might, perhaps, encapsulate a critical history of modern African culture in the story of these two exceptional periodicals. This volume is not quite that ambitious. It undertakes a detailed editorial history of two magazines, including their initial purpose, the evolution of their editorial philosophies, their publishing arrangements (including financial support and political complications), their relations with readers and contributors, and their influence on the creative and intellectual life of their time (a tall enough order in itself).

The special unanimity of the moment and of these media, however, gave each magazine's contents a special character. Indeed, for a time, the movements that grew around them seemed almost a single self-contained intelligence. In telling the life stories of these periodicals, therefore, one inevitably ends by offering journalistic history that becomes almost a composite intellectual biography, defining through *Black Orpheus* and *Transition* the body of creativity and thought that they helped bring into being.

There was already an excitement in the air when *Black Orpheus* and *Transition* began publication. Both Uganda and Nigeria were on the verge of independence. When *Black Orpheus* no. 1 appeared,

Nigeria had already produced an internationally known fabulist, Amos Tutuola, who by various critical lights was either a singular talent or a singular oddity, and in Chinua Achebe it would soon have a first-rate fiction writer whose productions were closer to the narrative conventions of the Western novel.[8] Although no comparable literary activity had occurred in East Africa, *Transition* had before it the example of *Black Orpheus*'s success when it appeared in 1961. And in both West and East Africa, the ideals of cultural recovery and artistic and literary experiment were very much in the air. The first proposal for an institute of African studies at the University of Ghana, Legon, had come as early as 1950, from Dr. Kofi Busia. The first professional East African historian at Makerere, Dr. Alan Ogot, had joined its faculty in 1959. There were thus already artists writing and scholars doing research, but isolation and lack of a common vehicle of communication obscured and isolated their work.

As a result, when *Black Orpheus* and *Transition* suddenly did appear, providing the new cultural and intellectual movements with vehicles of expression and communication, their influence was enormous. As editorial publicists, cultural midwives, arbiters of taste, moderators of debate, posers of intellectual challenges, and agents of unity and continuity, men such as Ulli Beier, Rajat Neogy, Gerald Moore, Jahnheinz Jahn, J. P. Clark, Wole Soyinka, Abiola Irele, Ali Mazrui, Ezekiel Mphahlele, and Paul Theroux had a far more central importance than an editor normally has. Conversely, the prominence of their leadership eventually made challenges to their ideals and directions inevitable.

Such challenges were likely for another reason as well. It required a force of personality, of character, and of will to hammer together the elements of a magazine that was not simply a storehouse for new culture, but a mill of creativity and debate. These were not mild or compromising men, and if they had been, it is unlikely that *Black Orpheus* and *Transition* would have become as successful as they were. The rancor with which these editors' critics opposed them in the end seems to have been a function as much of their personalities as of their convictions or their alleged editorial monopolism.

Some, such as J. P. Clark and Wole Soyinka, were primarily creative writers. Others, such as Ulli Beier and Abiola Irele, were not. (Neogy, though a poet, did not publish any of his own work after the first few issues.) Nevertheless, as editors, they all had a distinctive creativity. The task set before these men at this moment of intellectual and cultural history called forth their inspiration and originality—and also their drive, determination, and uncompromising sense of purpose. They would need both sets of qualities.

That the work of men such as Beier, Neogy, Soyinka, Clark, Mazrui, and Theroux was (and remains) controversial was no accident. They had set out to make waves, in an effort to see if those waves would stir up something new—something unprecedented in art and intellect. Like Odysseus when he opened Aeolus's bag of winds, both magazines in the end were faced with the task of finding a way to survive storms that their own actions had helped raise.

The story of the raising of those storms, which follows, is similar for the two magazines. Thematically, both magazines moved from an initial period of cultural self-definition (imaged by the names *Black Orpheus* and *Transition*) to a final period of militant repudiation of elements of their own past. Both progressed from the direction and control of outsiders to the direction and control of insiders (at a time when Africa itself was exorcising its political dependence). In their different ways, both Wole Soyinka and J. P. Clark were to attempt to shake off what Clark called "the legacy of Caliban," the vestiges of cultural dependence. Both magazines finally fell victim not to controversy, intellectual realignment, or political suppression, however, but to the practical difficulties of producing an internationally distributed periodical of high quality and broad relevance in economically disadvantaged contemporary Africa.

"BORDER OPERATORS"

I

"BORDER OPERATORS":
Black Orpheus and
Artistic Genesis

At the moment our literature in the European languages is of a frontier
kind. We are pioneers at the frontier, seeking a definition of ourselves and
the past from which we have come. The frontier lies between us and the
white man's technology, religion, mores, economies, etc. We try to address
him and ourselves at the same time.

> Ezekiel Mphahlele,
> "Writers and Commitment"

Well, Ulli Beier operated in a special field. He was a border operator—on
the border between the European and the local, the traditional. And he
could cross back and forth from one border to another and find things they
had in common. . . . Ulli was able to go back and forth like a smuggler . . .
from avant-garde European art and avant-garde European literature, which
at that time were still interested in myth and symbol, to modern and traditional African art and literature. This seemed like a common meeting
ground. For a time, just as it had been in Europe, this was a tremendously
fertile field for painters and writers.

> John Thompson

When Ulli Beier founded Nigeria's pioneer cultural journal *Black Orpheus* in 1957, there was hardly an acknowledged frontier between European and African art and literature at all. It was not widely conceded that anglophone black Africa *had* any modern art or literature. Only francophone African literature had credence, and that only as an exotic footnote to French literature.

Before Beier could begin his cultural smuggling ring, he had unilaterally to declare that there was such a border. He then set out to define the nature of the goods; to incite his students, friends, and acquaintances to produce them; to set the standards of valuation; and to search for customers in Nigeria and abroad. The early task of *Black Orpheus* was perhaps best defined in an unsigned review of the second issue of *Okyeame*, a literary journal established by the Ghana Society of Writers in 1961. The reviewer (probably Gerald Moore, who had reviewed *Okyeame* no. 1 in *Black Orpheus* no. 10) wrote:

> The function of periodicals in nurturing the new literatures in Africa and the Caribbean cannot be overstated. They represent necessary documentary proof of fashion and growth. Their function is not so much to preserve as to link. Often they stand at the very beginning of the development of local literature, setting up standards and providing a literary market for buyer and seller—the indigenous reading public and its artist. (*Black Orpheus* no. 14, p. 60)[1]

And what a market Beier created! Among those who owed their first publication, early critical recognition, or promotion to *Black Orpheus* were many of Africa's best-known writers: Gabriel Okara, Wole Soyinka, Dennis Brutus, Ama Ata Aidoo, Alex La Guma, Kofi Awoonor, John Pepper Clark. Francophone writers such as Aimé Césaire, Léopold Sédar Senghor, Felix Tchikaya U Tam'si, Flavian Ranaivo, and Jean-Joseph Rabearivelo were made available to anglophone readers, often for the first time, through translations in *Black Orpheus*. Among the artists given important recognition in the magazine were "Twins Seven Seven" (whose real name is Taiwo Olaniyi), Vincent Akweti Kofi, Valente Goenha Malangatana, Demas Nwoko, and Ibrahim Salahi.[2] In fact, the African artists, writers, and intellectuals who came into prominence from the late fifties to the late sixties were all profoundly influenced by *Black Orpheus*.

Abiola Irele, later an editor of the magazine and an important anglophone critic of the francophone writers, describes his own first acquaintance with the magazine as an undergraduate at the University of Ibadan:

> I discovered Césaire, Senghor, Damas, and all that through *Black Orpheus*. My interest in *négritude* was, in fact, through *Black Orpheus*: the translations of the poets and that sort of thing. That's one very important function that such a magazine can have, to introduce work from . . . the other side of the language wall. . . . So an extract from, say, Cheikh Hamidou Kane will be translated and that is a good way of letting people know what is happening even before the whole thing has appeared. . . . *Black Orpheus* performed that function very well. My perspective on black writing was really shaped, or determined if you like, by *Black Orpheus*.[3]

The Founding of *Black Orpheus*

Ulli Beier's background ought not to have fitted him especially for the task he was to set for himself in West Africa. An expatriate of German-Jewish parentage, he had come to Nigeria in 1950 to teach English literature to extramural students in Yoruba communities. Born July 30, 1922, in Gleiwitz, Germany (now Gliwice, Poland), Beier left for Palestine during World War II and was a student in archaeology before being held (from 1941 to 1946) in a British internment camp. He thereafter attended the University of London, where he received a B.A. in 1948. Beier was teaching English in South London and lecturing part-time at the university when he saw an advertisement for a teaching position in Nigeria. He knew nothing about Nigeria, he later said, but it was warm there, and anyway he was ready for a change. Suzanne Wenger, a young artist, went with him.[4]

His job in Nigeria was difficult and ill paid; his students, usually adults, tried under unpropitious circumstances to grasp an alien culture, adopt the valuation it placed on its "serious literature," and pass examinations imported from England. Ultimately Beier found a pedagogic strategy for conveying to his students the characteristics of English literature: he sought analogues with traditional African literature. He had studied traditional Yoruba culture and could understand the language, though he was never fluent. He began to teach English literature by making specific comparisons to Yoruba songs, tales, and epics.

With Robert Gardiner, the director of extramural studies at the University of Ibadan, as an important ally, Beier thus became one of a very small group who saw the importance of traditional art and literature in Africa.[5] In September 1956 this interest led him to attend the World Congress of Black Writers, sponsored by the first important black African literary journal, the Paris-based *Présence Africaine*, and held at the Sorbonne. With him there was Jahnheinz Jahn, a German scholar important as a systematic chronicler of black art

Ulli Beier, founding editor of *Black Orpheus*.
(Nigeria, c. 1962)

and literature from throughout the world. Beier and Jahn were galvanized by the congress. Beier, in particular, was impressed by the
literary movement that had grown up around *Présence Africaine*. He
later said:

> One could envisage that this could kindle a similar development in
> the English-speaking territories. . . . I started *Black Orpheus* with the

direct aim of translating some of these writers [Senghor, Césaire, Damas, U Tam'si] into English, so that they could be known in Nigeria and Ghana.

He hoped, he said, to stimulate a similar literary efflorescence in English-speaking West Africa and eventually to "provide a vehicle for the new writers who would emerge."[6]

Beier found funding, material, a printer, and a distributor with commendable dispatch. Though he credits himself with no such talent,[7] Beier has often been described by others as a natural entrepreneur. He got in touch with all of his Nigerian associates and wrote almost immediately to Gerald Moore, a fellow expatriate extramural lecturer, likewise interested in analogies between Western literature and traditional African literature. Moore, then in the far eastern part of Nigeria, alerted Beier to the first of their important new writers, sending in a few poems by his former student Gabriel Okara. Jahn, a diligent researcher, already had "drawers full of material."[8]

The Ministry of Education for Nigeria's Western Region, headquartered in Ibadan, temporarily helped Beier solve his funding, printing, and distribution problems. An education officer named Levi, who had encouraged Beier to found the magazine *Odu* (a scholarly journal of Yoruba studies) in 1954, explained to Beier that their ability to help had been fortuitous. Beier later said:

> The printers being extremely slow in Nigeria, the publication section always found it very difficult to spend their money. So, coming with my proposal in January, you know, about two months before the close of the fiscal year, they were only too glad that I offered to spend a thousand quid.[9]

Support from the ministry, however, also brought with it "fantastic problems" because, as Beier later reflected, a Ministry of Education is "just not geared for this kind of job . . . of distributing a magazine." Beier never quite knew with any confidence where *Black Orpheus* was available. Years later, on a trip to South Africa, Beier would ask a black staff member of the Johannesburg magazine *Drum* how much *Black Orpheus* was selling for there. His would-be informant replied: "I don't know, I always buy a stolen copy."[10]

The first issue of *Black Orpheus*, printed by the *Times* press of Lagos, appeared in September 1957, its layout, cover design, front page, and headings the work of Beier's first wife, Suzanne Wenger, with illustrations in the text by G. M. Hotop from the German edition of Amos Tutuola's *The Palm-Wine Drinkard*. Wenger's cover, an expressionistic silkscreen in violet ink on a grey field, inspired by a mask from the Dan region of the Ivory Coast, was to set the graphic tone for the magazine's first decade. Wenger used color more sparingly than Beier's second wife (and *Black Orpheus*'s second graphic designer), Georgina Betts Beier, later would, but there was the same bold simplicity of line and directness of effect characteristic of contemporary European graphic art. There were some marks of haste: the copyediting, often imperfect later, was passable, but one photograph, of a man demonstrating the Yoruba talking drum at the World Congress of Black Writers, unaccountably appeared in two places. The magazine's title, of course, was borrowed from Jean-Paul Sartre's famous 1948 introduction to Léopold Senghor's edition of poems from French Africa, in which Sartre compared the black poet's search for identity to Orpheus's descent into hell.

Black Orpheus was, Beier later said, "propaganda,"[11] designed, in a time still dominated by colonialist chauvinism, primarily to educate English-speaking Africans about the rest of the black world, and secondarily to inspire and encourage young writers and teach them about African traditional cultures other than their own. The first editorial announced:

> A journal devoted to contemporary African literature has long been overdue. The young African writer is struggling hard to build up for himself a literary public in Africa. All too often he has to turn to Europe for criticism and encouragement. It is still possible for a Nigerian child to leave a secondary school with a thorough knowledge of English literature, but without even having heard of such great black writers as Léopold Sédar Senghor or Aimé Césaire. One difficulty, of course, has been that of language; because a great deal of the best African writing is in French or Portuguese or Spanish. *Black Orpheus* tries to break down some of these language barriers by introducing writers from all territories in translation.

Beier added:

> *Black Orpheus* will also publish the works of Afro-American writers, because many of these are involved in similar cultural and social situations and their writings are therefore highly relevant to Africans.
>
> While it is the primary purpose of this journal to encourage and discuss contemporary African writing, we shall not forget the great traditions of oral literature of the African tribes. For it is on the heritage of the past . . . that the literature of the future must be based.
>
> (*Black Orpheus* no. 1, p. 4)

To these primarily educative ends, Jahn, Beier's nominal coeditor, contributed a report on the World Congress of Black Writers, and Moore and Beier contributed articles about West African poetry and Amos Tutuola's novels respectively, intended more to inspire classroom discussion than critical discussion.

Jahn reported the debate at the congress between Richard Wright and Aimé Césaire over the value of the African tradition in the face of modernization and exploitation, but the essential function of his article was its invocation of the congress's hopeful final resolution:

> This Conference urges Negro intellectuals and all justice-loving men to struggle to create the practical conditions for the revival and the growth of Negro cultures.
>
> . . . The conference urges all Negro intellectuals to defend, illustrate and publicize throughout the world the national values of their own peoples.
>
> We Negro writers and artists proclaim our fellowship with all men and expect from them, for our people, a similar fellowship.
>
> (*Black Orpheus* no. 1, p. 46)

Jahn's article explicitly tied *Black Orpheus*'s function to the goals of the congress and its sponsor: "We hope to continue with our own modest means the excellent work begun by the World Congress of Black Writers, and by the French literary journal, *Présence Africaine*, of bringing together authors writing in different languages, to a fruitful exchange of ideas" (p. 40).

Beier's conception of the African artist's cultural dilemma was more subtle. He wrote in "The Conflict of Cultures in West African

Poetry" of the symbolic significance of language barriers, which lead the modern African artist to use and sometimes glorify a European tradition that he must also, for his own cultural survival, systematically reject. Senghor, characteristically, was the "most powerful" such writer: "Senghor has become so much a European . . . that he can criticize European culture from the inside. He has gained so much perspective towards traditional African culture . . . that he can rediscover its value and proclaim its mission to the world" (no. 1, p. 21).

Publication in that first issue of Okara's poems, Beier's translations of two of Senghor's poems, Abedoye Babalola's translation of a selection of traditional Yoruba poems, and Beier's reviews, under the pseudonym Sangodare Akanji, of Camara Laye's *Dark Child* and Richard Wright's *Black Power* was further indicative of the magazine's simple goals of establishing links between anglophone West Africa and the black diaspora, educating Africans about their traditional culture, and promoting new writers and artists. Nevertheless, Beier's attitudes were not then strikingly at odds with those of the Western critics that *Black Orpheus* would, according to its first editorial announcement, seek to replace. He found Laye's narrative moving, but Wright's *Black Boy* bitter, and Wright's description of Ghana in *Black Power* only evidence that he was "temperamentally not well-suited to understand Africans" (no. 1, p. 50).

The Early Years: "Inspiration" and Discovery

Beier had hoped, he later said, that *Black Orpheus*'s influence would be largely "inspirational"—"to make people feel they were not alone, even if they were writing in a part of Africa where there were no other writers of their caliber." He also had in mind the role that the magazine might serve for Western readers: "If I were to start a magazine today," Beier later reflected, "I would probably have something very different. But ten years ago it had to . . . sell African literature abroad." Moore summed up *Black Orpheus*'s "indispensible" educational dimension for literature teachers interested in recognizing Africa's creative genius: "One would simply say, 'You will find this in *Black Orpheus*, number five.'"[12]

The issues that followed were to adhere to Beier's initial editorial philosophy. Beier featured, criticized, and reviewed writing from the rest of the black world–francophone and lusophone African, West Indian, and black American—but he also gradually introduced the first of a remarkable succession of new writers and artists from anglophone Africa. Ezekiel Mphahlele, then unknown outside South Africa, was represented in the fourth issue by his story "The Suitcase." Wole Soyinka, then a young playwright just returned from school in Britain, made his debut as a poet in the fifth issue. Alex La Guma's first short story appeared in the seventh issue. Demas Nwoko's paintings were first reproduced in the eighth, Vincent Akweti Kofi's sculptures in the ninth, Valente Goenha Malangatana's and Ibrahim Salahi's paintings in the tenth issue, in which John Pepper Clark's poems also first appeared. Lenrie Peters's and Christopher Okigbo's poems first appeared in the eleventh. Ama Ata Aidoo, Arthur Maimane, and Bloke Modisane contributed short stories to the twelfth issue; Dennis Brutus contributed poetry. And *Black Orpheus* also introduced a succession of other important intellectual voices; in the third issue, for instance, musicologist J. H. Nketia contributed an article about traditional Akan poetry.

27

Beier's editorial philosophy was never formalized or rigid. He was rather, he recalls, impelled by the spontaneous exhilaration of discovery: "What kept me going for ten years was simply the excitement of it. It was a wonderful thing being the first to read Soyinka's 'Death at Dawn' scribbled roughly on a sheet of notepaper. [To witness] the elation—euphoria of J. P. [Clark] after writing 'Song of a Goat'!!"[13]

The effort to report the inspirational accomplishments of the rest of the black world for anglophone West Africa continued in the second issue with an attempt to define *négritude*. The movement was exemplified by translations of the poetry of Césaire, Leon Damas, and Jacques Roumain; Beier ambiguously defined it as standing for "the new consciousness of the negro, for his newly gained self-confidence, and for his distinctive outlook on life" (no. 2, p. 22).

Beier's careful analysis of the poems followed, focusing on the poets' pain at dispossession and "longing for Africa." Roumain's "When the Tam Tam Beats" he called a "painful expression" of the "hybrid" nature of Afro-American culture; Damas's "Balance Sheet" an indictment of the "artificiality of manners," "false sentiments," and triviality of Western civilization (pp. 22–23). Damas's plaintive poem "Black Dolls" stood as a sort of centerpiece to the issue, expressive of the movement's overwhelming nostalgia and idealization. Damas's hyperemotional lines in retrospect suggest how inevitable was the reaction of *Black Orpheus*'s young Nigerian readers,[14] whose own literary attitudes were to be so very different:

> Give me back my black dolls to play
> the simple games of my instincts
> to rest in the shadow of their laws
> to recover my courage
> my boldness
> to feel myself myself
> a new self from the one I was yesterday
> yesterday
>   without complications
>   yesterday
> when the hour of uprooting came
>
>   (no. 2, p. 24)

The third issue (May 1958) introduced Afro-Cuban poets Marcellino Arozarena, Emilio Ballagas, Nicholas Guillén, and Luis Pales Matos, with a prefatory essay by Jahn that considered them from a folkloristic perspective as mirroring the mixed Catholic and Yoruba character of local Cuban culture and offering "a precise onomatopoeic representation" of indigenous dances ("Poetry in Rumba Rhythms," pp. 32–36). It also featured a poem by Guadelupan negritudinist Paul Niger (André Albert Beville). The reviews continued the West Indian emphasis. In the fourth issue, in addition to an essay by Georg Dickenberger introducing the poems of black American Paul Vesey (Samuel Allen), there were also reviews of three important West Indian journals by J. A. Ramsaran and a background essay on West Indian fiction by Randolf Rawling. The issue also published seven poems by Vesey, who had been identified closely with the *négritude* poets through his long exile in Paris.

Beier also gradually progressed beyond his somewhat incestuous reliance on friends and associates for West African material. The second issue had contained the first of two reviews of the art of Beier's own wife, Suzanne Wenger, signed by that wholly fictitious but indefatigable African intellectual Sangodare Akanji (Beier himself). The review was more an appreciation than a "notice," describing Wenger's unique acceptance among the priests of Obatala, the Yoruba creator god, and asserting, "She is not an artist experimenting with foreign forms; her relationship to Africa is a matter of basic attitude to life. . . . Suzanne Wenger has been rightly called the European counterpart of Senghor, because in her, as in the great poet, two cultures are a perfectly blended synthesis" (no. 2, p. 31).[15] In coming to Africa, Beier wrote, she had "stumbled on a world where fact meant nothing and meaning everything; a world which was not interpreted through logic but through poetry" (p. 30). The same reviewer, in the third issue, commented on two works by Jahn, *Rumba Macumba* and *Schwarze Ballade* (pp. 59–60). The first tougher, more controversial criticism came in the fourth issue, where Gerald Moore mounted a substantial defense of Joyce Cary's novel *Mister Johnson*, in response to Davidson Nicol's criticism of the book (no. 4, pp. 16–23).

Gabriel Okara, though a friend of the family in a sense, was the first independent contributor. Otherwise, the first few issues were written, translated, and compiled virtually entirely by the original triumvirate of Beier, Moore, and Jahn. Okara's collection and translation of material about the Ijaw creation myth in the second issue, Babalola's Yoruba material, and Beier's material about traditional art forms in the third and fourth issues continued the movement toward more immediate West African material. Ezekiel Mphahlele's moving story "The Suitcase," about a black South African's struggle between conscience and desperation, continued the movement toward modern anglophone material. Thereafter, Beier began regularly to introduce talented newcomers from English-speaking Africa.

His success in doing so is attested to in a taped Transcription Centre review of the eleventh issue. South African playwright and critic Lewis Nkosi, who had been with Mphahlele on the old *Drum* staff, praised the magazine for its eclecticism and its discovery of new poets who were "precise and musically adept." *Black Orpheus* was "full of exciting writing" and "truly representative of the negro race." [16]

However, Christopher Okigbo, Beier's former Nigerian colleague at the Mbari Clubs, unfavorably compared *Black Orpheus* to Neogy's *Transition*, of which Okigbo had become West African editor. "*Black Orpheus*," Okigbo said, "with its insistence on 'blackness,' rather tends to perpetuate the 'black mystique,' . . . blackness for its own sake." Beier imagined some mystical link between black Americans and black Africans, where there was really no specific "affinity," only a common search for roots. [17] *Black Orpheus*'s basic flaw, Okigbo felt, was that it would publish black Americans but not white ones. [18]

Jahn left as coeditor after the sixth issue (November 1959), following a brief visit to Nigeria to research a travel book, *Through African Doors*. Wole Soyinka and Ezekiel Mphahlele, then a disgruntled exile teaching English literature up-country, replaced him. The position of coeditor was sometimes nominal, involving less contact than a contributing editor might normally have and much the same function, and sometimes advisory, bringing a second or third perspective to the business of finding and evaluating new literary talent.

Mphahlele, for instance, introduced Beier to the work of Alex La Guma, Dennis Brutus, and the other South African writers, and led ultimately to Beier's 1964 visit to South Africa. Beier's "reviews editor," Oscar Dathorne, who was "in constant and lively contact with [The University of] Nsukka," brought Pol Ndu and Romanus Egudu to Beier's attention. Of Mphahlele and Dathorne, Beier writes, "We talked about the magazine continuously; we saw each other all the time—though we never had a formal meeting. Formal 'editorial meetings'—that's just not my style." [19]

Soyinka, too active in other areas to take on the role Beier had hoped he would, disassociated himself from the magazine after the thirteenth issue (November 1963), Mphahlele after the sixteenth (October 1964). Beier replaced them with Abiola Irele, a young Nigerian who would have an important influence on the magazine's future. Beier met Irele, then an associate editor for *Présence Africaine* specializing in anglophone Africa, in the summer of 1961 at that magazine's Paris offices. A former editor of the University of Ibadan's literary magazine, *The Horn*, through which he had met a number of the principals at *Black Orpheus*, including Jahn and J. P. Clark, Irele had useful contacts in both Paris and Lagos. Irele remained in Paris throughout his original tenure as coeditor, however, serving only as advisor and occasional contributor. He returned to Lagos and Accra a few years later, in time to join J. P. Clark in launching the second series of *Black Orpheus*.

Beier's "*Black Orpheus* Committee"—ostensibly advisors to the editors, but really, of course, more a list of sponsors and friends—also varied considerably over the years. In the beginning it included the *négritude* writers and their American colleagues: Marcellino Arozarena, Césaire, Damas, Senghor, Paul Vesey, and others. Later they were joined by alumni of the magazine. Once they had begun to make names for themselves through *Black Orpheus*, Beier would later ruefully comment, most writers had not "kept up the connection to the magazine that one might have expected," [20] becoming instead no more than signal flags to hoist over the magazine's masthead. Ghanaian writer Geormbeeyi Adali-Mortty, who contributed an important early review of Chinua Achebe's *Things Fall Apart* to the sixth issue (November 1959), joined the committee shortly thereafter, along with another early contributor, Nigerian scholar Adeboye Babalola. Jahn's retirement as editor at about that time also signaled his withdrawal for seven years from active involvement, even as a contributor. He, too, appeared on the masthead list. Later he would be joined there by Chinua Achebe, J. P. Clark, Alex La Guma, Gerald Moore, Gabriel Okara, Christopher Okigbo, and eventually Wole Soyinka, all premature retirees. Ironically, Beier's name, too, would finally be hoisted to the masthead of Irele and Clark's second series.

Editorial Evolution and Outside Support

There was, however, Beier was later to say, "a constant stream of new writers who . . . [were] very glad to be published in *Black Orpheus*."[21] In a proposal to the Rockefeller Foundation for travel funds in 1960, Beier reported that "more than half of the material on hand was written specially for this journal."[22] Once the magazine had gotten rolling, Beier later estimated, he accepted only about two manuscripts out of every ten he received and hardly ever solicited manuscripts.[23] By 1963, with new sources of support, *Black Orpheus* was even able to afford the luxury of paying its contributors.

Black Orpheus's growing circulation, which under Beier's editorship ultimately reached 3,500,[24] induced a commercial publisher, Longmans of Nigeria, to take over publication from the thirteenth issue (November 1963). Julian Rea, Longmans' Ibadan manager, was highly interested in Nigerian writing and was a close friend of Wole Soyinka's. He offered to act as publisher for Beier's center for artists and writers, the Mbari Club (which nominally "sponsored" *Black Orpheus*), and Beier "heaved a sigh of relief . . . because from then on I only had to deliver copy and read proofs; I did not have to do the layout in detail anymore. . . . Longmans saw the journal through the press and I no longer had to make those tiring 150-mile journeys to Lagos to nag, beg, cajole, bully, and threaten my printers." The Rea proposal did not go unchallenged at Mbari. Denis Williams felt strongly that Longmans was a colonial profiteer getting fat selling bad school textbooks throughout the former empire. Beier recalls:

> He felt we should take courage into our own hands and simply publish the magazine on our own, acting as a publishing house ourselves. Okigbo and Clark leaned his way, but not with sufficient conviction. I conceded Denis the argument, but I knew the problems involved and did not have the confidence that we had the managerial skills or the capital to handle this. . . . Besides I guess that the genuine good will of

Julian Rea, his sincere interest, overshadowed the thing he actually represented as a manager of Longmans. I have seldom been determined by ideologies; have always worked on the basis of personal relationships, across ideologies, institutions, boundaries, and races. This has been my strength—because it makes for lateral thinking—and my weakness, because it constantly lays one open to attack from *all* sides. Wole [Soyinka] being pragmatic on such issues supported me. Denis Williams felt so strongly that he resigned over it from Mbari. That was a very high price to pay.[25]

The Caxton Press in Ibadan replaced the *Times* press as printer, and Longmans regularized distribution, though they, too, Beier would later reflect, "were more geared to distribute school books."[26] *Black Orpheus* had also begun to come to the attention of the outside world, including two very different philanthropical organizations, the Rockefeller Foundation and the Farfield Foundation.

Robert July, assistant director for the humanities at Rockefeller, first met with Beier in Ibadan on February 26, 1960. Beier told July about two primary worries with regard to *Black Orpheus*: the haphazardness of distribution and the vulnerability of his subsidy from the Western Division's Ministry of Education; he estimated that he would need somehow to reach a printing of 7,000, efficiently distributed, to be self-sufficient. *Black Orpheus* cost, Beier said, about £500 for a printing, at that time, of about 2,500 copies. The program at the Rockefeller Foundation in those years, however, generally precluded support for periodicals and emphasized support to "key individuals." Moreover, it was felt by some that support ought to be administered through Beier's extramural employer, the University of Ibadan. That idea was abandoned, however, since Beier clearly wanted more, not less, autonomy.[27] Ultimately, in a grant-in-aid dated September 15, 1960, Rockefeller gave Beier support of a very different kind—$5,500 to enable him to travel throughout Africa. July thus encouraged an important feature in the development of *Black Orpheus*, the broadening of its base of contributors to other parts of Africa, but he did not underwrite the magazine's deficit. Beier planned a first trip to East Africa for winter 1961 (the year of

Transition's founding in Kampala), but admitted in a letter to July received on July 18 that he did not "know anybody in Kenya and Tanganyika," and only a few people elsewhere in East Africa. He was, therefore, open to suggestions.

His trips were a great success. In Khartoum, at the Technical Institute, Beier met two artists, Ibrahim Salahi from the Sudan and Denis Williams from the West Indies. Williams' consequent move to Nigeria was inspired by his meeting with Beier. In Kenya and Uganda he met short story writer Grace Ogot; her husband, historian Alan Ogot; and poet Erisa Kironde (who would soon be among *Transition*'s earliest contributors). In Mozambique he met architect Amancio Guedes and artist Valente Malangatana. In South Africa he met architect Julian Beinart at the University of the Witwatersrand, sculptor Sidney Kumalo, and *Drum* writers Casey Motsisi and Todd Matshikiza in Johannesburg. In Capetown Beier met with controversial *Black Orpheus* contributor Alex La Guma, who gave him the manuscript for *A Walk in the Night*, ultimately published by Beier's Mbari Press; he was also introduced to writers Richard Rive, James Matthews, and Alf Wannenburgh. Beier's trip to Brazzaville in the Congo was otherwise disappointing, but introduced him to the work of Felix Tchikaya U Tam'si.[28]

In Ghana, the Society of Writers was just bringing out the first issue of *Okyeame*. Efua Sutherland was starting her experimental theater. Vincent Kofi was planning a sculpture workshop for the cultural center at Kumasi. At Sierra Leone's Fourah Bay College, Beier met Eldred Jones. In Dakar he found Cheikh Hamidou Kane, whose *L'Aventure ambiguë* he called "an intelligent, sensitive book that ought to be translated immediately."[29]

Beier's connection with the Congress for Cultural Freedom and its parent organization, the Farfield Foundation, began at almost the same time. John Thompson, Farfield's executive director, had become interested in the South African writers and had met two *Drum* writers, Nat Nakasa and Lewis Nkosi, in Johannesburg. Ezekiel Mphahlele, more than a few years senior to these two wild young reporters, had been *Drum*'s literary columnist before his exile to

Nigeria and collaboration with Beier at *Black Orpheus*. Nakasa and Nkosi were full of praise for Mphahlele, whom Thompson ultimately recommended, sight unseen, to the Congress for Cultural Freedom in Paris, as a sort of roving African envoy. Mphahlele, in turn, later recommended Beier to Thompson.

Farfield, whose money came largely, and covertly, from the Central Intelligence Agency, had more freewheeling programs than Rockefeller. Political affiliation and ideology were not in question, Thompson recalls: Marxism was not thought to be much of a force in Africa. The fear was that political independence might bring instability; a cohesive intellectual elite might be a stabilizing force. "Our particular interest was in literary people," Thompson recalls. "We thought it would be important to aid them because it seemed to us, on the basis of the political experience of other countries, that literary intellectuals had been important. Our interest was in establishing an independent publishing program." He added:

> In those innocent days, incredible as it may seem, my theory was that if they were intelligent they were good. . . . I think now, looking back on it, that it was probably in the long run, indirectly and obscurely, part of American imperialism. Americans tended to take over these markets from England, but I certainly didn't know that then. As I look back on it, it was basically a missionary move. I would oppose it now. But it seemed like a good idea at the time. . . . There were no strings attached whatever.[30]

Beier, Mphahlele, Nakasa, and Nkosi did not know of Farfield's CIA connection until years later—any more than did the private philanthropies that had helped fund the Congress for Cultural Freedom. That awareness was not to come until 1967, when the *Encounter* and National Student Association revelations surfaced.

The Farfield grants were extremely useful to Beier, however, precisely because there were no strings attached. Although the money only amounted to a few thousand dollars a year, it enabled Beier to meet his deficit. Thompson signed the money over to Beier's Mbari Cultural Centre, by that time formally the owner of *Black Orpheus*, to be used as Beier saw fit. The Mbari Clubs, however, were largely self-supporting: a little café in Ibadan sold beer and lunches and sponsored entertainment in the evening. Upon this foundation, Beier built an edifice of art clinics, theater workshops, a publishing house (Mbari Publications), and ultimately the magazine. Thompson, although he insisted on detailed budgets, allowed Beier a good deal of freedom with expenditures. Like Rockefeller, Farfield also occasionally supplied Beier with travel money—again for the sake of broadening his acquaintance with the rest of Africa.

Along with the changes in financing, distribution, and the balance of its contributors came a gradual change in *Black Orpheus*'s approach. Beier still sought to teach English-speaking Africa about the art and culture of the rest of the black world, but his attitude toward *négritude* and its attendant ideologies was now more critical. In the formal proposal to the Rockefeller Foundation, he wrote: "We have been able to present the French African concept of 'négritude' and have it challenged by writers from other parts of Africa." The magazine's efforts, Beier predicted, would ultimately "force the French West African writers who have gathered under the slogan of 'négritude' to redefine their present stand and reexamine their concepts in the light of criticism from East, Central, and South Africa."[31]

Beier dismissed the idea that he had been acting as a cultural "missionary" at *Black Orpheus*, but he did exhibit predilections and preferences that shaped the first impetus of these literary and artistic movements, and he was criticized for his editorial choices. Some, Beier admitted, had said that he leaned in fiction toward stark realism—short stories of the kind written by South Africans Alex La Guma, Richard Rive, and Ezekiel Mphahlele; but African writers were often inclined to be "captious" and, like writers anywhere, to have antagonisms toward a whole array of their peers.[32]

Editors too, however, can be "captious," and Beier himself was certainly not without critics. Okigbo's comments about Beier's accession to the "black mystique" have already been mentioned. Okigbo's and John Nagenda's comments on *Black Orpheus*, however, were perhaps most critical of Beier's artistic standards. In fact, Okigbo called the work of one group of the Beiers' unschooled Mbari artists, reproduced in *Black Orpheus* no. 12 (1963?), "a disgrace, just a big shame." Beier's "greatest problem," Okigbo suggested, was in "not being able to . . . find a distinction between art and craft." Some of the Mbari works were "ugly" and ill executed. The interviewer, Dennis Duerden, asked if there wasn't also a bias toward work that was emotionally excessive or primitive. Okigbo replied that Beier was rather "very strongly attracted to work that's experimental," to "experiment for its own sake."[33] Nagenda agreed: the works in question were acceptable only as a record of experiments being tried; they were not "art as art." Later, academic artists such as Demas Nwoko and Babatunde Lawal were to criticize the participants in Georgina Beier's 1964 Oshogbo art workshop, the most notable of whom was Twins Seven Seven, as unschooled primitives. Most recently, of course, the school of poets that grew up around *Black Orpheus* has been criticized by younger Nigerian writers such as Chinweizu, Madubuike, and Jemie for imitating the techniques, themes, and deliberate obscurity of Western postmodernists.[34]

Perhaps it is unfair at this remove to carp about the imbalances of *Black Orpheus*'s various aesthetics. Beier was open to new artistic visions, and *Black Orpheus*, as Moore said, had "never been doctrinal."[35] Even so, there were imbalances. Beier's special circumstances and personal predilections did lead him to favor some literary, aesthetic, and critical attitudes over others. And if, as Moore commented, the "critical element" at *Black Orpheus* had "necessarily been subservient" to the creative, still each letter of acceptance, each initial contact with a potential contributor implied a critical judgment with powerful overtones. Each such judgment, in a part of the world where a Western-style critical tradition had only just begun, had overwhelming influence. Beier set the standard of valuation himself in this trade, which he initiated.

The remarkable efflorescence of art, literature, and criticism that grew up around *Black Orpheus* could hardly have occurred in the way it did without the efforts of this strong-willed man, who really had no axe to grind. He began these activities "more than anything else to please myself" and because they "put me in touch with all the writers and artists" and "gave me an exciting life and an exciting way of dealing with this literature." He brought to them enthusiasm, imagination, initiative. He was not inclined to equivocate in his judgments (as his letters to July show) or to question his own presuppositions, but as simultaneous booster and judge, he was nevertheless aware of the tenuousness of his relationship toward this new material. Still, one should not be surprised that he was not always successful in balancing the independence of his contributors and the objectivity of his own standards.

His objectivity was tempered by his reluctance to endanger his fragile hothouse. *Black Orpheus* would not, as Moore later put it, smother the first creative sparks in a critical blanket.[36] This unflattering scrupulosity, had it been widely recognized, might well have been taken as an insult, as indeed it was later when expressed in "Voices Out of the Skull" by Paul Theroux (no. 20, pp. 41–58). The rate at which accomplished writers deserted the fold perhaps indicates a need to escape from this protective atmosphere as much as from a patron driven by an artistic vision of his own. That they were able to move on to other things is a tribute to their, and to Beier's, success.

Although many of *Black Orpheus*'s artists and writers moved on to other spheres, there was still coherence to the magazine's collective accomplishments, and those accomplishments tell much about the relationship between the editors' standards and the artists' inclinations.

Poetry and Art in Beier's *Black Orpheus*

Beier's taste in poetry progressed beyond an initial inclination toward the *négritude* movement and its surrealistic poets, but even after he had begun to sponsor criticisms of *négritude*, Beier was to continue to favor complex poetry or poetry with an explicit social message.

The tenth issue, for instance, contained a selection of new Nigerian poems: four by Wole Soyinka, three by John Pepper Clark, and one each by Frank Aig Imoukhuede and Dorothy S. Obi. Obi's "Winds of Africa" and Imoukhuede's "Negritude" appealed to Beier primarily because of their themes. Imoukhuede, an Ibadan graduate on the staff of the Lagos *Daily Express*, crudely parodied the poetic devices and hyperemotionalism of Senghor, Damas, and their associates; Obi imitated them. Indeed it may have been the contrast, expressive of the hoped-for debate about *négritude*, that appealed to Beier.

Clark's poems appealed on both stylistic and thematic grounds. His "Imprisonment of Obatala," for instance, touched on an important theme of Suzanne Wenger's artwork, a central incident of Yoruba folklore referred to in a Lagos *Daily Service* review (the style of which seems suspiciously like Beier's) of Wenger's work, approvingly quoted by Beier (no. 7, June 1960, p. 35): "Is this the world of our fathers that we believed to be exhausted and degenerate, that is suddenly confronting us in a new disguise full of vigour and energy? Has our traditional culture still so much presence that it could excite and stimulate an important contemporary European artist?" Clark's poems, in this first *Black Orpheus* appearance, owed much to both the European modernist tradition of allusive subtlety and the traditional African concept of the private language of ritual.[37] The impression and the imagery were powerful, idiosyncratic, and often elusive.

Soyinka's disjunction of diction, syntax, metaphor, his purposeful obscurity, stemmed from an effort to see the poem's subject from fresh angles. In "Night," for instance, the speaker did not "dare / exacerbation from your [the Night's] subtle plough." But what does it mean to "dare exacerbation from" something? "Exacerbate" what? Why "from"? And how is the night a plow? Soyinka's "Death in the Dawn" took gentler liberties, imaginatively linking the speaker's accidental killing of a cock with a traditional ceremonial offering before a journey and a gory automobile accident. Such an interest in finding new imaginative applications for traditional myth and ritual was also typical of Beier's *Black Orpheus*.

That Beier did not worry about obscurity of allusion, syntax, or imagery is also attested to in his early publication of Christopher Okigbo. In a somewhat boosterish review of *Heavensgate* (then just published by Mbari Publications), Beier explained Okigbo's attraction:

> Okigbo is chiefly a poet for the ear. . . . The images change quickly and he hardly ever gives us time to build up a consistent and lasting vision in our mind's eye. But we can *hear* his verse. . . . Everything he touches vibrates and swings and we are compelled to read on and to follow the tune of his chant, hardly worried about the fact that we understand little of what he has to say. The obscurity of Okigbo's poetry is of course deliberate. (no. 12, p. 46)

Schooled on the surrealists and the expressionists, Beier depended on an intuitive emotional or psychological identification—texture rather than sense. His comparison of Okigbo and Clark is instructive. He imagined Okigbo "gradually chisel[ling] . . . a large chunk of experience"—"balancing, reconstructing" (p. 47); but Clark was "writing under a form of compulsion . . . like a 'pot all night on the boil.'" Beier imagined Clark "writing in a kind of explosion, under the extreme pressure of experience, writing only if cornered by life." Clark's poems were "heavy reading" because the poet's "harassed, tormented, and irrepressible personality is present in every line" (p. 48).

Beier's intuitions stemmed from impressionistic responses to language. He quoted Clark's "superb, unique description of Ibadan": ". . . running splash of rust / and gold—flung and scattered / among seven hills like broken / china in the sun" (p. 49). Beier, however, was as much attracted by Okigbo's subtle musicality as by Clark's "compulsive" imagery. Okigbo's disconnected lament and invocation from *Silences* ("Lament of the Drums"), which appeared in a later issue, is most memorable not for its elusiveness or allusiveness, but for its sprung rhythm, its subtle alliteration, its onomatopoeia, and its broken patterns of rhyme and near-rhyme. Beier responded intuitively rather than mechanically to a passage like the following from the final stanza of "Lament of the Drums":

> THE WAILING is for the fields of crop . . .
> THE DRUMS' lament is
> They grow not . . .
> THE WAILING is for the fields of men . . .
>   FOR THE barren wedded ones
>   For the perishing children . . .
> THE WAILING is for the great river . . .
>   HER POT-bellied watchers
>   Despoil her . . .
>   (no. 17, p. 17)

Beier was not, however, exclusively committed to thematic obscurity or disjunction of language. Dennis Brutus, a student athlete involved in protests at the University of the Witwatersrand when Beier first published two of his poems in 1963, then wrote simple unmetrical poems with an occasional stray rhyme, alliteration, or repetition, and a direct message. What appealed to Beier in "Kneeling Before You," for instance, was the combination of the personal and the political. It was "extremely restrained and disciplined." It was not "self pitying," and it was striking for its personal immediacy, in ironic contrast to the political situation (no. 12, p. 49).

> I knelt
> and answering, you pressed my face against your womb
> and drew me to a safe and still oblivion,
> shut out the knives and the teeth; boots, bayonets and knuckles:
> so, for the instant posed, we froze to an eternal image,
> became unpersoned and unageing symbols . . .
>   (p. 17)

With another of Beier's new poets, the Ghanaian Kofi Awoonor, the appeal seems to have been in the emotionally charged language, a succession of idiosyncratic apostrophes, most often invocations of traditional ritual:

> Sew the old days for me, my fathers
> Sew them that I may wear them
> for the feast that is coming
> the feast of the new season that is coming.
> ("The Years Behind," no. 13, p. 50)

> Make me a cane so that I can walk
> Can carry my crippled soul across the stile
> and enter the room where they are feasting all night
> ("The Longest Journey," no. 13, p. 52)

> Cannot we join the ceremony of our death
> and partake of the rituals?
> cannot we carry the remainder of our circumcision
> away with us beyond?
> the wind blows on the graves
> sweeping the sparky debris away
> cannot we find where they buried our birth chord?
> ("The Consummation," no. 13, p. 51)

Beier published seven of Awoonor's poems in the thirteenth issue, and another, "I Heard a Bird Cry," in the fifteenth (August 1964). In an appreciation of Awoonor's poetry masquerading as a review in the seventeenth issue, Beier praised his subtlety, understatement, and freshness of imagery. Of "The Weaver Bird," Beier wrote, "Nothing could be more different from the biting exasperated attack on Western Civilization in Senghor's *New York* or the explosive and revolutionary denunciations of Western values in the work of Césaire. . . . He looks at the arrogance of the Europeans in Africa and he can laugh! To him they are so many chatty and noisy weaver birds: destructive, to be sure, but something to be driven and chased away, rather than to be fought" (no. 17, p. 61).

On the surface, the poem does seem to contain the comforting moral that Beier ascribed to it, although some of the bird's characteristics and antecedents are a bit ambiguous and it performs an oddly sacramental function. Awoonor's poem is perhaps the best example of the qualities Beier sought combined in a single poem; subtle, ironic, allusive, ambiguous, its moral is passionately held but not easily reducible (despite Beier's attempt to do so) to one explicit allegory. Awoonor's common themes—tradition, rebirth, political change—were also those most central to Beier's *Black Orpheus*.

In some ways, Beier's approach to art was similar. As Okigbo and Nagenda had said, he favored experiment—but also art with an elusive private idiom, especially if, as in Demas Nwoko's Independence Day painting, there was also some indefinable public allegory. He simultaneously favored Europe's and America's introversive expressionists, traditional African art, and the naive school of the new popular urban African craftsmen. He was skeptical about academic artists, who were formally instructed in techniques they had not yet developed uses for—who were fed "dead knowledge." In a report to Ezekiel Mphahlele on the Mbari art workshops, Beier wrote: "Our first disadvantage in Ibadan has been that most of our students were art teachers from Nigerian schools—by and large the most difficult and lethargic material you can get." Beier believed that art was produced not through craft, though some "technical know-how" had to be taught, but simply by freeing the artist's psyche from the limitations of convention: "The main direction was given simply by rejecting everything derivative, literary, false, etc. Surprisingly, within three or four days some of the students got down to quite deep levels in their mind and produced quite powerful highly original images."[38] It is not surprising, therefore, that Beier favored either artists who had bypassed the university—traditional craftsmen and urban primitives—or complex Europeanized artists who sought to free something unnameable stirring at "deep levels" of the psyche.[39]

Demas Nwoko is an exceptional example. University-trained as a painter and an illustrator, Nwoko had learned theatrical set designing in Paris and later became an ingenious self-taught architect. Like the Mbari artists, his work seemed almost to reinvent at a stroke both artistic traditions, indigenous and European. One saw in it something of Gauguin, of Munch, of Chagall—and of traditional Ibo art: the geometric abstraction, the flattened or skewed perspective, the deliberate simplicity of representation.

Nwoko had been still a student in his final year of undergraduate study at Zaria, still largely unknown despite two local exhibitions, when Beier championed his cause in the eighth issue of *Black Orpheus*. He came to the attention of Beier and Wole Soyinka at roughly the same time. Soyinka asked Nwoko to design a set for his new play, *A Dance of the Forest*. With characteristic confidence in his own judgment, Beier devoted ten pages to Nwoko's work, including eight pages of glossy reproductions of his paintings ("Earning a Living," "Praying Woman," "Churchgoers," "Ogboni Chief in Abeokuta," and "'In 1959,'" with three detail plates). An introductory essay stressed the bankruptcy of taste among the new African elites and the artists' slavish imitation of inferior nineteenth-century European models. Meanwhile, indigenous African traditions were being neglected: "One cannot help but admire those few young artists who have not succumbed to these trends," Beier said. "Among these, Demas Nwoko is outstanding."

Beier stressed Nwoko's idiosyncrasy, his "great intensity of feeling," and his openness to the "deep levels" of the mind: "We are immediately aware," he wrote, "of ideas and mysterious presences behind the scene" (no. 8, p. 11). Nwoko's best paintings showed a "clarity and mastery of technique," both the "clear cut angular precision of Ibo masks" and the subtle ambiguity of "the worldwide artistic movements of the twentieth century," to which Beier had alluded in his earlier description of the Nigerian art scene (p. 10). One painting, in particular, seemed to combine subtlety of representation, abstract formal simplicity, and an intuitive evocation of intense emotion. Beier wrote: "The picture of three European officers seated in front of African soldiers is of almost unbearable intensity. Although the figures are in perfect repose one feels they must explode any minute into violent action" (p. 11). The conflict between the two ranks of figures is apparent, even if the resolution of the *Black Orpheus* reproduction makes it hard to perceive "unbearable intensity."

Beier's promotion of the work of another major university-educated artist, Ghanaian sculptor Vincent Kofi, was similar. Again an appreciative essay set about cataloguing subjective responses: "They are impressive, massive works, that seem lonely and out of place in the odd domestic architecture of Akuafo Hall. They all radiate a certain rugged, untamed power, that is expressed in the bulging, heavy forms, the rough surface, and the compact composition" (no. 9, p. 35). As always, Beier was not daunted by obscurity of reference. One huge sculpture, "The Crucifix," seemed to have nothing about it resembling a cross; Beier admitted that he found the statue "bewildering." Again, his approval of the work was based on its hybrid nature, its ability to strike new creative sparks from the two unwieldy masses of the European and indigenous artistic traditions. He wrote: "Some of our artists repeat feebler and watered down versions of their forefathers' work. Others, in their desperate desire to free themselves, get lost in their attempt to adopt and digest European forms. Only a few have attained the originality and power of Vincent Akweti Kofi" (p. 36).

However, Beier was perhaps best known for, and found the most detractors for, encouraging the deceptively simple works of the African popular artists. His point of departure, it seems, was the American pop art movement.[40] African popular art, Beier wrote in a beautifully illustrated article entitled "Naive Nigerian Art," was real popular art, produced by ordinary people, not by cynical manipulators of the public psyche. Beier's description of the Nigerian sign-painters was moving, romantic, and, his detractors might say, a bit condescending. These semiliterate country people were moved, Beier said, by a romantic attachment to the superficial pleasures of modern life:

> From remote Ibo villages . . . [he] often come[s] to large trading centers like Onitsha, Owerri, Port Harcourt. Here he is captivated by the bright "Highlife" of a carefree society. The city seems to him a world of unlimited possibilities: here people get rich quickly. Money is spent more easily. . . . These young men are not married off by their parents, to girls they hardly know. Here women are in fact available all

the time. There is beauty everywhere in delightfully straightened hair and high heels.

The life at home seems narrow and austere. The art of his forefathers he hardly knows or cares about. The magnificent power and seriousness of—say—Ibo Mo masks seem to him an unsuccessful attempt to attain realism. He is convinced that he can obtain better likenesses himself—after all, more likely than not, he has obtained a rapid results [correspondence college] course in drawing. . . .

Only his romanticism saves him from utter vulgarity. The chief influences on his art are cinema posters and commercial advertising. Yet to him these things are not cheap. They are transformed in his mind's eye into symbols of real brightness and glamour. To him they are the freedom he can now enjoy, the possibility of taking part in the new life, if only on its fringe. (no. 19, p. 31)

The world of the signwriters, "colorful and lovable and a little sad," is also chimerical. These things are not really bright and beautiful, Beier and his readers, both African and Western, know in their wisdom, and the signpainter's artistic success is entirely beyond the control of his own technical understanding: "Occasionally, there is an involuntary touch of surrealism: a tempting lady with bright blue skin. . . . Strange perspectives and foreshortenings . . . can create a peculiar surreal feeling of space. Charm and bad taste go hand in hand in the signwriter's art; surprisingly technical skill exists side by side with crippled anatomies and distorted perspectives."

Under the circumstances, perhaps the virulence of Beier's critics is understandable. Beier had saved his warmest praise for artists whose accomplishments were due more to accident than to talent; both the irony and the aesthetic power of their work, moreover, is entirely temporary. A little more knowledge of anatomy, a change in social circumstance would bring their careers to a sudden end, as indeed, Beier reported, it seemed likely might happen: "But for how long will he find clients for his fantasies? As Onitsha and Port Harcourt are becoming more bourgeois and respectable, even the barbers may want to have signboards that are slicker and less romantic" (p. 39).

Setting aside the charge of condescension, however, one must

certainly grant that the works reproduced are indeed, as Beier maintained, moving both in their ironic juxtaposition to the cult of technology and modernization and in their simple power of execution.
Beier's motives, moreover, seem primarily to have been connected to
his belief in the intuitive nature of all artistic expression.[41]

Most of the "primitive" artists that Beier introduced, of course,
were not anonymous signpainters but his own protégés—often the
products of his and Georgina Beier's Mbari art workshops. Perhaps
the best known of these was dancer, musician, artist Taiwo Olaniyi—
who adopted the name "Twins Seven Seven" in commemoration of
his auspicious birth. Olaniyi, in fact, was not discovered *by* Beier;
rather, he discovered Beier, appearing unannounced to dance at
Beier's farewell party for *Nigeria Magazine* editor Michael Crowder.
Both Seven Seven's costume and performance were utterly unique—
and, Crowder recalls, utterly lewd. As Crowder and choreographer
Peggy Harper walked out of the party, they came upon the mysterious young dancer again and invited him to come around to see
them in the morning. Beier, Crowder, and Harper all took an interest
in him as a drummer and dancer.[42] Beier provided a temporary job
and eventually encouraged Seven Seven to join the experimental art
school that Beier and his second wife, Georgina, were running in
Oshogbo.

At the Oshogbo art school, however, Seven Seven stubbornly
produced not paintings but elaborately detailed cartoons of mytho-
logical creatures that reminded the Beiers of Amos Tutuola's fiction.
He was taught etching and set to work illustrating Tutuola. Seven
Seven's talent was almost immediately apparent—perhaps because,
unlike the "naive" artists', it was neither malleable nor accidental.
Beier used vignettes by Seven Seven to illustrate number 18 (October
1965) and reproduced two etchings in number twenty-two (August
1967), explaining the genesis of Seven Seven's work in the latter
issue. He wrote:

> His manner of working is unbelievably direct. He does not think
> about form or composition. He has a lot to say and puts it straight
> down. You cannot persuade him to change a design, unless you per-

suade him to change the story first. A naive artist? Perhaps, but not an unconscious one. Seven Seven's etchings have been worked on. They often go through three or four phases of etchings. But when he works on a plate, he does not so much think in terms of *design* but in terms of clarifying his story. He looks for the right proportion of black and white, the right density of line as a writer looks for the right phrase—they are to him means of communication. His etchings are beautifully worked. They have a rich, velvety texture and his line is sensitive and alive and expressive like a line of Paul Klee's. The world he depicts is immensely rich and bizarre, utterly fantastic but never frightening.

Beier's detractors might again charge condescension: if not unconscious, Seven Seven's art is not charged with the weightiness or symbolic profundity of, for instance, traditional African carvings; it is strictly to entertain. "Story telling," Beier wrote, had become "an end in itself" (p. 48), and there was no artistic striving, unconscious or otherwise, toward "deep levels of the mind." Nevertheless, as Beier points out, Seven Seven was a unique embodiment of a culture in a period of transition—a culture accessible to a far wider audience than traditional Yoruba culture and cutting across artistic boundaries in a particularly appealing way.[43]

Fiction and Performing Arts in Beier's *Black Orpheus*

Black Orpheus's fiction, unlike its poetry and art, was not particularly "experimental," as Beier himself admits.[44] He generally printed either social realism by new writers or excerpts and sketches from established writers that are interesting primarily as evidence of literary development. As Bernth Lindfors points out, Gabriel Okara's "Okolo, or the Voice" in number 10 (pp. 38–44) is an early version of chapter 1 of Okara's novel *The Voice*.[45] Achebe's "The Voter" in number seventeen (June 1965) and Tutuola's "Ajaiyi and the Witchdoctor" in number nineteen (March 1966) bear indirect relationships to *A Man of the People* and *Ajaiyi and His Inherited Poverty*, respectively. Of course, extracts from new work by well-known writers such as Tutuola and Achebe were meant more to add luster to the magazine than to bring new things before *Black Orpheus*'s readers. Works in progress only whet the appetite for more substantial fare, although there is something to be said for Beier's publication of an extract from *A Man of the People*, which signaled an important change in Achebe's subject matter, toward contemporary politics. The extract published in number 15 from Cheikh Hamidou Kane's *Ambiguous Adventure* also served an important purpose. Though influential in francophone Africa, Kane was unknown and untranslated in anglophone Africa, and the piece's unusual narrative perspective (immersed in the protagonist's final vision, or delusion) must have been quite striking on first acquaintance—and baffling, outside the full context of the novel. Other established writers whose fiction appeared in *Black Orpheus* included Birago Diop, Mongo Beti, Cyprian Ekwensi, and Camara Laye.

Black Orpheus's novice short story writers focused on themes of individual alienation from a society somehow dysfunctional: corrupt, oppressive, vulgar, insensitive, or simply torn between old values and new realities. The quality of this writing was sometimes high, sometimes not. Once again, the number of important writers who contributed these realistic stories and sketches was impressive, but *Black Orpheus*'s fiction, unlike the poetry and art work, does not seem to have been informed by any distinctive new aesthetic. These were realists of the nineteenth- or early twentieth-century sort: close reporters of social reality whose themes often were simply emotional identification with the underdog or outcast.

Ama Ata Aidoo's early story, "No Sweetness Here," from the twelfth issue (1963?) is a case in point. Her narrative of a woman's painful separation from her husband and loss of her child under traditional social convention presented a rare feminist theme and an equally rare criticism of the cruelty of a traditional custom. Aidoo's careful detailing of village life gives the story its power, in spite of an ending that dissipates into sentiment (the mother's loss becomes permanent when the child is bitten by a snake).

Like Aidoo's protagonist, the main characters in these fictions, often by South Africans, tended to be the weak, the desperate, the impotent. The pitiable repressed young man in Mphahlele's "The Suitcase" in the fourth issue (October 1958), the educated black man humiliated and bullied in Bloke Modisane's "The Situation" in the twelfth issue, and the brutalized street tough bleeding to death in Alex La Guma's "Blankets" in the fifteenth issue (August 1964) are brothers in helpless suffering. Description in these stories was minute, precise, evocative. The key to their success or failure, however, was commonly in their use of dialogue, which often made the difference between bathos and sympathy. In "The Suitcase," for example, the amorality of the desperately poor is given pointed reality by one brief exchange on a bus. A man with a stolen suitcase faces discovery and one passenger advises against looking too closely into the matter. "'Oh leave him alone,' an old voice came from another quarter, 'only one man saw the girls come in with a suitcase, and only one man says it is his. One against one. Let him keep what he has, the case. Let the other man keep what he has, the belief that it belongs to the girls.' There was a roar of laughter" (p. 26).

Nigerian writers were less gloomy, more inclined to satire than to bitter irony, but the emphasis was still on hapless, victimized protagonists. In "The Honourable Member" (*Black Orpheus* no. 21), for instance, Kole Omotosho, then a student at the University of Ibadan, told the familiar story of an unambitious farmer whose wife pushes him into politics at great financial risk and then manipulates him into a succession of unscrupulous actions. Unlike the South Africans, however, Omotosho makes his protagonist a figure of fun and an object of ridicule. The candidate delivers an amusingly illiterate political speech, wearing a heavy cloth precariously doubled under his shirt to give him the pot belly expected of successful politicians. Moreover, the story does not end with humiliation and defeat. Instead there is the knowing wink of satire. The wife, the more subtle student of human nature, teaches the husband about "honour":

> It was a lengthy speech telling him he could not continue with that school boy idea of the goodies and the badies. This was not a boy scout game. It was politics. The game for the elders. And she played it for him as it should be played. . . .
> "What of God?" he asked.
> "We will buy a seat in the church," she answered.
> He was almost satisfied. He asked half-heartedly, "What of honour?"
> "Honour? If you do it, Onourable, it is honour." (p. 20)

The dialect was, of course, inconsistent, and the story's end product was perhaps only cynical deprecation, but Omotosho had at least succeeded in contravening the tradition of fatalism established by *Black Orpheus*'s South African writers.

Perhaps the most unique fictions promoted by the first *Black Orpheus* were not, however, in the two carefully wrought and very Western genres of social realism and social satire. Rather, they were the popular, semiliterate romances and adventure stories sold in Onitsha Market and the works of popular Yoruba-language novelist D. O. Fagunwa. The turning point in this movement toward African popular literature was the appearance of Beier's essay "Public Opinion on Lovers: Popular Nigerian Literature Sold in Onitsha Market" in the fourteenth issue (February 1964). Like his later appreciative essay on "Naive Nigerian Art" in number 19 (March 1966), this tentative excursion into popular fiction was written in a spirit of delight mixed with something Beier's critics might call condescension, but the primary tone was of pleasure in the shock of discovering something unconsciously revolutionary, breaking Western narrative conventions and familiar idioms. Beier took particular delight in the freshness of the language:

> The language of these pamphlets owes its peculiar charm and vitality to the fact that most of the authors do not really master the language. Their ideas about syntax and grammar are extremely hazy, though their vocabulary can be surprisingly large. The writers are not too familiar with English idioms and often new and charming expressions are coined, simply because they have misheard and reinterpreted an English phrase. Like:
> . . . head over feels in love
> . . . means of lovelihood
> . . . you are the apple of my heart
> . . . he is the sort of boy who would sell his mother for a dirty mess of pottage.
> Much of this writing has the freshness of innocence. The writer has no idea what is conventional in English language or thought, and he can be startling without intending to.   (no. 14, pp. 5–6)

The common theme of these "Onitsha Market novels," drawn from the clichés of American films and advertising (and in some ways resembling American pulp fiction), was romantic love, apprehended, as in the "naive" art described by Beier in the nineteenth issue, as a sort of cultural and social ideal. Some of its virtues and ideals, however, sounded more like vices, delightful perhaps in their ironic contrast to the ostensible ideals and virtues of the West, but hardly a fair reflection of a society in the throes of a social and cultural transformation.

> The subject matter of these novels and plays can best be described with the West African term "*Highlife*." Highlife is a reaction against the austerity of traditional African life. It is a way of life that believes in pleasure, music, drinking, free love, and ostentatious spending of money. The Onitsha writers speak about this new generation: schoolboys, teachers, drivers, clerks—people who have not yet gone very far in

being "Westernized," but who already find themselves in sharp opposition to traditional ways of life. It is significant that where traditional
people occur in these books they are always the villains and always
ridiculed.   (p. 7)

Beier's response to this new genre was impressionistic and immediate, rather than theoretical. His enthusiasm for the "tremendous
vitality" of these self-taught writers who "grab[bed] hold of the new
life with both hands" (p. 15) was analogous to his enthusiasm for
the highlife musicians, lorry painters, signpainters, and "rubber-cut"
artists. Caught up in the possibilities of this "vast reservoir of un-
trained but creative talent" (p. 16), Beier was rather more excited by
what he saw as unfettered creativity than he was patronizing or
condescending.

Beier's enthusiasm for Nigeria's "most popular writer," D. O.
Fagunwa, though he was "hardly known by name" outside Nigeria,
was analogous. Like Tutuola's, Fagunwa's animistic fairy tales and heroic mythologies were striking, from Beier's point of view, for their
originality:

> The true Yoruba flavour of Fagunwa's work . . . lies not in the mate-
> rial he used, but in the language, in the manner and tone of his story
> telling. . . . Fagunwa has the humour, the rhetoric, the word play, the
> bizarre imagery that Yorubas like and appreciate in their language. . . .
> He uses the language creatively and inventively, constantly adding to the
> traditional stock of imagery and enriching the language.

As an example of Fagunwa's use of language, Beier quoted a metaphor: "Love spread across his face, like palm wine overflowing a cala-
bash" ("Fagunwa, a Yoruba Novelist," *Black Orpheus* no. 17, p. 52).

Two of Fagunwa's narratives were reprinted in *Black Orpheus*,
"Igbako" in the fifteenth issue (August 1964) and "Kako" in the
nineteenth (March 1966), both translated by Wole Soyinka. Again,
however, part at least of the appeal of this material for Beier must
have been its exoticism, its incongruous juxtaposition to Western values. In "Kako," for instance, the hero proposes to desert his mistress
on the eve of their wedding for the sake of a demonic quest after a

talisman that brings power and prosperity. She tries to prevent his leaving:

> Our delay grew longer with the woman's desperate hold, and Kako grew truly angry. His face was transformed as he pulled out his matchet, saying, "Woman of death, witch of a woman seeking to obstruct my path of duty, know you not that before earth destroys the evil-doer, much good has already suffered ruin. Before God ajudges me guilty, I shall pass judgment on your guilt." And so saying, he slashed her amidriffs and it lacked only a little for the woman to be cloven clean in two. She fell to the earth twitching in the final throes of death crying the name of Kako. (p. 21)

Kako's sense of duty is perhaps reminiscent of the Old Testament, but it is otherwise inexplicable and unexpected to a modern Western reader.

Beier had also had remarkable success in encouraging the development of performing artists. They, too, like the market novelists, vernacular novelists, and "naive" artists, found a mode of creativity somewhere on the border between the traditional and the modern, the indigenous and the imported. Beier's successes in promoting, producing, or publicizing dancers, musicians, and theater troupes were exceptional, and have since been widely acknowledged. Oddly, however, he did not much use *Black Orpheus*'s pages to promote these efforts, preferring to publish translations of the Yoruba popular drama through Mbari Publications. Lindfors' retrospective index to the magazine (published in number 22) lists only three such entries under the heading "poetic drama," and no other heading applies to the theater arts. Under "literary criticism," only a few theatrical items are listed, and they review sophisticated modernists such as Clark and Soyinka.

One exception to this imbalance was the closing scene of Duro Ladipo's Yoruba-language tragedy *Oba Koso*, adapted and translated by Beier, which appeared in the fifteenth issue. Ladipo's Yoruba Folk Opera, which had been begun at Beier's Mbari Mbayo Club in Oshogbo, was, like Fagunwa's and Tutuola's fictions and Twins Seven Seven's art work, an important and widely praised effort to join traditional and modern aesthetic idioms—again, as with Fagunwa's novels, expressed in the vernacular. Beier's publication of the final scene of *Oba Koso*—in which Sango, the Yoruba epic hero, goes into exile, kills himself, is mourned by his wife (Oya) and his people (the Oyo), and ultimately is deified—announced to his readers that this work was more than entertainment. Its language merited the careful attention and reflection that one brings to a literary text. By taking *Oba Koso* out of the theater and putting it on the printed page, Beier announced that this was not simply song, but sophisticated verse.

The play's intensity, precision, and subtlety justified such elevation, but it is harsh treatment nevertheless for an editor to hurl his readers unprepared, as Beier did, into the final violent cataclysm of a complex tragedy. The images of Oya's final eulogy are both particularly beautiful and particularly mysterious:

> You are a small bird,
> But your song carries far through the forest.
> You are a small bird,
> Yet husband of all the queens.
>
> .   .   .   .   .   .
>
> The pounded yam will stay fresh for twenty years!
> Don't throw it away.
>
> .   .   .   .   .   .
>
> Let it not be heard that Sango
> Hangs at Koso from the Ayan tree
> From the Ayan tree of which drums are made.
> When the Dundun drum trembles—is it not Sango who speaks?
> When the Dundun drum trembles—is it not Sango who dances?
>
> (p. 45)

Nevertheless, Beier's non-Yoruba readers, though a bit muddled, may also have been anxious for more. That same year, 1964, *Oba Koso* went to the Berlin Theater Festival in West Germany; and 1965 brought a highly successful European tour.

The Critical Voice

It is perhaps an exaggeration to say that Beier "discovered" the writers and artists whose work he published in *Black Orpheus*. Moreover, the word has unpleasant connotations in Africa, told for too long that it had no history, or geography either, until Europeans came to provide them. Some of Beier's best-known protégés, such as Demas Nwoko and Vincent Kofi, already had a fair head of steam when he took up their cause. Others, such as Twins Seven Seven and Salahi, benefited from his critical promotion and attention but produced art impervious to anyone's influence. Finally, it must simply be said that strong-willed, idiosyncratic artists such as Awoonor, Clark, Nwoko, Soyinka, and others ought not to be remembered as "made men" owing their success to one early patron. It is hard to believe that someone with Soyinka's will, Nwoko's resourcefulness, or indeed simply with the talent that they all possessed would not have been able to create something beautiful, moving, provocative, and subtle without the prodding of even so imaginative a middleman as Beier. Beier seems undeniably to have had some influence with some artists and writers over the direction of their work, to have helped make some reputations, to have brought to light some otherwise neglected forms of creativity. His universal and far-reaching importance as editor and publisher of *Black Orpheus*, however, was probably in his dominance of the magazine's critical function, its role as arbiter of quality and analyst of the dominant trends, social implications, and core of representation in these new works of art, many of which were not easy of access to even the most sophisticated reader.

That Beier's was the dominant voice in *Black Orpheus*'s reviews and critical articles for most of the period of his editorial tenure was not apparent to any but a few readers—those who knew his pseudonyms. It appeared, rather, that the criticism of African writers and artists was being left largely to African critics, including, of course, the indomitable Sangodare Akanji. A fussy or precise reader might perhaps have noticed that Sangodare Akanji's name usually fell under neither of the two classes of signatures commonly appended to *Black Orpheus* articles—those listed on the masthead and those identified at the end of the magazine in the notes on contributors—a clue perhaps intended to suggest his real identity to the perceptive. Moreover, Akanji was well known in the Oshogbo area as Beier's name in the Sango cult; Omidiji Aragbabalu was also, Beier reports, a name associated with him in Oshogbo.[46] Perhaps, finally, one ought not to care whether a reviewer is African or non-African as long as his analysis is illuminating. One *ought*, however, to know when a reviewer is writing about a friend, associate, editorial colleague, or, as was twice the case, his wife. And one ought to know when an African magazine's critical dimension is dominated by expatriates, as, for a period at least, *Black Orpheus*'s was.[47]

A Western critic was on somewhat tenuous ground in judging these new non-Western writers, as is testified to by the approach that they were sometimes inclined to take. Paul Theroux's explanation for his critical scrupulosity in his pathbreaking analysis of the new anglophone African poets, "Voices Out of the Skull" (no. 20, pp. 41–58), for example, presupposes the delicacy of this situation:

> There are shortcomings in some of these poems: the language is sometimes stilted and archaic, the pathos pre-fabricated, the metrics diffuse, and the hyperemotionality hard to bear. I have not concentrated on the faults of the poems—one can easily be preoccupied with such things. People grow, the facade falls away, and nothing the critic says has much to do with the speed with which these affectations are dropped. Usually I have tried to find the very best examples of what I supposed to be the writer's intention, and then concentrated on his best writing.
>
> (p. 41)

The slight would have been easier to bear, perhaps, had it been made directly; Theroux's offhand deprecation left open the possibility that he might have said harsher things. Worse yet, he did not even keep his promise to concentrate on the virtues of five of the six poets reviewed (J. P. Clark, he had maintained from the first, would be a special case, meriting criticism). For all six poets, there was as much criticism as praise.

Moreover, the excitement over Theroux's casual slight made it easy to overlook the more significant thesis of his essay, that these poets, however African their material, shared a pervasive postwar Western theme—artistic and political individualism. Their theme, he wrote, common to all good poetry, was "freedom, the liberating experiences of reading and writing well" (p. 41). In Dennis Brutus's poetry, for instance, the individualism was starkly political, a protest against a system that uses black people as "stinking lubrication that helps the huge cogs of the economy to run smoothly" (p. 43). Brutus's poetry was remarkable not for its clarity or stylistic innovation, but for its political conviction:

> Brutus is whipped and he lashes back furiously. It is true that sometimes his punches are wild, sometimes he misses . . . but he swings enough times for us to see what he is aiming at. The man being stretched on the rack will be more concerned with his own pain than with the ingenious construction of the instrument of torture. (ibid.)

In Kofi Awoonor's poetry, Theroux saw not the public dimension always so insistently there—the struggle of a people to recreate their traditional cultural matrix in a new context. He saw only the individual's struggle for self-assertion in the face of philosophical and moral uncertainty, again familiar postwar Western themes:

> The conflict in the early poems comes when he is trying to "get born" without first dying—he seeks birth through desire, sexuality, excess. The reminder of death predominates over all our physical acts, so sexuality inevitably leads us back to thoughts of death. . . . A complete acceptance of death is not achieved even at the end of the book, although at the end we are a lot closer to discovering what it is in death that will redeem us or the poet. . . .
>
> Awoonor-Williams is waiting for the strengthened and confident second self to emerge and make an assertion. Until this happens the two selves will continue to grapple, the soul will shrink and expand, the flesh will weaken and tumesce. (pp. 49–50)

Of Clark, Theroux frankly confessed: "If [he] has a 'general theme,' it has escaped me"; but still Theroux made an effort to understand subjectively, as Beier had in his analysis of Vincent Kofi. And again, Theroux's theme was the poet's presumed self-absorption: "Ordeal. Ending on the edge of new agonies. Beginning again. And the poet wrapped only in nakedness goes on, deliberately, mostly conscious because he is half-carried by the nightmare winds, half carries himself with his own homemade, wild, tangle-wood tales" (p. 53).

Theroux, at any rate, was a well-informed observer of the modern African cultural renaissance. In the previous issue, however, Beier had commissioned Martin Esslin, a drama critic for the BBC in London who confessed himself utterly unfamiliar with modern African culture, to write a major review of the leading African playwrights, Soyinka and Clark, whose plays had come out in Oxford University Press editions. Beier's choice of Esslin, of course, presumed literary universality. In his article "Two African Playwrights" (no. 19, pp. 33–39), however, Esslin unobligingly admitted that he did not really believe that one could understand literature in most cases without a knowledge of "social conventions," most of which vary from one society to another.

Nevertheless, Esslin was led again and again in his essay to make judgments about the level of intensity in tragic situations whose social implications he did not understand. Of Clark's *The Masquerade*, he wrote, "The central issue of the play, whether it is indeed a sacrilege for a young girl to get married to the son of a mother who died in childbirth after having committed adultery, is difficult to grasp for an outsider" (p. 36). Of *Song of a Goat*, Esslin wrote, "The motivation of the tragedy, which is simply the husband's inability to engender a child, is far too simple and unoriginal to support the weight of full-scale tragedy across the generations. Moreover, the wife's seduction of the husband's younger brother is also, for my admittedly quite differently conditioned feelings, far too clumsily straightforward" (p. 37). The "husband's inability to engender a child" is "too simple and unoriginal to support the weight of full-scale tragedy"? In *Africa*, where parenthood is more important than wealth, and impotence is a calamity beyond naming? Esslin's ruminations simply show that his "quite differently conditioned feelings" were precisely what made it impossible for him to judge.

Further indicative of Esslin's incapacity to judge these works is his comment on their use of the English language as a medium of expression. He seems simply to have made the familiar uninformed assumption that indigenous African languages are national languages. He writes:

> I am, in my own mind, not quite clear as to the reasons that prompt African playwrights to use English in preference to their own rich and highly poetic languages. Is it that they themselves are more at home in English? In that case there might be strong arguments for concentrating on a realistic treatment of the life of English-speaking Africans. This would enable them to use an actual language, or different shades and idioms as spoken by different stratas of that particular—and surely immensely important—segment of their society. Or is it that African playwrights use English because they want a larger, more universal audience? . . . Or is it that, English being the language of the educated classes in Africa—or at least in ex-British Africa—and education spreading ever wider, English will become the *lingua franca* of educated Africans? . . . I, personally, do not know which of these assumptions is true. I merely throw them out as possible starting points for debate.
>
> (p. 35)

In fairness, Esslin had guessed many of the major issues involved in the use of English by African writers, but his ignorance of the history of the debate and the practical dimensions of the problem is obvious, and Beier's readers must have thought it quite odd to be presented in such an influential African magazine with pure speculation about an issue whose parameters were well known, immediate, and unambiguous. Beier's publication of Esslin, of course, was meant primarily as a symbolic announcement. A major Western critic was willing to devote a lengthy critical essay to these new writers: modern African drama had arrived and was to be taken seriously. More goods had gotten across the cultural border from Africa to the West, and

Beier had found an influential advocate there. What matter if another advocate might have understood the character of the merchandise better.

Like Theroux, Esslin, and Beier himself, O. R. Dathorne, who served as Beier's "reviews editor" after 1964, looked at these new African writers from within the framework of the dominant Western thematic prototype, the artist as spokesman for individualism. In a review of Soyinka's *Kongi's Harvest* in number 21 (April 1967), for instance, Dathorne wrote:

> It is the greatest pitfall of the African writer, and he constantly battles with it—the need to disregard tribe and create individuals. . . . [External] realities of contemporary African life can therefore be best experienced in terms of personal bewilderment. Where Wole Soyinka's *Kongi's Harvest* fails is that it never creates a single individual to express this.

Soyinka's drama, Dathorne said, "has only managed to create types. It is nevertheless entertaining theater, even at times disconcerting, but the overall effect is not one that makes any kind of universal impact. The effect is purely local" (pp. 60–61). Again, the presumption was that literature ought to be independent of the "local," of "social circumstance," and ought to aim, instead, at the creation of alienated individuals, standing in lonely opposition to their societies.

In consequence, Dathorne's critical judgments of new literature implied a clear hierarchy—literature that, as Erich Auerbach might have said, was long on perspective, on temporality, on point of view, on "the unexpressed background quality" (that is, modern Western literature) was superior to the other kind of literature defined by Auerbach, where meaning is "unmistakable," "unitemporal," free from the problematic subtleties of individual perception.[48] Literature that traces the progress of one character's lonely rejection is superior to literature that sees society as an organic whole and the individual as a part, functional or dysfunctional, of that whole.

Thus, when *A Man of the People* appeared, Dathorne saw it as superior to Achebe's earlier accomplishments, including *Things Fall*

Apart and *Arrow of God*. In his *Black Orpheus* review (no. 21, p. 61), Dathorne wrote:

> With this novel Achebe is beginning to show that he has serious claims to our attention. . . . For the first time he has shown himself to be aware of the difficulties of method, that novel-telling is *not* story-telling, that events change, assume different proportions with their shift into the future. He has not fallen for the easy line; when Odili turns against Chief Nanga it is for personal reasons not public high-mindedness; Odili can be taken as a type, the representative of the younger generation in their dramatic confrontation with the older, but he is very much an individual. (p. 61)

A Man of the People represented "a development of the West African novel, along with *Danda* and *The Interpreters* and T. M. Aluko's early short stories; in many ways a break with the whole tradition of creativity; a character, a person is laughing at a whole society." Dathorne added:

> Here there is no attempt to smother all distinction but to come to grips with the serious problems that face African writers; how to create individuals, how to stand *outside* the culture, how to ensure the flow of the movement of life from experience to paper. Here the past is not venerated but is seen as a series of groping, crumbling efforts towards the present. (p. 61)

His review of Okigbo's *Limits* in number 15 (August 1964) similarly praised that work for its dramatization of the individual's disaffected quest for self-affirmation. "Exploring the penetralia of the unconscious state of non-being," he wrote, it "narrates the progress towards *nirvana*" (p. 59).

Beier's own reviews, as we have seen, began by favoring *négritude* as an ideology and surrealism as an aesthetic. He moved beyond that to an interest in fostering an intellectual movement counter to *négritude*; however, he always favored an analogous complexity of method and relevance of subject matter. In art as well as literature, he preferred work that seemed to him to be open to the depths of the psyche, as perceived by Jung. He cared very little about traditional poetic structure or diction, conventional syntax, or strict logical consistency of image. Least of all did he care about straightforward representation. Beier's impressionistic method of critical response instead sought emotional identification with the artist as a sort of protagonist in a private psychological drama. Thus, J. P. Clark's "harassed, tormented, and irrepressible" poetry; Christopher Okigbo's and Kofi Awoonor's complex allegories of personal and societal spiritual rebirth; and Wole Soyinka's elusive phenomenological imagery · were particularly appealing, as were the narratives of the unschooled Onitsha Market novelists, whose literature was open to the depths of the psyche, in theory at least, simply because of an accidental underdevelopment of the mechanisms of artistic restraint and convention.

In attempting to define Beier's editorial leanings, this study has thus far concentrated on one kind of review: the cultural "booster article." Strictly complimentary, these were meant to promote rather than criticize the work of new artists and writers, protégés either of the Mbari Clubs, *Black Orpheus*, or Mbari Publications. They are useful, therefore in defining the positive dimensions of Beier's aesthetic, but they do not give a complete picture.

Beier's own early articles had been more informative than critical, but he soon began to write more pointed reviews of new West African material, usually behind the shield of one or another pseudonym. Tutuola's *The Brave African Huntress* was reviewed in the fourth issue (October 1958), Achebe's *No Longer At Ease* in the eighth (1960–61?—under the pseudonym Omidiji Aragbabalu), Ekwensi's *The Passport of Mallam Ilia* and *The Drummer Boy* in the ninth (June 1961), and *Jagua Nana* in the tenth (1961–62?). The criticism was restrained, however, and more than compensated for by Beier's overriding enthusiasm. Obi Okonkwo was perhaps, Beier admitted, a bit less "colourful," less "memorable" than his namesake in *Things Fall Apart*, but *No Longer At Ease* had strengths other than characterization, and here, at least, Achebe had ceased trying to "explain" or "justify" Africa to Europe. However, one could not help but notice that *No Longer At Ease* also initiated another change for Achebe, from a celebration and explication of traditional life to a bleak exposure of modern Africa's disjunction from its traditional mores, a theme that Beier had elsewhere been inclined to favor.

Beier admitted *Jagua Nana*'s chief fault, its improbable ending, but defended the novel in advance against a criticism leveled by many Nigerians at Ekwensi's first novel—that it was guilty of "representing them in a bad light" (p. 68). Such criticism of a writer could not be justified; Ekwensi had accurately depicted his characters, their world, their circumstances; and he had "refrained from drawing any morals." Moreover, "nobody in his right senses would assume that all people in Lagos are like that" (ibid.). However, the chief thrust of the article was its rhapsody of praise for Ekwensi's ability to catch the moral and social atmosphere that Beier would later describe in "Public Opinion on Lovers" (no. 14, pp. 4–16).

Beier saw the heroine of *Jagua Nana*, for instance, as an embodiment of the world of highlife, and again the chief attraction of that world for him seems to have been in its ironic contrast to the "dreary morality" imported from the West: "Jagua is a magnificent woman. She may be a harlot, but she is also an impressive woman full of warmth and charm. The author brings us completely under her spell and we fail to apply to her the dreary morality of our everyday lives" (p. 68). Beier similarly admired the character of the grandmother in Clark's drama *Ozidi* for her humanity, her intensity, and her amorality—the way in which she stands apart from the conventions of Western morality. In his review in number 22 (August 1967), Beier wrote (under the pseudonym Omidiji Aragbabalu) of the grandmother: "She is evil but magnificent. She stops at absolutely nothing" (p. 60).

If such a perspective, valuing the autonomous or disaffected individual, dominated *Black Orpheus*'s literary criticism, still it should be pointed out that Beier was not averse to allowing other points of view.[49] Number 17 (June 1965), for example, contained Abiola Irele's major critical essay about Achebe, differing in approach both from Beier's earlier article and Dathorne's later one. Irele saw Achebe's novels as classic tragedy, which implied "the working out in men's lives of a rigorous fatality that transcends the individual's ability to comprehend or to arrest its pre-ordained course of events." He emphasized not rejection of social convention but the fulfillment of traditional roles in a society under external stress. Thus, from Irele's point of view, *No Longer At Ease* is the *least* successful of the three novels and Achebe deserves credit in general primarily for his important social theme: "the tragic consequences of the African encounter with Europe" and "the disarray in the African consciousness that has followed" (p. 24). Achebe's truly remarkable creations are Ezeulu in *Arrow of God*, for his transcendence of the traditional code of behavior in a time of externally imposed change, and Okonkwo in *Things Fall Apart*, for his excessive conformity to that code, amounting in the end to a sociopathic perversion of it.

Beier, Dathorne, Theroux, and other critical writers sometimes showed a preference for the disillusioned styles of European modernism or for literary protagonists whose characters expressed ethical ambiguity or social dysfunction. Nevertheless, they were by no means blind to other features of these works, as Beier had shown in his review of *No Longer At Ease*, and again in his review of Awoonor's *Rediscovery* under the pseudonym Omidiji Aragbabalu in number 17 (June 1965).

Moreover, Beier's efforts to see similarities between Western literature and the new African, Caribbean, and Afro-American literatures were part of his larger purposes: bringing together Africa and the black diaspora, and promoting this literature to the wider world and to African readers schooled on the Western classics. Beier's success in educating anglophone Africa to the intellectual currents of francophone Africa and black America, and in promoting the works of new anglophone writers, both within and outside of Africa, is perhaps a primary legacy of his editorship of *Black Orpheus*. During his editorship, moreover, *Black Orpheus* had gone beyond even these ambitious objectives. It had become more a sort of international literary marketplace than a one-man smuggling ring. In the pages of the magazine one might read an influential South African critic (Mphahlele) on one of black America's best-known writers (Langston Hughes; no. 9, pp. 16–21). One might be introduced by a West In-

dian critic (Arthur Drayton) to the work of a new West Indian poet
(Cliff Lashley; no. 22, pp. 49–53). One might read new African
critics such as Abiola Irele or Theo Vincent (both later editors of
Black Orpheus). One might see a whole world of black literary peri-
odicals reviewed— Gerald Moore on the Ghanaian review *Okyeame*
(no. 10, pp. 66–67; and no. 14, pp. 60–61); Remi Jones on *Nigeria
Magazine* (no. 10, p. 71); Dathorne on *Bim* from Barbados, *Présence
Africaine* from Paris, and *Transition* from Kampala (no. 15, p. 60).
One might, for that matter, read essays that went beyond the circumscribed ends of what had been at first intended merely as a modest
literary review: as when Beier's ambitious article about traditional
Ibo and Yoruba art in number 8 (pp. 46–50) sought in a systematic
comparison to define the two cultures as well; or as in number 18
(pp. 60–61) when Dathorne took on J. P. Clark for his indictment of
the United States (*America, Their America*) and V. S. Naipaul for his
indictment of India (*An Area of Darkness*) in a head-on, *ad hominem*
attack (Dathorne described Clark and Naipaul as "two people making a song and dance about something that is really intrinsically at
odds within themselves" [p. 60], both "anxious to do a kind of so-
ciological striptease" [p. 61]).

Demise and Reincarnation

After 1965, however, although *Black Orpheus* was stronger than ever, Beier's influence among Nigeria's intellectual community had begun to wane. Some, who thought his methods highhanded, were hostile; others felt that the time had passed for one clever outsider to pull the strings; others simply began to concentrate exclusively on independent activities of their own. As Michael Crowder, editor of *Nigeria Magazine* from 1960 to 1963, has observed, "It's a very great art in Africa to know when to get out."[50] Perhaps Beier recognized that times had changed and that, as John Thompson said of him, "he had run out of borders"; but he was too strong-willed and successful to let go easily.

Mbari Ibadan, meanwhile, began to come apart, with Beier resigning as president of the club and editor of Mbari Publications in 1965 and concentrating on the Mbari Mbayo Club in Oshogbo (whose production of *Oba Koso* was then beginning its European tour). Both Beier and Soyinka felt that a proposed move to a new expensive building would ruin Mbari Ibadan and they left it in the hands of J. P. Clark, Demas Nwoko, Christopher Okigbo, and others, who modified its aims somewhat. Mbari's impetus in the performing arts was taken over by Demas Nwoko's theatrical experiments, while Beier's own interest shifted to Wole Soyinka's independent productions. "In Oshogbo," Beier writes, "I felt I had become *too* involved. I felt that [Duro] Ladipo [see p. 55] needed to be on his own entirely; but it was difficult to withdraw from either him or the artist group; in the end it could only be done by actually leaving Nigeria and moving to the other end of the globe."[51] Political events, meanwhile, moved inexorably toward civil war. At this moment of impending cataclysm, in 1966, Beier prepared to leave Nigeria. It was widely assumed that *Black Orpheus* would not survive his departure.

In fact, in a 1966 discussion of the magazine with Andrew Salkey, Beier and Moore expressed only mild grief at *Black Orpheus*'s presumed demise.[52] "Regret," Moore said, was the primary feeling, but perhaps after all there was "a kind of logic" in the magazine's death. Perhaps, separated from its original founders, *Black Orpheus* might become institutionalized, deadened. And at any rate, Beier added, perhaps the period for such a magazine had passed. *Black Orpheus* had achieved its original purpose and seemed no longer to be needed: "We need several different kinds of magazines now, . . . but we don't need a propaganda magazine any longer, because African literature has more publicity, at the moment, than it ought to have. . . . British publishers are snapping up African writing too fast, and very often bad writing, so . . . there's no point in boosting it." *Black Orpheus* ought perhaps, Beier suggested, to be succeeded by two journals. One would be a "very cheap and simply produced poetry magazine, where a young poet can see his work published within three weeks, and will not, necessarily, be given a world-wide distribution." The other magazine would be broader and more rigorous than *Black Orpheus*. "What you really need," Beier said, "is a really highly critical journal, . . . something that will become a tool for all the institutes of African studies, and all the English departments in Africa that are teaching African literature, . . . where a very hot kind of critical standard will be applied." Perhaps, Beier suggested, the magazine should even abandon *Black Orpheus*'s emphasis on what Okigbo had called "the black mystique"; perhaps it should simply be an international cultural journal, publishing anyone who met its high standards—something edited in Africa, but not strictly African in scope—to be called, perhaps, not *Black Orpheus*, but simply *Orpheus*.[53]

In spite of the universal assumption that it would die with Ulli Beier's departure, however, *Black Orpheus* did not do so, and Beier's editorial successors, though not entirely sympathetic with his ideas, had somewhat similar plans for the magazine. When Abiola Irele returned to Nigeria from Paris in 1966, he and J. P. Clark got together in Lagos to discuss the matter and decided to try to talk Mbari Ibadan, to whom ownership of the magazine had devolved, into reviving it. Clark and Irele held a series of meetings with the Mbari

committee early in 1967 to formulate plans for continuing the journal or otherwise establishing some kind of successor: "In fact," Irele
recalls, "we had thought of doing something else, that is of starting a
new paper that would incorporate *Black Orpheus*." The new periodical, "to be called something like *Mbari Review*," would enclose
Black Orpheus as a middle section devoted exclusively to poetry.
Eventually, however, these plans had to be scrapped, in favor of the
less complicated expedient of simply continuing the magazine with
its old title and format. Once Mbari had formally named them as coeditors, Irele and Clark did, however, decide to change the magazine's overriding editorial goals. They hoped, that is, to make the
magazine a vehicle for the "very hot kind of critical standard" that
Beier had called for. *Black Orpheus* would abandon its role as a booster
of African culture: "We felt that there was no point any more in pre-
senting African literature as new literature that had to be defended and
all that—*Black Orpheus* could now serve as simply a critical journal,
like any other, this literature having more or less arrived."[54] The magazine did not, however, embrace Beier's most ambitious idea—to abandon its emphasis on the black diaspora; in fact, if anything it became
more specialized in its appeal to Africans, since Clark and Irele began
to give each new number a single thematic focus, usually of pointed
relevance to the contemporary African creative scene.

The new editors' managerial plans were equally ambitious. Irele
and Clark were anxious to guarantee the magazine's permanence
with proper distribution, proper accounting, and a permanent staff.
They realized that their African audience would always come from a
small intellectual elite. Subscription receipts, therefore, would be
limited. They needed either substantial advertising revenue or external support. Longmans of Nigeria had helped Beier, but they informed the new editors that they could not continue to do so. The
Farfield Foundation, whose African activities had by then been taken
over by Frank Platt, offered to pay for a permanent, full-time editor.
Clark encouraged Irele to accept the job, but Irele decided that he
could not spare the time from his own writing. Shortly thereafter the
controversy at *Encounter* revealed Farfield's substantial CIA support,

however, and although the effect of that revelation on *Black Orpheus* was minimal, Irele was glad that he had decided not to pursue the Farfield suggestion.[55]

Another imaginative effort to secure outside funding was equally unsuccessful: Clark and Irele approached the federal government and offered to "sell a substantial part of . . . every edition" to the foreign ministry, who might "then distribute it to various embassies and missions around the world." When that idea miscarried, they fell back on Mbari's modest funds, but arranged for Aig Higo, an associate at Mbari and Heinemann's Nigerian representative, to serve as managing editor. Heinemann would take over distribution from Longmans. Like the coeditors themselves, Higo was unfortunately already badly overextended, however, and the distribution of the magazine "was never properly done."[56] Higo, Clark, and Irele, scraping together what time they could from other activities, were assisted only by a clerk at Mbari Ibadan, whose services were only occasionally available. The first issue of the magazine, now a collector's item, was poorly produced and badly printed.

Momentum and Redirection: The Focus of the Second *Black Orpheus*

The combination of the new editors' redirection of the magazine and the momentum left over from Beier's final years made the first new issues (renumbered as volume 2 by Clark and Irele) really exceptional. In spite of the civil war, the editors put together issues at once controversial and scholarly, full of new things yet carrying on in the best tradition of Beier's editorship. Volume 2, number 1, for example, contained an obituary announcement and tribute to Christopher Okigbo, killed a few months earlier in the Nsukka sector fighting on the secessionist side. That Clark, a federalist, could print such a tribute indicates the extent of *Black Orpheus*'s effort to be regarded as neutral. Okigbo had, moreover, left his last powerful poem, "Path of Thunder," written before the outbreak of war and remarkably prophetic of the turn of events, in Higo's hands before leaving for Biafra.[57] Well-connected in the government and aware of the various maneuvers during the Ironsi regime (Ibo-hegemonist and anti-Ibo, pro-unification and anti-unification, and so on), Okigbo had also shown the poem to Beier but had decided not to publish it at that time for fear it might be inflammatory.[58] Its appearance in *Black Orpheus* 2, no. 1 was a dramatic announcement of the new *Black Orpheus*'s ambitious aesthetic aspirations and of its intention to remain neutral. The section entitled "Elegy for Slit Drum," for instance, seemed to stand as a stark commentary on the bitterness of the war. A musical, ironic passage, its one-word refrain ("condolences") was as if in formal ritual of apology to the gods for all that had come to pass:

> CONDOLENCES . . . from our swollen lips laden with condolences:
>   The mythmaker accompanies us
> The rattles are here with us
> Condolences from our split tongue of the slit drum condolences

One tongue full of fire
One tongue full of stone
   Condolences from the twin-lips of our drum parted in condolences

. . . .

We should forget the names
we should bury the date
the dead should bury the dead—condolences . . .

(2, no. 1, pp. 8, 10)

Under the heading "Poems Prophesying War," along with Okigbo's poem, Clark and Irele also published Ken Tsaro-Wiwa's poems, again from the Biafran perspective, though they were more personal, an emotional comment on the irrationality and random cruelty of war.

To further add to the controversiality of the first issue, Irele persuaded Clark to overcome his reluctance and publish "The Legacy of Caliban," a major critical essay of his own, in the new magazine. It represented an absolute about-face for *Black Orpheus*, questioning the dominance of European literary aesthetics, European languages, and European arbiters of quality in modern African literature. The African writer, Clark argued, had been required to please two audiences, the European and the African; and the European, for political and economic reasons, had monopolized the arrangement:

> For a variety of reasons the European sector has been more articulate and of overwhelming influence upon African writers. Jealously, it holds fast to its claim of being the original owner and therefore the natural custodian of the European language the African is using in his works. These in turn belong to the tradition of literate literature which again goes back to Europe. The very machinery for publication and distribution of African works is to be found chiefly in the capital cities of Europe. Then, of course, there is the old economic supremacy. . . . Finally, there are the agents of this ubiquitous complex operating right in the midst of the African sector, and ironically the scouts and promoters of new talents are often to be found among their ranks. The net effect is the imposition of their standards upon African writing.
>
> (2, no. 1, p. 28)

The reference to *Black Orpheus*'s old regime was unmistakable, as was the announcement of a radical break with the magazine's critical emphasis. Complexity of language was not to be the supreme standard of quality, as if any literate African were a *rara avis*; and there were to be no more left-handed compliments to alleged primitives who discovered an original aesthetic idiom all unawares. A number of writers enshrined in the literary pantheon would therefore have to be reevaluated; many of Moore and Beier's favorites came in for sharp criticism, among them Tutuola, the Onitsha Market novelists, Okara, and Joyce Cary. The approach was not exclusively critical. For example, praise was accorded Tutuola's "natural gifts," his "faithful-[ness] to his vision," and his "complete lack of self-consciousness." But Beier's brand of praise was attacked. Tutuola was to be admired in spite of, not because of, his linguistic eccentricities:

> Here is no original language as such, but one found everywhere in Nigeria in the letters and "compositions" written among a vast group of people who for various reasons have not proceeded beyond a certain stage of school. It is a level of English considered "vulgar," half literate by all sections of Nigerian society, and it is for this reason parents disapprove of their children reading Tutuola!   (p. 37)

Clark added:

> "Naivete," made so much of by the adulators of Mr. Tutuola and incidentally by the followers of the Onitsha market novelette, is not enough; language has to be "moulded" by the artist with skill and consciousness. Mr. Tutuola, who lacks both of these qualities in his early work, sacrifices something of his natural charm and power by trying to acquire them in his later works. It is as if the Onitsha market novelist were to aspire to the equipment of an Achebe! . . . Such predilection and weakness do not make him "purely African," and far from contributing to the man's magic fascination for us as a compulsive story-teller, actually detract from it.   (pp. 37–38)

Dylan Thomas's mild reference to *The Palm-Wine Drinkard* as "a brief, thronged, grisly, and bewitching story . . . written in English by a West African" was seized upon ardently as a "first public admission of prejudice by a prominent literary figure in Britain," on the grounds that the final phrase was gratuitous and condescending.

Highest praise, in contrast, should be reserved for a writer such as Achebe, who could serve almost as a "highly accomplished notary," slipping easily between the extremes of West Africa's linguistic schizophrenia—between traditional proverb and standard English, everyday language and poetic diction, pidgin and the "para-English" of black colonial interpreters. The task of the African writer was no easy one:

> The African writer thus occupies a position not unlike that of the ambidexterous man, a man placed at the unique and advantageous position of being able to draw strength from two separate equal sources. His is a gift of tongues. So equipped, he should be able to meet the exacting demands of both sectors of his audience. But if he fails he will end up like Caliban crying: "I shall be pinch'd to death"—and goodness knows the critics can be vicious, even like Prospero and his pack of spirits forever hounding Caliban. (p. 39)

The new *Black Orpheus* meant to specialize in careful, dispassionate scholarly work as well; and volume 2, number 1, therefore, featured an article by Nigerian composer and musicologist Akin Euba that offered a rigorous, eloquently straightforward definition of the African musical idiom (pp. 44–47). Musicology was a relatively new subject for the magazine and emphasized the editors' determination to broaden *Black Orpheus*'s range of interest, as did their commissioning a report by Jamaican writer Lindsay Barrett on Demas Nwoko's efforts to create a practical modern African architectural style. The article did not match Euba's for clarity or balance, and the illustrative photographs were poorly executed and reproduced, but Clark and Irele did deserve credit for championing Nwoko's pioneering work (pp. 40–41). Evidence of the editors' determination to maintain Beier's pan-Africanism was a review by a young Nigerian secondary school teacher, Akin Osunbunmi, of Okot p'Bitek's "Song of Lawino"—though again the critical style was immature. The most propitious item of all in the new magazine, however, was probably an announcement of Clark and Irele's plans for "the year's fare" (p. 15). The next two issues, in a departure from Beier's format, were to focus on single themes: 2, no. 2 would be "a special issue on traditional African literature"; 2, no. 3 would be "political."

If doubts lingered about *Black Orpheus*'s future, the appearance of the second new number, nearly on time (dated June–September 1968) and impressive in its contents, if shabby of aspect, set them to rest.[59] Irele, who by now had taken up residence at the Institute of African Studies in Legon, Ghana, tapped the institute's director, J. H. Nketia, for an article on Akan drumming every bit as impressive as Euba's essay on music in 2, no. 1. The article was not pathbreaking, perhaps, since Nketia's work was already somewhat known, but it was absolutely exhaustive, combining clarity of expression with scholarly rigor. Its description of the expressiveness of traditional drumming, of the place of drumming in traditional society, of how the drummers were able to encode and transmit tonal speech, and of the tenacious memory and keen perception required of a good drummer was inspirational rather than analytic.

The remainder of the second new issue continued Nketia's effort to map, analyze, and preserve, through careful scholarship, the topography of traditional culture. Robert Armstrong, the American scholar directing the Institute of African Studies at Ibadan; Wanda Abimbola, a lecturer and researcher at the University of Lagos; and Clark himself offered extensive translations of three important traditional Nigerian literatures: the Idoma, Yoruba, and Ijaw. Clark's work with the Ozidi saga, of course, had been an important source of material and literary influence in his own writings. Armstrong and Abimbola, former colleagues at Ibadan, had more traditional backgrounds as linguists, and Armstrong's articles featured the impedimenta of fussy scholarly footnotes. Armstrong's and Abimbola's translations were printed side by side with the Idoma and Yoruba originals, but Clark's appeared only in English translation, because of difficulties in finding a typescript suitable for reproducing the Ijaw text. The only vaguely controversial note to that issue was a letter objecting to some small matters of interpretation in Clark's earlier "Legacy of Caliban" (p. 45).

The third issue (undated but appearing early in 1969), however, was again remarkably controversial. While the civil war continued to grind toward its inevitable conclusion, straining relations among African intellectuals, Clark and Irele printed a special issue on politics and literature. Again the list of contributors—Ali Mazrui, Ezekiel Mphahlele, Gerald Moore, Okot p'Bitek—and the breadth of approach and subject were exceptional. The quality of the issue, however, hid the fact that it, too, was subject to the climate of growing political acrimony.

Gerald Moore, for instance, who had contributed to Beier's final issue a long essay that sought to define a common naturalistic theme in black poetry, was induced by Clark to write an article entitled "Poetry and the Nigerian Crisis" (2, no. 3, pp. 10–13). Moore's theme, as he wrote with reference to Clark's poem "Casualties," was the political astuteness and detachment of Nigeria's poets. "Such writing," Moore commented, "carries us into the very skin of the present hour. The task of reconciliation, hardest of all, awaits them. But when so much else has failed Nigeria, her poets have not, I believe, failed her" (p. 13). In addition to Clark, Moore particularly praised Okigbo for seeing in the events preceding the war "omens of a more radical crisis" (p. 11) and Soyinka for his "ironic impressionistic poems . . . that get at the meaninglessness of war" and his criticism of the "glib optimism" that had made conflict possible (pp. 13 and 10, respectively). Moore, writing from the borrowed perspective of J. P. Clark, the only one of the major Nigerian poets "in a position to speak of events which have taken a new plunge of horror" (p. 13), could not have guessed that Soyinka, languishing in a cell in Lagos, would later condemn Clark in *The Man Died* for waging a single-handed campaign to discredit him. No evidence of such a campaign surfaced in *Black Orpheus* 2, no. 3; nevertheless, in retrospect Moore's praise for the highmindedness of the Nigerian poets certainly rings hollow.

The other three articles on politics and literature, Okot p'Bitek's "The Poet in Politics" (pp. 29–33), Ali Mazrui's "The Patriot as an Artist" (pp. 14–23), and Ezekiel Mphahlele's "Writers and Commitment" (pp. 34–39), for the most part avoided present conflicts. Mazrui's article was speculative, Mphahlele's was theoretical, and Okot's considered only the poet's traditional political role in East Africa. Mazrui's article crowded together a succession of value judgments and broad generalizations, and in one offhand aside seconded Clark's criticism of Tutuola and his Western admirers: "*The Palm-Wine Drinkard* was widely applauded abroad as a great achievement in creative fantasy and unusual diction. Yet, many African critics regarded the external applause as an attempt to patronize naive attempts by an under-educated African" (p. 16).

Mphahlele set himself the academic task of reading the works of a number of more or less Marxist theories of literary commitment (Trotsky's *Literature and Revolution*, Lukács's *The Meaning of Contemporary Realism*, G. V. Plekhanov's *Art and Social Life*, and John Mander's *The Writer and Commitment*) and considering their implications for Africa. His conclusion, however, was provocative. He praised the Afro-American poets and the *négritude* poets, as well as Awoonor, Brutus, Dipoko, Okara, and others for their strong political and social themes. Although he stopped short of agreeing with Trotsky that all art should be "virtually collectivist" and "incompatible with pessimism" (p. 39), he hoped that African literature would not follow the modernist prototype:

> No black hero in African fiction is stricken with *angst* which makes him dash about like a trapped fly. Perhaps he is the typical hero of western literature, perhaps he is the supreme example of modern man as modern literature sees him, because the western world today is a disintegrated because a differentiated one. So it produces disintegrated personalities. We have not yet created societies like this in Africa, and the heroes of our fiction cannot yet be seen as possessing what one may call the intensive "other individuality" of a Kafka or a Camus hero. The African hero is still very much part of a communal world. (p. 39)

Okot p'Bitek's "The Poet in Politics" defined, as had Nketia's article on Akan drumming, the important political role of traditional artists—in this case the Acholi poets. Their songs of abuse, insult, sarcasm, or of praise, celebration, or jingoistic nationalism set a precedent for poets taking an active hand in politics and demonstrated how the colonial order had, in distorting traditional authority, petrified traditional poems, turning them into museum pieces rather than living forms (pp. 29–33).

Along with the first number of volume two and the last few issues under Beier, these two thematic issues of *Black Orpheus* (2, nos. 2 and 3) constituted the magazine's zenith. It had attained nearly all that it had set out to attain: it was controversial, scholarly, imaginative, independent, broad in scope, and influential; it had succeeded in making a name abroad both for African literature and for itself. It had also gradually abandoned its propagandistic approach. It is particularly ironic, therefore, that at this point, with exceptional promise of success in spite of the enormous practical difficulties brought on by the civil war, *Black Orpheus* began to come apart at the seams. Irele and Clark had continued, after their earlier failures, to look for ways to find permanent support: practical problems of printing and distribution had delayed the 1969 issues. In the end they decided to take the step that the Rockefeller Foundation had encouraged and Beier had resisted nearly ten years before: they sought and obtained university sponsorship.

Early in 1970, Irele returned to Nigeria and joined the faculty of the University of Ife, which was setting up its own university press under the direction of Hans Zell. Irele and Zell had long discussions that resulted, late in 1971, in final arrangements being made with Higo and his associates at what was left of Mbari Ibadan to formally transfer *Black Orpheus* to the new Ife University Press. In the meantime, however, it was suddenly and unexpectedly announced that Ulli and Georgina Beier were returning to Nigeria from Papua, New Guinea (where they had been getting up a remarkable new cultural program very much like the original Mbari Clubs), and that he would become director of the Institute of African Studies at Ife! The news precipitated a crisis at *Black Orpheus*. Clark wanted nothing further to do with Beier.[60] Irele felt that his return would be of no consequence: Beier would have no direct control over the magazine. The arrangement with Ife University Press had called for Irele and Clark to remain as editors, aided by a panel of associate editors drawn from the other Nigerian universities. The other members of Mbari agreed with Clark, however, and the deal with Ife was aborted. A whole new set of negotiations were entered into with a new sponsor, the University of Lagos.

The turn of events was especially damaging. First, as a result of the dispute between Irele and Clark, Irele left the magazine, taking with him a fair amount of material that would have appeared in *Black Orpheus* and publishing it in his own new journal, the *Benin Review*. Second, publication of one issue of *Black Orpheus* after another was delayed while discussions about the magazine's future continued. A special issue on "the novel in Africa" was delayed again and again, finally appearing as "volume 2, number 5/6," advertised with some justice as a double issue, since it had been expanded from about fifty pages to eighty-nine. It was not dated, but probably appeared late in 1970. Volume 2, number 7, also undated, did not appear until 1972, offered only the usual fifty pages or so of material, and made no editorial apology for the delay. The first issue after Irele's departure, the occasion for Clark to begin a third volume, was dated "January/June 1974"; the second, delayed for over a year, bore the number "2/3" and the ponderous date "October/December 1974, January/June 1975." Clark, with more and more unversity responsibilities, simply did not have the time to keep the magazine going. The first few issues of volume two, he admitted (no. 7, p. 60), had really been the work of his wife, Ebunolowa Bolajoko Clark.

Even as first Irele and then Clark gradually withdrew from active direction of the magazine, however, it continued, in spite of everything, to produce some impressive successes. Momentum, or reputation, may have been responsible for this, but one must not neglect to credit the accomplishments of these last half-dozen issues of the magazine. *Black Orpheus* continued especially to buoy its reputation for independence of outlook and diversity. Volume 2, number 5/6, for instance, went after its theme, "the novel in Africa," from a number of directions. Gabriel Okara, who had been a beneficiary of Beier's early and assiduous promotion, and whose reputation Clark had otherwise been inclined to deflate (especially in "The Legacy of Caliban"), was praised diligently in a critical essay by J. Shiarella, the title of which was given in both the index and the text as "Gabriel's Okaras The Voices, a Study in the Poetic Novel" (pp. 45–49). The author, a lecturer at University College, Nairobi, was somewhat hampered by an admitted ignorance about Okara's technique (his article ruminated at one point about whether Okara composed in Ijaw and then translated into English), but the article did succeed in justifying its claim that Okara's novel constituted an important experiment in a hybrid form of expression.

Donald Ackley's strong praise for Wole Soyinka's *The Interpreters* in the same issue (pp. 50–57) was also surprising in light of Clark's presumed hostility toward its subject. Moreover, Ackley, an American academic from Western Michigan University, praised *The Interpreters* precisely for qualities that might have appealed to Beier: its complexity and its Joycean reflection of cultural disharmony and personal alienation. Drawing on an earlier review by John Thompson in *African Forum* (Fall 1965), Ackley's analysis of the plots, subplots, characters, and themes of this notably "difficult" novel was exceptionally lucid, and it focused on the novel's expression of modern Africa's ethical and intellectual impasses—Egbo's struggle to decide between a hereditary title and his government job, "between the ugly mud-skippers of this creek and the raucous toads of our sewage-ridden ports" (p. 53); Sekoni's high ideals and their defeat by cynical, corrupt bureaucrats; Sagoe's "philosophy of shit" and religion of "drink lobes," and the hypocrisy of the party organ newspaper he works for, "located amidst garbage and ironically labelled *The Independent Viewpoint*" (p. 54). Like many of the critical arbiters of *Black Orpheus*'s former incarnation, Ackley stressed the moral purpose of the dissident individual:

> To interpret is to create anew, to transform experience into meaning. It is what the individual, and above all the artist, must do. But it takes a power, a commitment, that requires courage. And none of the characters achieve that in *The Interpreters*. Kola, the painter, senses his inability, but does not conquer it. (p. 55)

Ackley also emphasized Soyinka's rejection of *négritude* and his definition of the artist as a lonely voice of dissent:

> While in many respects similar to European existentialism, Soyinka's view represents a reaction against the cultural and historical myopia of

African intellectuals. It rejects on the one hand the "narcissism" of *négritude*. . . . It rejects on the other hand the preoccupation with the past which has deluded the African into thinking that independence represents the end of Africa's problems. . . . It is, above all, thus, a call for commitment to and confrontation with reality.

Soyinka's "philosophy" may not find wide-spread acceptance. . . . But there is little doubt that the novel which grows out of that view of Africa and the African is brilliant, both in conception and execution. Few African writers, if any, have provided comparable work. (p. 56)

Volumes two and three of *Black Orpheus* also continued to print material that tended toward a reevaluation of modern African culture, in implied antithesis to the magazine's former predilections. Thus, for instance, Ebun Clark contributed a long academic article with two and a half pages of double-columned endnotes reevaluating the relative places in the modern Nigerian theatrical canon of Hubert Ogunde and Duro Ladipo (3, no. 2/3). Ladipo's Yoruba Folk Opera, of course, had been another of Beier's major enthusiasms. Now, however, *Black Orpheus*'s subeditor offered a dissenting evaluation: far from being a valid modern expression of a traditional popular art form, Ladipo's brand of traditional drama was westernized and intellectualized—accessible only to a small educated elite. Ladipo's work was only "most popular in the minority theatre of the intellectuals, particularly the expatriate intellectuals who largely created his theatre; and their influences can be seen in his use of western production structure." (The reference, of course, was unmistakably to Beier.) Ogunde's theater, in contrast, had been improvised, eclectic, and topical, offering a great variety of material inexpensively to large audiences. Clark granted Ladipo his chief accomplishment, the preservation in a sophisticated modern idiom of a traditional form expressing traditional values, but criticized him for offering it in a Western theatrical setting under the influence of Western expatriates (pp. 59–85).

Volumes two and three of the journal still offered uncontroversial scholarly work like Euba's and Nketia's earlier articles; Euba, in fact, contributed another deliberate, precise piece of scholarship to 3, no. 1 on "The Potential of African Traditional Music as a Contemplative Art." Euba was particularly interested in tracing, in a non-judgmental fashion, the shifts in artistic forms and standards that would be necessitated by the adoption in modern African music of the Western paradigm of a passive audience whose role is contemplation of, not participation in, the musical performance. Euba also offered a marvelously cogent definition of the various levels and kinds of interaction between Western and traditional African musical idioms (pp. 56–59).

Black Orpheus 3 also continued to direct single issues to specific themes of relevance, as it was put on the inside front cover, "to the arts of Africa and related lands." Number 2/3, for instance, was a special issue compiled by American Quincy Troupe on Afro-American art and literature. The emphasis was on cultural kinship—shared traditions, shared social concerns, and personal relationships among artists.

Perhaps the most significant fact about that issue of *Black Orpheus*, however, was that it seemed destined to be the last. It appeared well behind schedule, one of only four issues to appear in the five years since Clark and Irele had begun their unfortunate negotiations with the University of Ife. The magazine hopefully styled itself as coming out twice a year (under Beier it had generally come out twice, sometimes three times, a year) and made one final apology for its tardiness:

> We apologize to our subscribers and readers for the delay in the appearance of this number. *Black Orpheus* has been suffering from the usual publication delays that at present plague most journals in this country.
> To ensure that we meet our publication commitments, we have made this edition a combined one, and it really is a double number. The next edition will also be a combined issue and will appear in June 1976.
> We hope to regularize our editions by the end of 1976, and ask for the indulgence of our readers.   (3, no. 2/3, inside back cover)

Clark's hopes were not realized. He went on sabbatical in 1975, quitting his editorship of *Black Orpheus* and leaving the final arrangements with the University of Lagos Press somewhat up in the air. A new editorial board had to be formed and a temporary editor appointed while a permanent editor was sought by a special university committee. After repeated failures of consensus, a new editor, Theo Vincent, was appointed by an editorial committee reformed under the chairmanship of Michael Crowder in 1976. The appointment finally became official in 1977.

Vincent set to work on a new issue to focus on traditional literature in indigenous languages, as 2, no. 2 had. The material was hurriedly compiled and sent off with accompanying English translations to a British printer in an attempt to circumvent the printing delays that had been so harmful in the final years of Clark's editorship. The issue ought to have appeared in November 1978. In fact, however, it did not appear for over three years—the victim, Vincent has said in an interview, of the confusion attendant upon the British printer's unexpected liquidation.[61] Somehow, in the haste of sending out copy and correcting galleys and proofs, originals and proofs had been lost. In the long interval between 3, no. 2/3 and the first new issue of volume four, *Black Orpheus* continued to accept subscription requests and to solicit renewals from subscribers who would not see a new copy of the magazine for six years.[62] When *Black Orpheus* 4, no. 1 finally did appear, it had—in its graphic design, its contents, and, apparently, its editorial philosophy—lost all continuity with its illustrious predecessors.

Black Orpheus's Fourth Series

Theo Vincent's indigenous vernacular literary material was not what, after so many delays, broke a by then murky surface in 1982. Instead, complained Abdul R. Yesufu, who reviewed the first new issue for *Research in African Literatures*, Vincent had appropriated for *Black Orpheus* 4, no. 1 nearly the full proceedings of the 1978 University of Lagos Conference on the Interrelationship of the Arts in Nigeria. Yesufu, a faculty member at the University of Benin, went on to decry the absence of creative writing in the new issue. Had the new editor, he asked, found it "convenient to fall upon a ready-made package of papers?"[63] The charge was almost, but not quite, unfair. Beier and his successors had never published conference papers, but Rajat Neogy's special issue on the first East African Writers Conference in 1962 had been a crucial step in *Transition*'s intellectual maturity.

The trouble was that the Lagos conference was no such first-of-its-kind event, had no such historical significance. Moreover, though some papers were first-rate, others were either unsuitable for the magazine's audience or below its old standard. Their inclusion, moreover, seemed an accidental backward glance toward the themes and principals of the earlier *Black Orpheus*es. Some of the writers had been close to Beier and his colleagues; others, though they had not, referred to that group explicitly.

Michael Crowder, for instance, in "Patronage and Audience in Nigeria," commented on the fragility of the public and the sources of subsidy for Nigerian art, literature, and serious entertainment. Crowder's was a cogent, factual argument for creating indigenous art forms, for state support, and for the need for artists to "meet their [urban] audience halfway" (4, no. 1, p. 73). There was, however, also oblique, soured reference to Beier:

> Indeed the development of the contemporary arts in Africa was deformed in its early days in that not only was its main source of patronage and audience from an alien culture but in many cases the very live-

85

lihood of the artist . . . depended on expatriate . . . decisions. This fact has accounted for the success of "intuitive" artists like Tutuola or Twins Seven Seven whose appeal as being "authentically African" attracted European audiences who preferred to think of Africa not as a modernising continent but an exotic one. (p. 71)

Nor was Crowder alone in slighting allusions. Dele Jegede, from the Center for Cultural Studies at the University of Lagos, whom Vincent described in the notes on contributors as "very well known for his cartoons in the *Daily Times*," repeatedly referred to Beier in his article about art education, "'Made-In-Nigeria' Artists: Problems and Anticipations." Though Jegede furnished Beier's own best descriptions of his work at Mbari, Jegede's allusions were touched with cynicism:

> Meanwhile those who have had a meeting of education and whose primordial artistic talent had been untapped by the school system were at Oshogbo, Ile-Ife, and elsewhere, waiting along with their illiterate counterparts for the arrival of Ulli Beier . . . to remove the mote from their artistic eyes and ignite their dormant talents. (p. 36)

Beier's characteristic dismissal of schooled artists (and of the location of a new art school in Zaria) was characterized a few pages later as an instance of "pent-up venom against the system" and of condescension to Zarian artistic traditions. Beier's scanted principles were superseded by no more enlightened solution in Jegede's article, however, which merely asserted the premise that art must develop in school art classes.

If Jegede's article lapsed back into the attitude to art education that had preceded Beier's and Wenger's experiments in the sixties, neither was there much new to *Black Orpheus* 4, no. 1 as a whole. Where the conference papers shone, it was not in thesis but in descriptive detail. Peggy Harper's argument was a familiar one—that African aesthetics could not be divorced from "socio-religious purpose" (p. 1). The weight, even elegance, of her paper lay in its descriptions of masquerades among the Gelede, the Tiv, and the Kwangh-Hir. Raphael Ige Ibigbami, of the University of Ife's Fine

Arts Department, was thorough and lively in his disquisition on "Traditional Pottery in Yoruba Culture," detailing the varieties of pottery, their unexpected purposes, the proverbs surrounding their manufacture and use. It was hard not to give credit to the careful study and observation behind such writing. And yet this remained academic conference writing. Yesufu's estimation was fair after all. Who, skimming through a new magazine presuming to call itself *Black Orpheus*, would find in such material the excitement of the old days?

Other articles, moreover, were even more academic or did not offer Harper's and Ibigbami's intriguing detail. Tunji Vidal, for instance, from the Department of Fine Arts of the University of Ife, detailed "The Tonemic and Melodic Character of Yoruba Principal Chants" in a way unlikely to inspire browsers in a new cultural review—except perhaps those who could invest interest in an argument *against* "basic phonemic tones" occuring "within the context of the diatonic scale, a seven-tone scale with half steps," and *for* "an anhemitonic pentatonic, a five-tone scale without half steps" (p. 20). At another extreme was director, playwright, critic, and scholar Kalu Uka's "Approaches to Theatre Reviewing As Art Education (Suggestions to Nigerian Reviewers)," an essay whose simple purpose was to hector young semi-educated local literary columnists and radio and television announcers for panning the wrong plays.

Theo Vincent had indeed, as Yesufu charged, found a smooth, and shallow, strand for launching *Black Orpheus* 4. Now that it had overcome "the problems" (no more explicitly alluded to elsewhere), the magazine, Vincent wrote, would "retain its character of being a venue for publishing creative and critical works on the black world" ("Editor's Note"). So much, no more, for editorial philosophy! Vincent's own reprinted conference contribution, on "Theatre and Audience in Nigeria," was workmanlike and reasonable, if not startling—but its argument for a middle ground between Nigeria's wildly successful popular dramas and its ill-attended "high-brow" literary ones lacked the challenge and toughness that had sometimes characterized his predecessors on *Black Orpheus*'s editorial stool. That, indeed, was the lapsed opportunity of *Black Orpheus* 4—its missed chance to pose new challenges for contemporary African culture.

It was an inauspicious start in other ways as well. As mixed as were the magazine's contents, its editing was worse. Errors abounded on nearly every page. And this from a magazine announcing an increase in the subscription rate for its biannual issues, inclusive of postage, to 8.00N for Nigerian, and $16.00 for American, subscribers. No veteran *Black Orpheus* subscription-seeker, moreover, could miss the lack of reference to lost subscription fees. "*Black Orpheus* wishes to assure all subscribers," wrote Vincent on the page containing publisher's announcements, "that it will appear regularly." "We would like," he added in the "Editor's Note," "to express our appreciation to our numerous subscribers who, in spite of our disappearance from the shelves for a long period, had the faith to continue renewing their subscriptions."

A second new issue, following on the heels of the first, was in some ways more promising and self-defining. In other ways it was not. For one thing, it had shrunk to fifty pages, from the ninety-three of *Black Orpheus* 4, no. 1. For another, it left, as had Vincent's first new issue, a primary impression of a backward glance at the old *Black Orpheus*es. At any rate, it at least included both creative writing and critical reflection that had not been begged from someone else's cooking shed. But the choice of some articles, stories, and poems continued to show a failure of editorial (as opposed to authorial) timeliness and originality nearly as great as had the borrowing of the Lagos conference proceedings for 4, no. 1.

Darwin Turner's "Revolt and Tradition in Literature by Afro-Americans in the U.S.A., 1960–1973," for instance, was the thoughtful overview that one would expect from a scholar of his stature. Nevertheless, it was again apparently a reprinted conference paper, written for an academic audience (addressed explicitly to "scholars" in its concluding paragraph on p. 33). And it focused not on current writing but on the period of the "black arts" movements in the sixties and early seventies, a special interest of Beier's and Irele and Clark's *Black Orpheus*es.

An equally competent article by Marlene Mosher of Tuskegee Institute, "James Baldwin's Blues," found in that writer (whose works Turner distinguished from the "black arts" writers and labeled as in another, "traditional" stream) a pervasive reflection of the spirit and attitude of blues lyricism. Baldwin's ideal for coping with racism, Mosher argued, like the blues, valued the hard road of understanding over escape or avoidance. Her thesis was thus broadly revelatory of a major black American writer and relevant to the African experience. Nevertheless, hers was another academic recapitulation of the work of a figure whose role during the magazine's earlier heyday might have been seminal and defining. (A Baldwin interview had been the lead in *Transition* no. 12 in January/February 1964.)

Black Orpheus's most promising creative work, on the other hand, was in fact a poem by a black American writer, Denver Sasser, whose style reflected the "black arts" movement's revolution in sensibility. Sasser's "Black Space Girl," moreover, had a sophistication of idiom and metaphor that belied its droll undercutting of its own voice. Its subject, interracial love, might seem an odd choice for a new periodical dedicated to "the black world," but the "black arts" movement, as Turner pointed out, had become concerned more and more after the late sixties with "affirmations of love as a necessary foundation for the new Black community," rather than with "denunciations of oppression" (4, 2, p. 33).

Sasser's poem, in any case, was a step toward establishing a standard of quality. A witty, headlong "rap," heedless of any conventional aesthetic other than extended simile or exaggerated conceit, Sasser's iconoclastic voice recalled those of Imamu Baraka and Ted Joans. The speaker's white lover is a pale "amateur white astronaut," exploring "the wet, hollowed underside of Venus" (p. 12). An ironic reflection, the poem ambiguously acknowledges and repudiates "affirmations of love":

> Earth seems an unmade bed receding in the
> green distance of your beautiful yet false light,
> in the white hot heat of your grimace as G's pull
> out of shape your encroaching, voyaging heart

as you blast off into eternal space to probe &
discover & send back rock samples & litter
with your soul's junk and white pollution this
incredible breathing pulsating
black hole in space.

(p. 13)

There was, on balance, promise in *Black Orpheus* 4, no. 2's black
American material, if the magazine could overcome its academic
cant. Its African material, however, both creative and critical, seemed
less promising.

A critical rehabilitation of the mostly unvalued Togolese popular
novelist Felix Couchero by Sabit Adegboyega Salami, for instance,
was handicapped by its quotation of passages from that author's
work that offered no convincing evidence of the novelist's argued sophistication. It was further handicapped by an inexcusable profusion
of errors, some seemingly authorial, some editorial, some typographical. The book reviews in *Black Orpheus* 4, no. 2, moreover, including one by Vincent himself of a reissue of Beier's *Introduction to
African Literature*, were mostly remarkable for their blandness.

The creative voices that Vincent now sought to add to the
crowded mixed chorus of neo-African writing, almost as if in response to Yesufu's *RAL* review (which in fact had not come out yet
when *Black Orpheus* 4, no. 2 went to press), were equally only a
qualified success. Two new voices were raw and amateurish; a third,
Bona Onyajeli's, though it had once had some strength, was now a
neglected echo of *Black Orpheus*'s past. Onyajeli, whose poetry, according to Vincent's note, had appeared in both *Black Orpheus* and
Nigeria Magazine in the sixties, had suffered a stroke in 1974 and as a
result had fallen into silence and obscurity. His poems in 4, no. 2, the
leads to that issue, were from a manuscript "composed during the
civil war while he was working in the War Information Bureau" and
had been "rescued from the garbage heap by his sister" ("Notes on
Some of the Contributors," p. 50). The first, "The Minstrel," was
doubly a backward glance at that difficult period for the magazine. A
wake and eulogy for former *Black Orpheus* and *Transition* stalwart

Christopher Okigbo, written upon his death in the war, it echoed in nearly every passage memorable lines from Okigbo's "Heavensgate." Onyajeli's other, more self-defined contribution, his "Poems for Meiro," was also evocative of African writing in the early sixties, combining African elements with Christian (biblical) motifs, litany with indigenous call-and-response. Onyajeli's poetry was perhaps more than a relic of the past; nevertheless, his accomplishment in these poems placed him a rung below famous contemporaries writing in styles that his own work recalled. He was not a lost Okigbo or Okara.

In turn, the two new African writers in *Black Orpheus* 4, no. 2, Abiodhun Ehindero and Chinjara Hopewell Seyaseya, were rungs below Onyajeli. Seyaseya, a Zimbabwean student trying his hand at short fiction, offered a melodramatic "love" tragedy hardly surpassing the Onitsha Market novelists in sophistication and lacking their compensating ingenuity. Ehindero's verse had the attraction of its occasional reference to African proverb (in "Abiku" and "The Chameleon and the Lizard"), but its form and mood borrowed not from contemporary African but from nineteenth-century British verse.

The new magazine stands thus, as of this writing (in 1984), in a difficult and ambiguous position. There were doubts, of course, that the second *Black Orpheus* would survive, and doubts that it would bring anything new to African culture. It did not, however, face the barrier of nearly seven years of lapsed promise. It was able, moreover, quickly to establish itself as a claimant, if not to direct succession, at least to continuity and progression. It was a new *Black Orpheus*, but it had grown out of the ashes of the old one and it quickly established its own character and pretensions. The succession to the third *Black Orpheus*, of course, was even more direct. The fourth could claim no such continuity. Its first two issues did not establish a distinctive editorial voice; nor did they entirely create a new edge of creativity. *Black Orpheus* revived is, so far, neither one of the old *Black Orpheus*es nor something new. If it wishes to retain the influence or distinction of its predecessors, it will eventually have to face that challenge.

The Influence and Importance of the First Two *Black Orpheus*es

Between 1957 and 1975, the variables in *Black Orpheus*'s equation changed so much that it is hard to compare the ambitions, methods, and fortunes of its various principals. Some clear differences do, however, stand out as regards the intellectual climate and its effect on the magazine's editorial history. When Beier, Moore, and Jahn founded *Black Orpheus*, the fact that they were cultural outsiders was advantageous, giving them credibility and independence and making it possible for Beier to attempt what he saw as the magazine's main role, his "cultural smuggling ring." For a time, the intellectual climate precluded explicit public criticism. Beier's real influence as a critic was therefore in his editorial role, his power to open or shut what was almost the only door to local or international critical attention. His editorial role was analogous to the method for guiding the Mbari art workshop students that Beier had described in his letter to Mphahlele (see above, p. 44).

By 1965, however, the climate had changed. The writers and artists whose recognition Beier had helped spur were now well known and influential,[64] and inclined to be critical of outsiders in their midst, as well as of each other. *Black Orpheus* became less a booster magazine for new writers and artists and more a showcase for the variety of talents and diversity of viewpoints of an increasingly established intellectual elite. In such a climate, the original *Black Orpheus*'s dependence on the cultural outsider, and on postwar Western standards and preoccupations, was now clearly out of place. It seems inevitable that the direction of *Black Orpheus* (or, for that matter, of *Transition*) should have fallen to cultural insiders and that, as a result, *Black Orpheus* and the intellectual community that had grown up around it should be increasingly caught up in controversy—aesthetic, social, political, and personal.

When it got caught up in this new intellectual climate, first under Beier and then under Irele and Clark, *Black Orpheus* really reached the height of its accomplishment. There was a danger, of course, in thus dropping its position as a neutral publicizer and promoter and beginning to join the fray, but the original *Black Orpheus* was not to last long enough to suffer from its newfound controversiality.

A more threatening change had been the gradual worsening of the managerial climate: it simply was becoming harder, especially during the civil war, to cope with the practical difficulties of printing and distribution. Moreover, where Beier had been an active and deft manager, Irele and Clark preferred to be relieved of those burdens and concentrate on purely editorial functions: communicating with contributors, editing copy, planning new issues. Eventually, practical difficulties put the magazine on the critical list.

In its editorial philosophy, *Black Orpheus* also changed. Beier's original interest in establishing routes of cultural commerce, together with certain personal aesthetic inclinations, led him to seek in the new African culture a "universalism" of expression whose standards and themes were unconsciously predicated on contemporary Western aesthetic preoccupations. Irele and Clark sought to open *Black Orpheus* to antagonistic standards, to reconsider the judgments, the choices, the influence of the first *Black Orpheus*'s proprietors. It is not necessary to choose among the three editorial regimes. In very different social and intellectual climates, with very different ideals, inclinations, talents, and problems, each set of editors and editorial contributors made valuable contributions to the genesis of modern African art and literature. If *Black Orpheus*'s fourth regime, under Theo Vincent, is to deserve to inherit the name *Black Orpheus*, it must be ambitious enough to try for similar accomplishments.

Beier's practical success, moreover, stands in sharp contrast to *Black Orpheus*'s fate in other hands. Beier accomplished the difficult tasks of founding the magazine, attracting a school of accomplished contributors, building its reputation and theirs, finding financial support, and expanding distribution—all without really being able to devote more than a fraction of his attention. He had taught a variety

of subjects full-time in six different towns each week while editing
Black Orpheus and had also been intensely occupied at various times
with *Odu*, the Mbari Clubs, Mbari Publications, and Duro Ladipo's
Yoruba Folk Opera. *Black Orpheus* nevertheless came out regularly
for ten years and its influence grew. After Beier left, the magazine's
appearance became unpredictable, its production and distribution irregular. Its editorial choices became more provocative and its critical
columns more open to controversy, but the erosion of its financial
base forced the magazine into a downward spiral. In contrast, *Black
Orpheus*'s consistency and regularity under Beier insured that its influence would persist.

Beier's tastes, sensibilities, and beliefs had had a substantial impact on African literature and art. One can hardly criticize him for
that: he had wanted to "start something," and he succeeded. Though
his influence has sometimes been exaggerated by his admirers, it was
undeniably present in the work of the new writers and artists, if only
because of his power to shut and open doors. Most often, doors were
opened for artists and writers whose work was complex, problematic, elusive, and intuitive. It would be as wrong, however, to say that
Beier's influence tended to circumscribe creativity as to suggest that
he was simultaneously father, mother, and midwife to the new artists
and writers. They found critical acclaim with his help and benefited
from his efforts to bring together the world of black culture, but
Beier was no Svengali. If he had been able to make people artists,
playwrights, novelists, or poets, he would probably have begun by
making himself one.

Nor did Beier's influence compress the horizons of this new culture. Though he favored one kind of creativity, it was a peculiarly
open-ended kind. Erich Auerbach perhaps best defines the adaptabil-
ity to a variety of experiences, traditions, and viewpoints of the literary and artistic aesthetic that Beier favored. He writes (with specific
reference to Virginia Woolf):

> What takes place here . . . is precisely what was attempted every-
> where in works of this kind (although not everywhere with the same
> insight and mastery)—that is, to put the emphasis on the random

occurrence, to exploit it not in the service of a planned continuity of action but in itself. And in the process something new and elemental appeared: nothing less than the wealth of reality and depth of life in every moment to which we surrender ourselves without prejudice. . . . In this unprejudiced and exploratory type of representation we cannot but see to what an extent—below the surface conflicts—the differences between men's ways of life and forms of thought have already lessened. The strata of societies and their different ways of life have become inextricably mingled. There are no longer even exotic peoples. It is still a long way to a common life of mankind on earth, but the goal begins to be visible.[65]

Auerbach's reference is to the modernistic perspective in fiction, whereas Beier's influence tended chiefly to encourage an African modernism in poetry and art. Nevertheless, there is a similarity of effect, and *Black Orpheus*'s enduring aesthetic contribution may indeed have been that it made this goal of "a common life of mankind on earth" through an increasingly interrelated world literature a little more "visible." No mean accomplishment for a mere "border operator." Beier, in reflecting on his role during those years, recalls a candlelight procession he later saw along a beach in Brazil:

> Yoruba descendants went to pray to Yemanja, Yoruba goddess of the sea. As they were singing her *Oriki* facing the sea, a counter-procession appeared from behind, the Catholics . . . carrying the Virgin Mary—protectress of sailors . . . hoping to draw guilty sailors away from the African ritual. But the *Orisha* worshippers saw it differently. They turned around and were merely delighted that "the Virgin had come to greet Yemanja." They said their prayer to Mary and turned back to their ritual with Yemanja. They did not see the frontier that the Catholic Church had seen.

Beier adds, "We at the time were blissfully ignorant of borders and it was this that gave me and still gives me my irrevocable sense of belonging."[66]

"MY CONTRIBUTION
IN IRON AND STEEL"

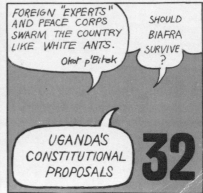

II
"MY CONTRIBUTION
IN IRON AND STEEL":
Transition and Intellectual
Controversy

To Whomsoever It May Concern:

I write these words in sorrow. Rajat Neogy, editor of *Transition*, and Abu Mayanja, constitutional lawyer and politician, have been arrested and put in detention. So far as we know this is not a case of detaining someone who has been plotting to overthrow the government. It looks more like a detention of people for being intellectually honest. If I am wrong I hope the Uganda government will publicly correct this impression, and bring the accused to trial.

I personally know of no two people who have contributed more to the intellectual liveliness of Uganda than Rajat Neogy and Abu Mayanja. I did not always see eye to eye with either of them. In fact Abu Mayanja and myself have been on opposite sides in almost every debate in which he and I have taken part in the Main Hall of Makerere. And the differences between us were real. But Uganda's reputation as an open society was secure for as long as there was one Abu Mayanja free to speak out his mind, and one *Transition* leading the rest of Africa in sheer intellectual verve.

There is a sense in which intellectual freedom is indivisible. On a day like this I feel lonely and shaken.

—Ali Mazrui

When Ugandan President Milton Obote arrived at the Commonwealth Prime Ministers Conference in London in January 1969, the burning issue raised by the journalists who besieged him there was the unhealthy trend throughout East Africa toward the oppression of the minority Asian population. He came with answers and evasions prepared. A few journalists, however—British, American, East African—surprised him by asking instead about the arrest in Kampala on October 18 of Rajat Neogy, editor of *Transition*, a lively and controversial intellectual and literary magazine Neogy had published in Kampala since 1961. The attention of the Western journalists was partly circumstantial: Neogy's wife, Barbara, was the daughter of a well-known American sports figure, basketball coach Joe Lapchik, and was a former *Vogue* model with friends in the international press corps.

Obote was aware that the young editor's arrest had gotten some press coverage in London and New York. Protest letters had arrived in Kampala via overseas airmail as well. Nevertheless, the questions somehow found him at a loss. He denied that *Transition* had been suppressed at all: in fact, he rather liked *Transition*, read it himself. He had not found it to be critical of the government (the reporters had been primed to unearth a connection between Neogy's arrest and certain articles critical of the Ugandan government's recent proposals for a new constitution). Rather, Neogy had been detained for his involvement with "certain organizations."[1] Obote added, "Were it not for these organizational ties, Neogy would be sitting in the editor's chair today."[2]

To Neogy, languishing in a 5½-by-7-foot cell in Luzira Prison, it was all quite unreal. His arrest had been sudden, arbitrary, and psychologically disorienting: "Like death, you think it only happens to other people." For five months his world was limited to his cell, except for an hour or two of exercise in a compound the size of a badminton court. He was not allowed to speak with the warders or the trustees who brought his food. He was not allowed paper or pencil.

First his reading materials were censored, then the "privilege" of reading was withdrawn altogether. There were periodic surprise searches of his cell to make certain that he had found no ways of circumventing the prison regimen. Brooding over his arrest later, after his release, Neogy began to wonder if there had not been a pattern to *Transition*'s relations with Obote's government all along—a pattern of surveillance and intimidation, eventually leading to suppression— a pattern beginning even before the magazine had completed its gradual evolution from its early concern with cultural matters to its later interest in politics and society.[3] Perhaps *Transition*, for many years dogged by accusations of implication in a conspiracy with the American CIA, had in fact itself been the victim of a conspiracy.

The Founding of *Transition*

Neogy had begun *Transition* with other than political purposes. Impressed by the success of Ulli Beier's Nigerian review *Black Orpheus* in stimulating a modern literary and cultural movement in West Africa, Neogy meant to try something similar in East Africa. Valeria Hume, who worked with Neogy from the beginning, later recalled the magazine's inception: in January 1961 she had begun to hear about this fellow Neogy—twenty-two years old, a bit of a "beatnik." The descriptions of his bohemianism, she presumed, must be colored by Kampalan provincialism. She finally met Neogy at a friend's house: "I remember well. . . . We were sitting round the children's supper table, and he walked in. Big head, lots of hair, and eyes. And he sneered, but then he should. He spoke, but I couldn't understand a word. . . . I gathered that he was planning to start a magazine. An independent, intellectual magazine, about culture and the African creative scene and all that. I admitted a past involved with college newspapers and the Socialist Student Press in London." Neogy promptly invited her to help him: "You go out and sell advertising and when you've sold enough, we can go to press."

"But what are we printing?" Hume, still hazy, asked.

"Don't worry about that, just sell the space."

She had the job of advertising manager—unpaid, without even a petrol allowance:

> And there I was, high heels, net stockings, red umbrella and all, parking a large Peugeot Station Wagon all over Kampala, finding offices I never knew existed, climbing endless staircases, and explaining with absolute sincerity how this new cultural magazine was going to be invaluable in the promotion of plastic bags, foam rubber cushions, tractor tyres, and fish and chips.
>
> Maybe it was the red umbrella or that they were so short and I was so tall. In any case we scraped together the requisite number of pages from advertisers, all on spec.[4]

What little money Neogy had from Hume's solicitations and his family permitted no extravagance. Recently returned from England, where he had attended the University of London, Neogy's chief experience consisted of student editorships and a bit of free-lance journalism.[5] Educated at the English-speaking Gowan Primary School because his family, one of only six Bengali families in Uganda, did not understand Punjabi, the majority Indian language there, Rajat Neogy had acquired his Cambridge School Certificate at thirteen and had left before his fifteenth birthday for further schooling (and a bit of knocking about) in England. As an Indian Ugandan, he found Makerere College closed to him, a "non-African." An uncle, K. D. Gupta, however, was Indian Education Officer for all of East Africa and was at the head of a movement to improve the education of Ugandan "Asians" and thereby qualify more of them for matriculation abroad. Gupta's educational movement, in fact, was the spearhead of a major effort to improve the lot of the mass of East African "Asians."

Neogy's parents had been sent to Uganda by the Aga Khan himself in 1938, under a four-year contract to serve as headmaster and headmistress of separate Muslim secondary schools; they had remained, living in a succession of faculty bungalows in Old Kampala, because the war and German U-boats had severed their link with home. Not long thereafter, Neogy's father became a British civil servant, leaving the Aga Khan's employ to head the faculty of Nakivuvo Primary School, then just opened by future Governor Sir Andrew Cohen (he who would later be the young *kabaka's* special nemesis).

"Starched Brahmins" (the name *Neogy*, a title rather than a caste or occupational name, means "the king's favorite minister"), in spite of their relationship to the khan's modernophile followers, the Neogys were defined by the rigorous strictures of their caste. Merely crossing the shadow of a Hindu "untouchable" required a ritual bath. As members of the educated elite, as members of an exalted caste, and as Bengalis, they were at the periphery of Ugandan Indian life. Neogy's mother also inflicted successive religious and philosophical enthusiasms of her own upon him. He went to Catholic primary

Rajat Neogy, founding editor of *Transition*.
(New York, 1965)

school and, later, Protestant Sunday school, but still attended Hindu temples "whenever a visiting deity from India appeared." "By seventeen," he writes, "I was a well-established atheist with a bent towards Meister Eckhart's mysticism. I read the English (Penguin) translation of the Koran at eighteen and at that time decided if I were ever to choose a religion it would have to be Islam and no other." The only Africans the Neogys knew, beyond those with claim to special elite status, such as the family of the young *kabaka*, were their own servants.

When Neogy returned to Uganda from England, after five years of something that was hardly exile, it was not with the intention of founding an avant-garde intellectual magazine. Indeed, he had no intention of staying. He had just married his first wife, a Swede, and planned only to introduce her to his parents, show her Kampala, and then leave for Greece. Somehow, he got caught up in the intellectual currents of the moment, however. His friends, he recalls, were mostly Ugandan nationalists. His interest in political science (which he had studied in London), his journalism, and his poetry were behind what happened next, almost accidentally. On the same day, a few months after his return to Kampala, Neogy's first son and his magazine *Transition* were both born.[6]

Wole Soyinka later recalled one of the newborn: "I was in Kampala shortly after its [*Transition*'s] birth and remember well the editorial office situated in Rajat's home, its entire space taken up by a smooth slab of wood, supported on piles of bricks. All the labor originated from this desk" (Editorial, *Transition* no. 45, p. 4). Neogy found the cheapest printer in Uganda, an Italian refugee from the Congo (Zaire) with "a French wife, three children, and an army of Congolese employees to support." The printer spoke no English, Neogy neither French nor Italian. Valeria Hume and the Italian's wife tried to interpret: "But he, patient Signor Pessina, set every letter of the early *Transition*s by hand, purely at sight from the typed copy, without understanding a single word, and errors occurred wildly." Every morning they collected "garbled" proofs and corrected them, and eventually four or five successive revisions, over brandies in a nearby bar. The brandy might, indeed, explain some of the equally wild errors that eluded these two inexperienced proofreaders. J. E. Goldthorpe's article on "Race Relations in East Africa," for instance, would have appeared without its first ten paragraphs (and three footnotes) and would have begun with the dangling phrase "and so on," had not Neogy caught the omission between printing and binding. The missing page had to be printed front and back on a single sheet of cheap, thin, unbleached paper and was bound in with a subscription offer as pages 31 and 32. The printer's type was limited, so only two pages could be printed at a time before the type had to be dismantled. Material came in erratically, then stopped altogether. A last-ditch effort produced enough advertisements to fill up the final, middle page of the first issue. It had only been three months, but the production time had "seemed endless."[7]

The first issue was egregiously arty, bohemian, meant to challenge conventional sensibilities and to provide a medium for the editor's own feelings of alienation. Neogy himself contributed a Joycean prose poem of inexplicable intent entitled "A Man Beat the Earth With His Two Fists" (p. 37), a pair of poems after the manner of the surrealists (p. 37), and another poem in the style of the concrete poets (p. 8). There was also a column of editorial reflection—random, tentative, offhand—entitled "Notes From a Dangerous Man's Diary" (pp. 48–49). It began, "Sort of free-wheeling with thoughts and typewriter; more for discipline and to lessen temporary madness. You will have to excuse rough-shod style and apparent confusion which is not confusion, but truths viewed at various perspectives and sometimes imprisoning prisms."

What emerged in the first editorial column was a crudely expressed, half-formed philosophy of perception and illusion, vision and alienation—along with an affirmation of intellectual freedom; of radical, surrealistic modes of artistic perception (as against purely rational modes); and of the value of the "outsider"—by which Neogy seems to have meant the intellectual or creative person, not the racial, ethnic, or social outsider. There was a painful self-consciousness in Neogy's self-definition:

> Society as it is, for what it is, totally unacceptable to me for obvious reasons. It cannot be changed; there is no satisfaction in Utopian intellect. I do not want to change it. I am an Outsider. I *accept* my inaccessibility to others. I don't make a fetish of *being* "outsider." Senti-

> mentalists of a finer order will call my 'condition' the painfulness of truth. But pain and joy do not come into this. Since I am surrounded by stupidity and am not Selfish (because not possessive or acquisitive materially or spiritually) I have a certain duty. . . . I have to add my contribution, in iron and steel; i.e. in permanence. (p. 49)

Neogy had begun with an "odd analogy" for the collective intellect, which seems in retrospect a good enough image for *Transition* itself: it was to be "a pair of rails" on which the wagon of intellect "may travel for certain distances" (p. 48). *Transition*, in a sense, was meant to be a vehicle, an engine—not, as *Black Orpheus* had at first been, a sort of exhibition hall for new culture. And it had better be fashioned from "iron and steel"—it would have need enough of strength and resilience in its dynamic career.

That the featured contributor to the first issue was Gerald Moore, who had founded *Black Orpheus* with Jahnheinz Jahn and Ulli Beier, was meant perhaps to signal continuity—to identify *Transition* in some manner as the East African *Black Orpheus*. One of Moore's contributions to that issue, in fact, was a retrospective tribute to *Black Orpheus*. Moore's other contribution would have made unlikely *Black Orpheus* material in the light of Ulli Beier's apparent tastes in fiction, but it fitted Neogy's inclinations well, offering a detached, realistic recollection of a dream in which the dreamer witnesses a suicide he is unable to prevent and in which his effort to summon the police turns into an unreal mockery.

Even more appropriate, perhaps, was an article by Ivor Jennings, "Is a Party System Possible in Africa?" whose subject, if not its style, hinted of Neogy's future preoccupations. Jennings's article had none of *Transition*'s later style of irreverent controversiality; nevertheless, he gave no easy or theoretical answer. A Cambridge University professor who had helped draft Pakistan's constitution in 1955, Jennings argued that political parties in newly independent states tended to be superficial, loosely organized, and liable, therefore, "to breakup on policy or personality" (p. 11). When inevitable disputes occurred, there was confrontation rather than debate or fair exchange of opinion within a system of checks and balances between the government and an independent opposition party. Specific constitutional safeguards were therefore necessary to protect the rights of minority ethnic, political, tribal, or religious groups—"their lands, their language, their share of government jobs, their educational system"— and such safeguards could not be replaced by the abstract assertions of a "bill of rights," which would be dependent on goodwill and the retention of a sophisticated independent judiciary.

Precisely these issues, similarly argued, were eventually to precipitate the controversy through which *Transition* was to run afoul of Milton Obote's government. In October 1967, Abu Mayanja, an opposition party leader, made similar assertions, with more pointed reference to Uganda, that ultimately landed both him and Neogy in jail. To extend the irony, another controversial article in the first issue of the new magazine was a discussion by Dr. J. E. Goldthorpe of "Race Relations in East Africa" (pp. 31–36), which was to be the ostensible topic of Obote's news conference at the 1968 Commonwealth Conference and also eventually figured as an issue in Neogy's detention.

The rest of the contents of the first issue, however, were incongruous with Neogy's bohemianism and his effort to stimulate controversy. Though lively enough in their different way, they tended toward the scholarly. Neogy seems to have been torn between providing a more thoughtful alternative to the political, social, and economic reporting of the tabloid press and providing an outlet for young artists, poets, and story writers as *Black Orpheus* had done. A publisher's announcement, headed "Culture in Transition," began,

> This journal appears when East Africa is undergoing various and exciting changes. It is a time when idealism and action merge with various degrees of success. It is also a time for testing intellectual and other preconceptions and for thoughtful and creative contributions in all spheres.

A promotional leaf bound into the magazine also stressed the need to "give perspective and dimension to affairs that a weekly or daily press would either sensationalize or ignore," but added that *Transition* would also be "a monthly reflection of the cultural and social scene in East Africa." Its "constant aim" would be to "search [for] and encourage writers and poets from East Africa."

Although Gerald Moore had strongly implied in recounting *Black Orpheus*'s achievements that *Transition* would seek similarly to stimulate creative cultural activity, there were no new artists or writers (apart, perhaps, from Neogy himself) unearthed in the first *Transition*. The editor made up the deficiency by taking *Transition*'s description of itself as a "review" quite literally—publishing no fewer than eight reviews in the first issue. There were, for example, reviews of Graham Greene's *A Burnt-Out Case* by Roland Hindmarsh ("The Congo of the Mind," p. 41); of Jean Genet's *The Blacks* by Ben W. Mkapa, then a final-year honors student at Makerere College ("What Black is Black," pp. 39–40); of Langston Hughes's *An African Treasury* by former *Drum* editor Tom Hopkinson ("Afro-English," reprinted from the London *Observer*, p. 38); and of Robert George Reisner's *The Jazz Titans* by *Transition*'s "beatnik" editor himself. Neogy's was more homage than review: "Bird [Charlie Parker] was a negro of genius," he wrote. "I have seen those who truly know music weep when they have spoken of him" (p. 40).

And that was the first *Transition*: a bit academic, a bit controversial, and a bit bohemian, with the flavor of a young man's disillusionment barely concealing his idealistic aestheticism. Its tone was far from the knowing cynicism of the issues that were to follow a few years later.

It cannot have been the modest contents of the first *Transition*, but something about it—perhaps its tone of naive cultural alienation—deeply offended some Kampalan sensibilities. Though the headmaster of a local secondary school offered to hawk it on Main Street, and though they sold all but a few copies (unsalable because the cover's "classy matt paper" too readily absorbed grimy handprints) of the 2,000 in that original impress,[8] there was hostility and resistance: "The Jazz Club was nearly turned out of its home in the

Lugogo Sports Club when the manager discovered *Transition* was being sold to its members. Nasty, left-wing literature, and very likely pornographic too." At a bar where Neogy was trying to peddle copies to the lunchtime crowd, an angry Englishman snatched one and "ceremoniously tore it up," saying, "That's what I think of your trash!"[9]

Cultural Midwifery: Editorial Philosophy in Early *Transitions*

True to his, and Gerald Moore's, promise, Neogy plugged away for the first dozen *Transitions* or so at the task of finding, promoting, and encouraging artists and writers in East Africa, whose creative development had lagged, in part, because the creative climate was less propitious than that which Beier, Moore, and Jahn had found in West Africa. It was not until 1964, three years after the founding of *Transition*, that the publication of *Weep Not, Child* by the East African Publishing House was to establish James Ngugi (now Ngugi wa Thiong'o) as East Africa's first serious novelist. The Makerere Student Dramatic Society, an important pioneer in drama, did not produce its first play until 1961, the year of *Transition*'s founding, and its first new *African* play was not staged until November 1962, at the Uganda National Theater. It was Ngugi's *The Black Hermit*.

By the time the fifth issue appeared (in mid-1962), Neogy had already begun to rethink his initial editorial policy. For the first four issues he had stuck to the concept of *Transition* as a straightforward literary review. Then, on the cover of the fifth issue, the subhead on the lower right-hand corner that had announced a commitment to "Poetry Prose Criticism" was replaced by the single word "Monthly." He had been concerned from the first, Neogy said to Lewis Nkosi in a panel discussion of *Transition*, that he was operating in a place where there was simply not much literary activity emerging—a literary desert, as another commentator, Alan Ogot of the University of Nairobi, called East Africa. East Africa's slow literary development, it was thought, might be a function of its relative powerlessness, the retardation of its political struggle for independence serving as "active discouragement to expression, at any level," Neogy told Nkosi.[10] When East African writers did begin to appear, some of them in the pages of *Transition*, the nationalistic ferment then served, Neogy

112

thought, not so much to restrain creativity as to cause it to flow along unexpected channels.

Neogy did have some initial success in his efforts at cultural midwifery. In the second and third issues he published two stories— "And this, at last," by John Nagenda, then a final-year honors student at Makerere and editor of the college literary magazine *Penpoint*; and "The Return" by Ngugi, also a final-year English student at Makerere and also connected with *Penpoint*. Both men were to play important roles in East Africa's literary development.

Nevertheless, that Ngugi and Nagenda were both inherited from a student literary magazine was indicative of Neogy's predicament. As Ogot and Nagenda were to point out three years later, if *Transition* were to avoid becoming a sort of secondhand *Black Orpheus*, rediscovering writers coming to prominence in the pages of Ulli Beier's review, then it must publish young East African writers; yet it must also prevent itself from degenerating, Ogot pointed out, "into another kind of *Penpoint*"—another school magazine for Makerere.[11] Abiola Irele later commented, "One sensed the pull toward a restricted university periodical that the Makerere lecturers, thrilled with the appearance of an 'intellectual' magazine on their doorstep, were exerting on those early numbers."[12] If *Transition* were not to be a stepchild, it must find its own voice, its own school of contributors.

Transition's first story, Nagenda's, though well fashioned, did not point new directions. It was, in fact, merely a setting, without real plot, for an old man to deliver one of those romantic eulogies of the African past for which the anglophone writers were criticizing the negritudinists. The old man, from a warrior clan, spoke to a young reporter: "You town boys, what do you know? Have you uncovered the empumupu, that heart-like object growing at the end of a stalk which itself is at the end of a bunch of ettooke? And this empumupu was made up of layer after layer of itself which you went on pulling off until the core lay gleaming and naked and infant-brown in your hands. And you smelled it, and it smelled like fecundity. The matoke garden was more than a garden of food, it was our mother" (*Tran-*

sition no. 2, p. 5). Nagenda's evocation of the past was powerful, standing as it did symbolically for something numinous and universal; nevertheless, his dialogue and narrative context were clumsy and artificial. Though promising, Nagenda's story was not much more than good school writing.

Ngugi's story was both more promising and more mature. Though still a student, he had already published five stories (in *Penpoint* and the *Kenya Weekly News*), and his first *Transition* story did strike out on newer ground, confronting the bitterness and the sense of personal estrangement and irrevocable loss left behind by the independence struggle head-on in a way that prefigured Ngugi's treatment of these themes in *A Grain of Wheat* (1967). In "The Return," Ngugi's protagonist, carrying home on his back a bundle that seems to contain "the bitterness and hardships of the years spent in detention camps," as if he were Christian "carrying his load of sin on his Pilgrim's Progress to the Cross" (p. 5), finds in the end that self-sacrifice and struggle have not vindicated him but merely cost him his place in his village and his wife. There was sentimental idealism in this—youthful alienation of a kind similar to Neogy's own. But Ngugi's final affirmation was nevertheless striking for its maturity— for its denial of polemic, its affirmation of life in spite of loss and estrangement, and, again as in *A Grain of Wheat*, for its reaffirmation of commitment: "This was truly his 'Return,' and as he peered into the future, as he became aware of the beauty of life, in spite of its hardships, he could see no possibility of his going away again" (*Transition* no. 3, p. 7).

After the third issue, *Transition* shifted its attention back toward criticism. As Neogy later said, there simply wasn't much creative writing going on. Then, too, the magazine, though hardly off the ground, had begun to attract the attention of the literary world outside Kampala. At roughly the same time that Neogy had begun his effort to stimulate new creativity through *Transition*, the South African literary critic and writer Ezekiel Mphahlele had independently begun an effort in Nairobi to encourage artistic and literary activity through the formation of a club for writers and artists, the Chemchemi Centre, roughly patterned on another Ulli Beier brainchild in Nigeria, the Mbari Clubs. With the launching of these two complementary projects, the club in Nairobi and the magazine in Kampala, it seemed a propitious moment to bring writers from elsewhere on the continent together in East Africa, both to stimulate East African writers and to give an awareness of East Africa to writers from South Africa and West Africa. Mphahlele was able to arrange the conference because, in addition to directing the Chemchemi Centre, he was also a representative of the Paris-based Congress for Cultural Freedom. Four years later, Mphahlele's introduction of Neogy to the Congress for Cultural Freedom was to bring Neogy deep pain and embarrassment when that organization's CIA links were exposed, but at the time Mphahlele seems to have been completely unaware that he was, in effect, employed by the CIA—as was Neogy unaware.

The immediate effects of the writers' conference on *Transition* were, first, to put a solution to its financial problems within reach (since Mphahlele offered funding from the Congress for Cultural Freedom), and, second, to deflect the magazine, for a time, away from the tasks of raising political issues and promoting new writers and toward the more prestigious task of sorting out the aesthetic preoccupations of the visiting writers, whose reputations had already begun to be established—Nigeria's Chinua Achebe, Wole Soyinka, Christopher Okigbo, J. P. Clark, and Gabriel Okara; Ghana's Kofi Awoonor; South Africa's Bloke Modisane, Arthur Maimane, and Mphahlele. The idea, in principle, seems to have been to inspire serious writing and criticism by example, to demonstrate that anglophone black Africa had sophisticated modern writers by assembling them in Kampala. East Africans might be galvanized by the demonstration. Still, one temporary effect of the conference on *Transition* was simply to magnify the influence of *Black Orpheus*.

Once the excitement of the writers' conference had died down, Neogy put Mphahlele's subsidy to good use. *Transition* had actually suspended publication with the third issue in January 1962, Neogy's initial capital having run out,[13] but he managed to get the fourth issue out by June, five months overdue, and the fifth appeared a few months later with an extensive report on the conference. Thereafter, the writers and critics who had gotten their starts in *Black Orpheus* or through Mbari began to be conspicuous in *Transition*. The first of them, the poet Christopher Okigbo, had met Neogy at the conference and talked with him about the possibility of *Transition* expanding into West Africa. Though the magazine was then actually only a few months old, such ambitious plans were made feasible by the support from the Congress for Cultural Freedom. In the end it was settled that Okigbo would become the West African editor, using his Mbari contacts and his position as Nigerian representative of Cambridge University Press to drum up contributors and secure a foothold there that would, it was hoped, eventually allow circulation to expand significantly.[14]

Okigbo's first contributions to the magazine, landmarks in African writing, were his poems "The Limits" in number 6/7 and "Silences" in number 8, introduced by an acknowledgment, à la Eliot, of the influence of an international gallery of famous writers: Raja Ratnam, Malcolm Cowley, Stéphane Mallarmé, Rabindranath Tagore. This sort of eclectic internationalism was right up Neogy's alley. Unlike Beier, Neogy never intended his to be a magazine with primarily African or pan-African parameters—as Okigbo himself pointed out.[15] *Transition* was meant to have a universalist flavor as well as an international audience.

Okigbo's Eliotesque poem "Heavensgate," as well as "The Limits," had already appeared in chapbooks from Mbari Publications, and his "Four Canzones" had appeared in *Black Orpheus* no. 11, but "Silences" marked a new complexity in his style, an unraveling of meaning and image that was eventually to find full expression in "Path of Thunder." The first section of "Silences," "The Lament of the Silent Sisters," found its first publication in *Transition* (the second section, "Lament of the Drums," appeared in *Black Orpheus* no. 17 in November/December 1964), its appearance indicative both of

Neogy's venturesome spirit and of the temporary disequilibrium of the new magazine's aesthetic. Okigbo's nebulous, introspective pilgrimage was a long way from the intense political soul-searching of the protagonist of Ngugi's "The Return."

Still, *Transition* was making an important contribution to African literary development in publishing "Silences"—especially since this was not a final, finished version of the poem, but poetry in the process of creation. The final version of "Lament of the Silent Sisters" was to be very different from the *Transition* version. The original:

> We are the dumb bells
> outside the gates
> In the hollow landscapes;
> without memory we carry
>
> Each of us an
> Urn of native
> Soil, of not
> Impalpable dust.
>> (*Transition* no. 8, p. 15)

became, in the final version:

> DUMB-BELLS outside the gates
> In hollow seascapes, we carry
> Each of us an urn of native
> Earth, a double handful anciently gathered.
>> (*Labyrinths* [London: Heinemann, 1971; rpt. 1979], p. 41)

The original:

> . . . The Kingfisher gathers his ropes in the distance:
> The salt water gathers them inward.
>
> —Will the water gather us?
>
> —Silences fade in my stomach like galloping antelopes.
>
> —Will the water gather us?
>
> —As deep and profound as scented shadows,
> Silences are loud like mountain waterfalls.

—Will the water gather us . . .
Gather us . . . gather us . . .

(Transition no. 8, p. 15)

became:

The Kingfisher gathers his ropes in the distance
The salt water gathers them inward
The dipping paddle blades, the inconstant dolphins
The salt water gathers them inward.
Will the water gather us in her sibylline chamber?
And our silences fade into galloping antelopes.

(Labyrinths, p. 42)

The change in Okigbo's style from the restrained clarity of voice, delicate suggestion of image, in the earlier version, to the internal contradiction and syntactic disjunction of the later version was crucial to his development as a poet. The "galloping antelopes" in the original, for instance, made a simple, evocative metaphor for the way near silence fades into deeper silence. In the final version it had become a teasing paradox—a silence that could somehow "fade" into harsh sound.

Transition no. 8 also revealed two other young writers—one a completely unknown East African, Rebecca Njau; the other a South African "coloured" writer, Richard Rive, just emerging into prominence as a member of the group of South African writers that *Black Orpheus* and Mbari were bringing to light. Rive was then known as the author of a few realistic stories. *Emergency*, just completed, was not yet published. *Quartet* was about to appear from the East German firm Seven Seas. Rive had been invited to the Kampala conference, but had not actually participated. The South African authorities had withheld his passport, and he had not gotten to Kampala until a few months later. Still, the conference had, in this way, been the oblique catalyst in his acquaintance with Neogy.

Rive's story in *Transition* no. 8, "Moon Over District Six," was a slum-New-Year's-Eve sketch, of minor importance and sometimes nearly incoherent with clumsy dialect. However, it did introduce to

Neogy's readers the mood of ironic desperation, the intransigent action and sordid characterization of the new South African writers:

> "I say, paal, buy us two one and fours," said a flashily dressed dandy in pink socks who wanted to jump the bioscope queue.
> "I'm a'ready buying five tickets," lied a frightened stranger.
> "O'ny two man," pink socks insisted.
> "But I'm a'ready buying five," said the nervous stranger.
> "It's New Year an' I'll rip you' guts," said pink socks who had no knife. "You'd better buy it an' don' talk a lot."
> "A'right," said the frightened stranger.   (p. 11)

Rive's story was also significant in that it established a parallel, a model elsewhere in Africa for the kind of barren realism emphasizing powerlessness in the face of political and economic necessity that was to color much East African writing—including, of course, Ngugi's and Rebecca Njau's.

Njau's play "The Scar," in the same issue, was overwhelming in its presentation of social determinism, and yet there was also something more—the broaching of a controversial feminist theme, then as now a delicate subject in Africa. Neogy had not quite "discovered" Njau; she had already gotten "The Scar" performed on Radio Uganda and was even reported to be working on a novel. But the subject of "The Scar," female circumcision, powerfully emphasized the clash of modern and traditional values, and its treatment, at once realistic and symbolic, prefigured *Transition*'s own later tone, style—its combination of toughness and controversiality, with an emphasis on cultural symbols as well as social or political facts.

Njau's was, it should be noted, the first creative work to attempt the subject that Ngugi was to make central to *The River Between*, and hers was the more controversial treatment, placed as it was within the deliberate context of female emancipation. The heroine, Mariana, like many of Ngugi's early heroes and heroines, seemed to speak for the author's own point of view. A reformer encouraging the young women to shun the initiation ceremonies and working to change the social and economic relations that keep women in bondage, she advises Nini, a young follower beginning to waver because of social pressure: "You are a brave girl, Nini, why should this worry you? Women must be free to eat, talk, and walk freely. Who will free us except ourselves? Do you want to remain in bondage forever? Do you want to die a slave of man?" (p. 25).

Njau handled the conflict between old ways and new quite skillfully, with a dramatist's knack for embodying confrontation in terse dialogue:

> FIRST WOMAN: What does an unmarried woman like you know to teach others?
>
> SECOND WOMAN: You have taught our girls to talk and laugh and argue with men! Do you want them to remain unmarried like you?
>
> MARIANA: I want them to free themselves from slavery; I want them to respect their bodies and minds[;] I want them to break away the chains that have so long bound them. (p. 25)

That the play degenerated into melodrama by the end, a revelation of Mariana's scandalous past resulting in the failure of her leadership, was not fatal to its theme, and Mariana's final speech, expressive of regret at broken ideals, was, in its powerful use of images from East African life (ending with the circumcision scar itself), a striking announcement to *Transition* readers that the magazine intended its literature to be tough, controversial, unflinching, and uniquely East African. There was also an echo of Prospero's speech in *The Tempest*:

> My time is over; the sheep-fold is open; enter and take the lambs; you have won the battle. My life has been a dream; I have been floating in the air and clinging to things like a bat; but now I'm down, my wings are broken; I can float no more. My scar is wounded afresh; it will heal no more; I can hide it no more. (p. 28)

Oddly enough, Lewis Nkosi, reviewing this issue of *Transition* a few months later, was to complain of the magazine's lack of "consistency, a sense of purpose." Okigbo's poem, he thought, overshadowed everything else—which was hardly a fair estimation of Njau—and though he praised Okigbo's aesthetic eclecticism, he criticized him for importing alien themes and attitudes. Okigbo was "both stimulating and irritating—irritating because he seems to me to represent a consciousness which is rooted in a European pessimism and despair, without showing us its connection with an African subsoil from which one would expect his poetry to spring."[16]

Nevertheless, with the appearance of *Transition* no. 8 Neogy was entitled to boast of a significant milestone in light of "the high mortality rate of literary magazines"—*Transition* had survived its first full year. He also announced, rather sheepishly, that it was no longer a monthly (only seven issues had appeared in the first year of publication, at any rate) and that subscription and single-copy rates would have to be increased "to pay for the enlarged bi-monthly," from fifteen Ugandan shillings to twenty-three for six issues. Subscribers who had signed on at the old rates were "having their subscriptions readjusted" (p. 3).

The fourth issue, in June 1962, had introduced as the magazine's graphic symbol an illustration of one of the famous Benin bronzes, the "horn-blower," and now Neogy announced that this had been intended to symbolize "what we hoped might be achieved through the pages of *Transition*: a closer understanding and sharing between East and West Africa"—in the service of which ideal he proposed to produce a separate West African edition of *Transition*, to be edited by Okigbo. It would be quarterly and would share its literary material with the parent Kampala edition, varying only in the inclusion of "political and other non-literary material" drawn from West Africa. Another addition to *Transition*'s "far-flung" staff was Kofi Awoonor, "the Ghanaian poet and lecturer in English at Achimota." Though Neogy had, he said, often been on the brink of "financial disaster," the help of "friends across the seas" (presumably the Congress for Cultural Freedom) had made it possible to "consolidate and renew our publishing efforts" (p. 3). Beginning with the tenth issue, in September 1963, *Transition* was even able to shed its first skin—abandoning its familiar cover, a simple geometrical pattern of rectangles, in favor of a fresh design for each new issue.

Ngugi's, Nagenda's, Rive's, and Njau's pieces had perhaps been false starts for *Transition*, in that no coherent literary movement with the magazine at its center had sprung up around them. Nevertheless, Neogy was still not ready to turn aside from his interest in literature. *Transition* did continue to publish interesting new writers from throughout Africa, but it did not spawn a school of writers who bore some active, coherent, organic relationship to one another as writers, as *Black Orpheus* did. Some *Transition* writers had simply made their mark elsewhere,[17] but the larger reason for the magazine's artistic disunity and misdirection seems simply to have been that *Transition*'s new writers were too few, too separate, and therefore too little affected by mutual influences.

In *Transition* no. 9, for example, Tchicaya U Tam'si's poem "The Hearse" appeared (translated from the French by Gerald Moore), months before U Tam'si's first *Black Orpheus* appearance. But it was the *Black Orpheus* appearance that made the larger impact, perhaps because U Tam'si's surrealism, like Aimé Césaire's, could strike no root in East Africa, whose own young poets—David Rubadiri, Okot p'Bitek, and later Taban lo Liyong—were to be so simple and matter-of-fact. Perhaps U Tam'si's themes of death, illogic, and distortion appealed to Neogy's bohemianism; perhaps the poem's note of nameless national mourning and betrayal struck some respondent chord; nevertheless, U Tam'si's style did not win allies or imitators in East Africa.

"Sticks to Blindmen": *Transition's* Literary Growing Pains

During the period beginning in 1963 in which Neogy made his most consistent effort to build a literary movement around *Transition*, there continued to be a lack of cross-fertilization. Nevertheless, the magazine remained self-consciously literary, reviewing and publicizing writers who were appearing elsewhere (with a tough-mindedness often missing from *Black Orpheus*), trying hard to find new writers of its own, and fanning the flames of various literary controversies. Its major accomplishments, a few years later, were to be in very different spheres (primarily, that is, in its ironic analysis of symbolic elements in African politics and society), but there were signal contributions to African literature as well—in a style that began even then to hint at a somewhat different future for the magazine. His literary issues, Neogy has commented in a recent interview, were meant to serve as "sticks to blindmen," a tactile, physical probe of the difficult path of new nationhood ahead.[18]

In *Transition* no. 10 (September 1963), for instance, Neogy put poems by ten different young poets together in a special section ("Ten Poems From Ten Poets"). It was a fascinating collage, intended, to borrow again his recent metaphor, to sweep *Transition's* poetic blindman's stick across as wide an arc as possible. The blindness, in this instance, was meant also to be color blindness, and Neogy's special section emphasized his desire to liberate *Transition* from what Okigbo was later to call *Black Orpheus's* reliance on the "black mystique."[19] It was no easy feat to accomplish. There were, to be sure, poems from the group associated with *Black Orpheus*: Africans Dennis Brutus and Kofi Awoonor, and Beier's expatriate coeditor, Gerald Moore. But Neogy was publishing Brutus and Awoonor nearly simultaneously with their first publication in *Black Orpheus*. There were, moreover, also poems by a group of unknown Indian poets that, if not entirely successful, were at least interesting technical experiments. There were poems by three other expatriates, and a poem by the Cameroonian poet Mbella Sonne Dipoko, who was more or less single-handedly "discovered" by *Transition* and had already had three poems ("Creative Hope," "Transient Night," and "Promise") in number 6/7 (October 1962).

Though Dipoko was to become a poet of some importance, it must be said that his early *Transition* poems are striking neither for their subtlety of theme nor for their technique. The mood, central image, and idea of "Our Life" in *Transition* no. 10, for instance, are similar to, and less successful than, the images and themes of another young poet in that issue, Kofi Awoonor. In "Our Life," as in two Awoonor poems published by Beier at roughly that same time, "I Heard a Bird Cry" and "The Weaver Bird," a bird becomes the unifying symbol expressing a longing for the traditional past, a criticism of the colonial experience, and mixed feelings of hope and apprehension about the future. Dipoko's "ailing bird," however, who "made its agony / a song blown through the air" was compared to the people's "winged hope":

> As in the cities we said the same prayers
> As in the villages we espoused ancestral myths
> Transmitting our frustration our life our mortality
> To the young country of tomorrow and day after tomorrow
> Flattering ourselves with the charity of the blood-donor's love.
>
> (p. 20)

Awoonor's contribution to *Transition* no. 10 was modest enough (and only eight lines long), but his impassioned call in this poem, "The Years Behind," for the remaking of the "old days" was central to his work. Beier also chose this poem for inclusion in Awoonor's first *Black Orpheus* selection. Again, although Awoonor's poetry profited most from Beier's assiduous promotion (in *Black Orpheus* and an Mbari chapbook), it must be noted that Awoonor's promise was recognized almost as early in Kampala as it was in Ibadan. Promotion and literary "propaganda," which Beier quite deliberately undertook, did not fit Neogy's style or universalist presuppositions. One of the things, in fact, that most hindered his efforts at building a unified literary movement around *Transition* might well have been his rejection of what Okigbo was to call "blackness for its own sake."[20]

Like Awoonor's "The Years Behind," Dennis Brutus's "Sabotage, 1962" appeared in *Transition* no. 10 almost simultaneously with Brutus's first appearance in *Black Orpheus* no. 12 (1963); and Brutus, like Awoonor, must be said to have owed much of his early recognition to Beier's assiduous promotion. Nevertheless, one must again credit Neogy's early recognition of an important writer and his selection of a work central to that writer's early direction. In "Sabotage, 1962," Neogy had chosen a poem remarkable for what were to become Brutus's hallmarks: his conciseness, the physicality and sexuality of his imagery, his revelation of tightly controlled but painful emotion. Like many of the new East African writers, Brutus's style was terse, direct:

> Here, thunderheads rear in the night
> dominating the awed quiet sky;
>
> on the quiet-breathing plains
> fractured metals shriek abandoned wails;
>
> my country, an ignorantly timid bride
> winces, tenses for the shattering releasing tide.
> (p. 21)

Two of the Indian poets, G. S. Sharat Chandra and Sukhi Singh, showed promise of originality. Chandra's "Expiations" was a series of images piled, heedless of syntax, upon the familiar theme of death's inevitability, but the images for death were sharp and unexpected ("the intersection we just took / when the green lights blinked," "that song in the coffee bar which / inspite your coin and banging fists, never played"). Singh's "Of Former Love" was a sort of poetic cubism, cutting the metaphors apart and putting back together contradictory or illogical pieces. It ended with a clumsy eroticism bound to stir controversy:

> I saw her private hands,
> Womb-gloved, protected, self-raped,

Stroke her transparent heart.
Hair-dunes in desert waist,
And I, the outside part.
(p. 22)

By the time Dipoko's "To Pre-Colonial Africa" appeared in *Transition* no. 13 (March/April 1964), his poetry, though still showing affinities with Awoonor's, had much matured; but again it was a poetry seeking single metaphors for the swindle of colonialism: a diver returning with a strange catch ("glittering, their liquid lustre gave the illusion of pearls"), a trader bringing useless trifles:

So did our days change their robes
From the hide of leopard skin
To prints of false lions
That fall in tatters
Like the wings of a whipped butterfly.
(p. 32)

Dipoko's combination of Brutus's crude intensity with Césaire's incongruity promised greater things to come, from a poet whose images could disorient, shock, and sting.

If Dipoko was one of the few who could be said to have made a name for himself through *Transition* in that period when so many writers were making fast starts in East Africa and elsewhere in Africa, he was nevertheless not the only one whose promise Neogy recognized early. Though Awoonor, Brutus, Wole Soyinka, Okot p'Bitek, Taban lo Liyong, and David Rubadiri, for instance, scored major successes elsewhere, they all got started at roughly the same time and all wrote for *Transition*.

Okot p'Bitek, for instance, contributed a study of Acholi folk tales to number 6/7 (October 1962), a study of Father Placied Tempels' *Bantu Philosophy* to number 13 (March/April 1964), a study of "The Self in African Imagery" to number 15 (July/August 1964), an impressive study of "Acholi Love" to number 17 (November/December 1964), and a poem, "Return the Bridewealth," to number 24 (1966). *Song of Lawino*, which established Okot's reputation as a serious poet, appeared in the same year as "Return the Bridewealth." Taban's ironical meditation on graduate study at Howard University in the United States, "The Education of Taban lo Liyong," appeared in the same issue. A casual send-up of formal education, delightful in its style of offhand irreverence, Taban's piece fit *Transition*'s tone well: "That girl," his misanthropic persona reflects, "she has a waspish waist, and two Vat 69s stuck on her chest" (p. 16). Nevertheless, much of Taban's early growth as a writer came in the United States.

Even so, there was an importance to the publication, in an East African journal, of these young writers, who were, after all, on the verge of a remarkable literary effusion. Neogy had not brought forth fresh literary currents, but they were coming forth all around him, and by 1964 Neogy was publishing material that was indicative of the depth and complexity of this new literature.

Grace Ogot is an example. Though she had already made an appearance in *Black Orpheus* (11, 1962), she was hardly well known. The appearance in *Transition* no. 13 (March/April 1964) of her story "Ward Nine" was as tough an announcement of the magazine's iconoclasm as Njau's "The Scar" had been in the eighth issue (although lacking the earlier piece's social militancy). Ogot, a nurse married to historian Alan Ogot, wrote with the practical aim of detailing the corruption that she had seen in her own profession. "Ward Nine" was a thorough, immediate, realistically detailed account of venality, brutality, and insensitivity to suffering in public health care, a theme that might also strike home to readers elsewhere in Africa.

Ogot's skill was her ability to inspire sympathetic identification with human suffering, but what was striking about her narrative was precisely what was to be striking about *Transition* itself a few years later in its more political heyday: its tough-mindedness and the resultant force of its indictment. What one remembered about the story were its revelations from beneath the veneer of health professionalism: the protagonist's helplessness as he lay bleeding and uncomfortable, ignored by the nurses because he hadn't bribed them; the doctors' callousness; the nurses' lies and efforts to punish the man by not feeding him or bringing him a bedpan. Just as later in *Transition*'s more political period, Neogy's new writer did not spare readers the impolite details of human pain and degradation.

Another illustration of Neogy's preference for material that would shock conventional sensibilities was his publication in no. 23 (1965) of a West African folktale, rendered in ballad stanzas by a former expatriate lecturer at Ibadan named Paul Edwards, that told the story of the progressive dismemberment and disfiguring of a village belle's spectral lover. The poem's two final stanzas were gruesome enough for any reader:

> They came to a man who had no face
>   Who sat beside the way,
> And he stopped beside that faceless man,
>   And gave his flesh away.
>
> She knew now what was that man's name,
>   No need had she to ask;
> And in his bed in the narrow earth
>   She performed her wifely task.
>
> (p. 31)

With other writers such as U Tam'si or Soyinka, however, it seems to have been a taste for the avant-garde—appealing to the bohemianism Howe later described—that moved Neogy. Wole Soyinka's first contribution to the magazine, coming when he had already begun to establish himself in Nigeria as a playwright, poet, and Beier's coeditor at *Black Orpheus*, was his poem "Luo Plains," an appropriate choice both for its East African setting and for its combination of striking diction with concrete immediacy of image. In addition to an evocation of heat, vastness, and drought, there was also a hint of the erotic in the linking of the landscape with a woman's body:

> Lakemists
> On her shadeless dugs, parched
> At waterhole. Veils. Molten silver
> Down cloudflues of alchemist sun . . .
> A lake's grey salve at dawn?

That dawn
Her eyes were tipped with sunset spears
Seasons' quills upon her parchment, yet
The hidden lake of her

Forgives!

(*Transition* no. 13, p. 17)

Yet if the poem's theme and style fit the magazine well, and if Soy-inka's recognizable name lent credibility, Neogy nevertheless needed to find more material from outside the *Black Orpheus* camp, and especially more uniquely East African material, if the magazine was to find its own literary voice.

There was less to be said, therefore, in favor of Neogy's publication of another influential Nigerian, novelist Chinua Achebe. Achebe, like Okigbo, contributed a work in progress, but there were fewer important differences between the chapter of Achebe's third novel, *Arrow of God*, that Neogy published and the version eventually published in book form by John Day than there had been between the earlier and later versions of Okigbo's "Silences." Achebe's excerpt for *Transition* no. 9, projected as the second chapter of his new novel but eventually published as the third, was close for the most part to the final version: there were to be corrections of typos, a few minor changes of wording, changes in one character's name ("John Mac-millan" became "John White") and in another's title (Clark, previously a "young administrative officer," became a "young political officer"), but the only major change was to be the transposition of Winterbottom's diatribe commencing "One thing you must remember about the natives . . ." from the beginning to the end of his recollection of the feud between Umuaro and Okperi. Neogy was thus printing an excerpt from a nearly finished book by an established writer whose work was continuing along a line that he had already laid down with the publication of *Things Fall Apart* in 1958.

Neogy's major opportunity to publish an influential East African writer at the beginning of his literary development came a few years later with the emergence of Okot p'Bitek, who until that time had been working under the sponsorship of Makerere College's Department of Extramural Studies in his home Gulu region toward the preservation and revitalization of traditional culture. Okot's contributions to *Transition*, together with Ogot's, Njau's, and Taban lo Liyong's, brought Neogy closest to the goal of which he and Mphahlele had talked—that of creating a unified East African literary movement.

Okot's early contributions, for instance, were exceptionally revealing of the literary development that was about to take place. "Acholi Love," for example, was defined in revolutionary counterdistinction to the Western concept of romantic love, the chivalric ideal. Sexual attraction among the Acholi, Okot said, was physical, immediate, direct. A young man might simply take by the arm a woman he had just seen for the first time on her way to the well and say, "I want you!" A contest of wills would follow in which he tried to storm her defenses through a series of prescribed arguments, inducements, and sham physical assaults. This intentional reversal of the concept of love absorbed by the African elite from their European mentors was made more pointedly ironic by the matter-of-fact way in which Okot described Acholi practices that, from the Western point of view, were moral anathema. At one point in the ritual of courtship, for instance, the young woman's mother "now begins to bring much pressure on her, and to urge her to go to the man's hut, and find out if, as the Acholi say, *he is alive*. The desire for childbirth was so strong, and the implications of inability to produce so grave, that it was absolutely essential to know, right from the start" (p. 31).

Okot's first *Transition* poem, "Return the Bridewealth," like "Acholi Love," concentrated on his familiar early theme, central also to *Song of Lawino*: the rejection of old ways for new and the cultural infection and putrescence that follow. As in "Acholi Love" and *Song of Lawino*, the theme is sexual. A man's wife has deserted him. He wishes to remarry, but neither he nor his parents can afford a second bride price. He must ask that the first bride price be returned. The poem hints at a larger cultural symbol as well—of a "bride price" stolen from Africa by the colonial interlude. Nevertheless, there is no room in this simple poem for the ironic complexity, invective, misunderstanding, and cultural distancing that characterized *Song of Lawino*. Instead, the protagonist's first-person voice simply frames an acrid portrait of the new husband:

> He marches past me, stumping the earth in anger, like
>   an elephant with a bullet in his bony head!
> He does not look at me
> He does not touch me, only the butt of his weapon touches
>   my knee lightly,
> He walks away, the sacks of cotton on his behind rising and
>   falling alternately,
> Like a bull hippo returning to the river after grazing in the
>   fresh grasses.

When the woman returns the bride price (in a bank check), the protagonist's comment is only, "They say the doctor has cut open her stomach and removed the bag of her eggs / so that she may remain a young woman forever" (p. 53).

Neogy thus opened up to his readers the essence of Okot's forceful message about the bloated sterility of the "modern" ways that were eradicating the African tradition. Though the poem had no complex ironic voice to match Lawino's in *Song of Lawino*, in publishing "Return the Bridewealth," Neogy had taken a large step toward placing *Transition* at the center of East Africa's nascent literary revolution.

Courting Controversy: Literary and Political Debate in Early *Transition*s

In the years between 1963 and 1966, Neogy began gradually to turn away from creative literature toward literary criticism and political controversy. In doing so, he seems to have been making a conscious decision gradually to relax his primary commitment to the pursuit of "Poetry Prose Criticism" in order to develop a facet of the magazine that had been growing in prominence from the first few issues—its role as a platform for debate.[21] In getting caught up in the literary and political controversies that followed, Neogy ultimately fully committed himself to a new role for the magazine, one that seems, in retrospect, to have much more closely matched his own inclinations and the intellectual climate.

Neogy had already shown some inclination to political and social controversiality. Jennings's article on political party systems in Africa in *Transition* no. 1 had been followed, in *Transition* no. 2, by a "Transition Profile" of Julius Nyerere and a defense by Nyerere of one-party government that evoked the familiar picture of elders in traditional Africa sitting under a big tree and talking out village problems until consensus was reached. Nyerere's arguments were otherwise equally straightforward—and completely inimical to Neogy's own beliefs. There was a temporary need, Nyerere argued, for the suppression of free speech and assembly, since political independence and economic disadvantagement constituted a "time of emergency." A review in the same issue by Geoffrey Engholm, a British economist teaching at Makerere, spoke for the other side, denouncing similar arguments in defense of Nkrumah's one-party state ("Kwame Nkrumah and the Future of Africa," pp. 36–37).

Transition no. 3 featured an editorial by Neogy decrying "the strong and widespread anti-Indian prejudice which exists among Africans" ("Race Attitudes," pp. 38–39). *Transition* no. 4 featured both a somewhat skeptical perspective on pan-Africanism by Alan

Rake, whose book about Tom Mboya had just appeared in the United States, and an assault by Mboya on the narrow-mindedness and unfairness of expatriate commentators on African politics, delivered as an address in Paris (pp. 29–30 and 11–14, respectively). Rake had, of course, for some time been an expatriate contributor of articles about Africa to international publications. Mboya's contribution to *Transition* no. 8 followed Nyerere's lead in defending "African socialism" as having a strong traditional basis in the African social structure and in African conceptions of communalism and charity. Mboya rebutted Rake on the subject of pan-Africanism. An exchange of letters between Mboya and C. N. Omondi of Nairobi in *Transition* no. 11 (pp. 5–6) debated the issues further. The term "African socialism," Omondi argued, was simply being used to cover "half-way systems" and convenient distortions of Marxism.

This sort of editorial evenhandedness, even on issues about which Neogy had strong feelings himself, was to be an important feature of Neogy's *Transition*. *Transition* no. 11 was most notable, however, for its introduction to *Transition* readers of someone who was to become perhaps the writer most clearly associated with the magazine's distinctive style, Makerere University political scientist Ali Mazrui. Mazrui recalls the electricity of his first meeting with Rajat Neogy, shortly after arriving in Uganda to take up his teaching post at Makerere: "Rajat had a brilliant knack for 'sensing talent' in the room! He thought he 'sensed' me." Neogy promptly gave Mazrui two new books, Joseph Kariuki's *Mau Mau Detainee* and Mboya's *Freedom and After*, which Mazrui proceeded to review from the almost eccentrically original context of Thomas Carlyle's *On Heroes, Hero-Worship, and the Heroic in History.*[22] Mazrui's article initiated *Transition*'s first key series of political controversies, which will be taken up in due course in this account. In the meantime, however, there were equally virulent literary controversies to consider.

With a prefatory disclaimer, Neogy also published an article by Obiajunwa Wali entitled "The Dead End of African Literature" in *Transition* no. 10. A former intimate of the first generation of Nigerian writers, Wali wrote from Northwestern University in the United

States, where he was engaged in graduate studies, to reprehend the proceedings of the Kampala African writers' conference. Judging from the report in *Transition* no. 5, Wali declared, the conference seemed to have gone nowhere. It was exemplary of nothing more than the esotericism, elitism, and pro-Western bias of the new African writers. Beyond debating a few "sterile concepts such as 'négritude' and the 'African personality'" (p. 13) and offering the new African writers a chance to become acquainted firsthand with the overseas patrons who were their only real audience (p. 15), it had accomplished nothing. That, Wali argued, was inevitable in light of the nature of this new literature: "African literature, as now understood and practised, is merely a minor appendage in the main stream of European literature. Both creative writers and literary critics . . . read and devour European literature and critical methods" (p. 13).

Wali's examples were, perhaps, a bit haphazard and ill-defined, but his impudent indictment was nevertheless arresting, and Neogy printed it even though his own reaction to the writers' conference had been quite different. Where Neogy had been enthusiastic and exhilarated, Wali was coolly derogatory; this new literature, he wrote, lacked "blood and stamina" and could only have meaning to those "steeped . . . in European literature and culture" (pp. 13–14). Unless it reformed, dropped its adherence to European aesthetics, the new African literature was doomed to virtual irrelevance and ultimate dissipation. Wali was particularly adamant on the subject of language. An African literature neither could nor, for social and political reasons, should be written in any other than an indigenous African language: "Until these writers and their western midwives accept the fact that any true African literature must be written in African languages, they would be merely pursuing a dead end, which can only lead to sterility, uncreativity, and frustration" (p. 14).

Although he had predicted that Wali's article might "cause some anxious heart-searching among the younger writers of this Continent" (p. 3), the reaction must have surprised even Neogy by its stridency and persistence. The uproar, in fact, did not die down until two years later. By then, Chinua Achebe, Austin Shelton, Ezekiel Mphahlele, Gerald Moore, Wole Soyinka, Denis Williams, Paul Edwards, John Clare, Jan Knappert, Peter Nazareth, and R. L. Wigglesworth had all added their motes to the controversy as it unfolded in one issue after another of the magazine.

Achebe and Mphahlele had, in fact, already engaged in a little preliminary sparring in the issue preceding that in which Wali's first article appeared. When the glare of Wali's ill-mannered searchlight fell on them, in fact, these two leading figures in the movement Wali denounced were engaged in precisely the "sterile" pursuit of which they stood accused, the debate over the relevance to anglophone Africa of the francophone concept of "*négritude*." Mphahlele, Achebe had charged at the Congress of Africanists in Accra, sounded as if he favored an analogous tying of literature to primarily social or political ends. Mphahlele replied: "Our writing can only be valid if it interprets contemporary society in a mode of expression that hits on the intellectual, emotional, and physical planes of meaning. What more can you ask of a writer, of an artist, of a musician?" "What more," Achebe snapped back, "can you ask of a toy train when you have wound it and set it on the rails? Nothing."[23]

Mphahlele, stung, was disinclined to take invective lying down. He was at pains to reassure readers of *Transition* no. 9 that he had not meant to prescribe social or political roles for artists and writers; that, in fact, he rather thought Achebe's own writing felicitously exemplary of an appeal to the "intellectual, emotional, and physical planes of meaning." He refused, however, to let Achebe have it all his own way:

> Let writers follow their own temperament, by all means. But they should not start squealing when they are being told that some of their tam-tam poetry or some of their verbal violence is just so much gas, or that some of their sedate prose is mouldy and stinks, or that people have their everyday concerns even while they are acting out the conflict of generations. Otherwise if writers want to please themselves and themselves only, the peak of Mount Kilimanjaro is very near, or they can charter a space ship.   (no. 9, pp. 7–8)

Still, if the invective was pyrotechnic, the substance of the disagreement seemed susceptible to compromise and resolution.

It was otherwise with Wali's manifesto to the new anglophone writers and that was the reason for the vigor of their rebuttal. Mphahlele was among the first to respond, pointing out in a long precise letter inaccuracies and inconsistencies in the details of Wali's argument (where, in fact, Wali was vulnerable) and scolding him for concentrating on Western apologists for African literature, such as Ulli Beier, rather than on the literary texts themselves. On the language issue, however, Mphahlele won fewer points, merely pointing out that foreign languages had united the African nationalists, whereas African languages would have separated them, and that, at any rate, writers were not responsible for promoting languages. Should writers "leave off writing and engage in linguistics" (p. 8)? A critic must merely accept the writer's mode of expression and judge his writing on its merits as writing.

Gerald Moore, in the same issue, stressed the impracticability of Wali's linguistic proposals, adding that African writers had, in any case, found ways of bending the English language to their own peculiar needs:

> If there are distinctively African modes of thought and experience a real writer will fight his way to expression of them in a language which gives him a hearing (and a living). If the words are not there, he will put them there, as countless other writers have done before him, as Achebe does in *Things Fall Apart*. At all events let us not lecture him.   (p. 9)

Wole Soyinka's ironic comment simply affirmed the writer's right to be left alone. "I learn a great deal about my opinions every day," he wrote, "and it was a new revelation that I 'do not consider Yoruba suitable' for any of my plays. But what about Ibo? May I know what Obi Wali has done to translate my plays or others' into Ibo or whatever language he professes to speak?" (*Transition* no. 11, p. 9). Denis Williams, equally terse, agreed that it was nobody's business choosing a writer's language for him. And anyway, "Why write novels, plays, *etc.*, south of the Sahara? . . . Nothing, surely, could be more un-African" (p. 9).

By the time Wali had framed his reply, published in *Transition* no. 12, three Western academicians, John Clare, Austin Shelton, and

Paul Edwards, had reinforced the creative writers' first reactions. Shelton, then senior lecturer at the University of Nsukka, penned a facetious review of the novel that he presumed Wali meant to write and for the occasion invented a typical non-Ibo fan of this new Ibo-language novelist: "I had the wonderful experience of hearing Nana Ngwazi, an Itsekiri-speaking man, say that 'as soon as I learn to read Igbo, I'm going to buy that book!' What better compliment could the author receive than such forthright praise from his fellow Africans?" (p. 8). Jan Knappert's letter in *Transition* no. 13 recommended Swahili as the hoped-for language of African unity (p. 8).

Wali's response was recapitulation. He had not criticized the new writers as writers or attempted to "bully" them into changing their language of expression, he wrote. "But I insist that any African writer who chooses to write in a foreign language must face the implications of his choice, the most important being that his works belong to the literary traditions of the language of his choice, for he cannot eat his cake and have it" (*Transition* no. 12, p. 7). Language, he argued, brought with it unavoidable cultural correlatives. To pretend otherwise was "self-deceit" (p. 6). Writers, moreover, had a responsibility to open new paths for others into the use of vernaculars.

In another magazine perhaps the quarrel might have died there, but not in Neogy's *Transition*. There was a year's respite, but in 1965 the conflict broke out again with the simultaneous publication in *Transition* no. 18 of Achebe's careful reply to Wali ("English and the African Writer," pp. 27–30) and a new thrust, in a somewhat different direction, by a somewhat chastened Wali ("The Individual and the Novel in Africa," pp. 31–33).

Achebe, speaking in a sense for all the writers Wali had criticized, won back most of the ground Wali had gained in his earlier surprise assault. Like Mphahlele, Achebe pointed out that though English was a mixed heritage as curse and blessing, it had been an important factor in African unity, cultural as well as political: "On the whole . . . [colonialism] did bring together peoples that had hitherto gone their several ways. And it gave them a language with which to talk with one another. If it failed to give them a song, it at least gave them a tongue, for sighing" (p. 28). Moreover, in most of Africa the colonial languages continued to be necessary. "Where," Achebe asked, "am I to find the time to learn the half-a-dozen or so Nigerian languages each of which can sustain a literature? I am afraid it cannot be done." For good or ill, the language enjoying nationwide currency was English. "Tomorrow it may be something else, although I very much doubt it" (p. 28). A writer must accept what he could not change.

Achebe's final point, perhaps his strongest, was that there were a number of positive consequences of the necessity for the Nigerian writer to write in English. It was, first of all, a worldwide language, which meant that an African writer might have access in English to an international audience. It was also, as a result of wide dispersion, a remarkably malleable language. It was therefore possible, within limits, to modify English to suit African modes of expression, to make it thereby a vehicle for the African sensibility. Achebe had, in fact, tried to do this himself, as he demonstrated through reference to his newly published novel *Arrow of God*. English, far from crippling the African writer, opened new possibilities for him. As further examples of efforts to mold English to the requirements of an African aesthetic, he cited Christopher Okigbo's *Limits*, J. P. Clark's "Night Rain," and even Amos Tutuola's *Palm-Wine Drinkard* (which Wali had accused the Kampala conference participants of neglecting).

For the African writer, Achebe pointed out, there must be a tension between the acceptance of this alien tongue as it was, *as* an alien tongue, and the determination to use it, to modify it, to transform it:

> So my answer to the question, Can an African ever learn English well enough to be able to use it effectively in creative writing? is certainly yes. If on the other hand you ask: Can he ever learn to use it like a native speaker? I should say, I hope not. It is neither necessary nor desirable for him to be able to do so. The price a world language must be prepared to pay is submission to many different kinds of use. The African writer should aim to use English in a way that brings out his message best without altering the language to the extent that its value as a medium of international exchange will be lost. (pp. 29–30)

In this literary controversy, as in earlier and later political ones, Neogy's delight in the passionate duration of the exchanges and his absolute readiness to provide a forum for all comers were instrumental in bringing all of the chief participants to rethink, refocus, and sharpen their perspectives on key issues. If one result of the long interchange had been to stir up intense reader interest, another had been to inspire from Achebe an important critical statement of far-ranging implications.

In turn, Achebe's pointed response deflected Wali's ideas onto a new tack. In adhering to the formal conventions of the Western novel and its social ideal of isolated individualism, Wali asked in *Transition* no. 18, were not the rising generation of African writers vitiating the African traditions of communalism and social hierarchy underscored by indigenous narrative forms? Was that not the real meaning of the character Clarence in Camara Laye's *The Radiance of the King*? Of Obi Okonkwo in Achebe's *No Longer at Ease*? Of Okolo in Gabriel Okara's *The Voice*? There were differences among them to be sure, and the problem could be looked on merely as a challenge, Wali meekly admitted, but his tone was pessimistic.[24]

This new pair of contributions was thrashed out, too, in succeeding issues of *Transition*, again drawing Austin Shelton into the fray, as well as fresh combatants, among them O. R. Dathorne and Judith Gleason. It would be tedious to follow the debate too far, and although much more was to be said on both subjects, in *Transition* and elsewhere,[25] Achebe's cogent defense of his own literary practice effectively capped that discussion. Wali's mildly stated new thesis lapsed temporarily into irresolution.

By this time, moreover, literary controversies were constantly springing up in the magazine, and the threads tended to get crossed and tangled. The issue in which Achebe's and Mphahlele's preliminary sparring over *négritude* appeared also contained a depreciation by Wole Soyinka of the new national theaters in Kampala and Ibadan, which he saw as formalized, rigid, misguided (and expensive) imitations of an inappropriate Western prototype. To the thirteenth issue (pp. 16–17), Okot p'Bitek contributed a startling re-assessment of Father Placied Tempels's pioneering study of Bantu philosophy,[26] which for Okot was, though an important first move-ment in the right direction, nevertheless based upon a number of dangerous and unsound premises—that, for example, all of Africa's psyche could be known by studying one isolated ethnic group and that, more alarmingly, an outsider could perceive an African world view of which Africans themselves were ignorant. "It is," Okot wrote, "to say the least, unhelpful pride to start off by holding that a people do not know what they believe, or cannot express it; and that it is the student who, after discovering it, will tell them what this belief is" (p. 16).

In this critical essay, as in his earlier creative writing, Okot was offering *Transition* readers a glimpse of a striking new attitude that he had taken in his own researches among the Acholi. One must ap-proach traditional Africa humbly, Okot made clear; one must learn diligently and only then begin to make something new out of what had been found: "The role of the student of traditional philosophy, it seems to me, is, as it were, to photograph as much [as possible] . . . and in as great detail as possible, the traditional way of life, and then to make comments; pointing out the connexions and relevances of the different parts" (p. 16).

There was also in this period a series of remarkably thoughtful reviews of new literature that were neither in *Black Orpheus*'s style of enthusiastic promotion nor in Wali's style of out-of-hand detraction. Though these reviews tended to be academic, and were clearly root-ing for these new writers to succeed, they were deliberate and re-strained in their assessments. One might particularly cite as examples Lewis Nkosi on the new Ghanaian writers published in *Okyeame* (in a survey of little magazines in *Transition* no. 12); David Cook's re-view of three Soyinka plays; Donatus Nwoga on Mongo Beti's *Mis-sion to Kala*; M. M. Carlin on Ngugi's *Weep Not, Child*; and J. P. Clark on "Poetry in Africa Today."[27] Even at the peak of the magazine's in-terest in political and social issues there were literary articles of real importance, such as J. P. Clark's "Another Kind of Poetry," which took a hard, precise look at the techniques and literary forms of indigenous oral poetry (*Transition* no. 25, pp. 17–22), and Gerald Moore's "Time and Experience in African Poetry," which sought to trace an existential theme in work of established writers such as Awoonor, Clark, U Tam'si, and Lenrie Peters (*Transition* no. 26, pp. 18–22).

By the beginning of 1966, indeed, *Transition* had come to be a regular vehicle—in a way that *Black Orpheus* under Beier had perhaps never been—for literary criticism that was tough, far-ranging, and contentious. Virtually every issue aired some new analysis, sparked some new critical confrontation. And there was in this literary criticism a stance of ironic disputation, a willingness to take chances, a delight in controversy for its own sake. Wali was not the only writer who enjoyed stirring things up. O. R. Dathorne, for example, in *Transition* no. 20, settled with Wali's article in *Transition* no. 18 thus:

> The tacit assumption is frequently made that African literature was fathered by Senghor and mothered by Achebe, that négritude, the old and the new, and black versus white were its first progeny and Ngugi, Rive, Nkosi, and Awoonor-Williams, its grandchildren. There have been muted suggestions that there were various bastards who did not toe the family line and a good school of critics and a bad school of critics sprang up, to tell us that the bastards were the real offspring or vice-versa. (p. 5)

There was, in fact, something contagious in the magazine's irreverent, contentious (and sometimes extravagant) style. In *Transition* no. 24, for instance, Christina Ama Ata Aidoo reviewed Mukwugo Okoye's *African Responses* in a voice typical of the magazine's collective tone. Okoye, she said, had tried to write a sort of *100 Amazing Facts About the Negro*, as if the way to defend black cultures was to accumulate disconnected trivia. But white contempt was based on prejudice, not ignorance:

> He has gone to a great deal of trouble to prove that the Black Man is omnisocial, omnisophical, omniloco, and omni-god-knows-what-else!

> . . . Everything has been discussed, everything except the most burning question in the negro's history so far, to wit, how the negro shall free himself today.

Okoye's neologism "Omnigro" and his dedicatory poem came in for special ridicule. She quoted the poem at length, asking sarcastically, "Can you beat that?" ("Looking Back With Pride," p. 56).

"Sour Milk": Neogy, Mazrui, and Theroux Fashion the *Transition* Style

While the literary controversies were thus gaining momentum and breadth of application during the period from 1963 to 1966, the social and political debates ushered in by Mazrui's article in *Transition* no. 11 were also gaining in force and extension. Indeed it was Mazrui's eclectic, unpredictable style that was perhaps most emblematic of *Transition* in the mid-sixties, as Abiola Irele pointed out in a review of the first thirty-one issues.[28]

The identifiable elements of the Mazrui style were there from the first: the thematic paradox; the violent yoking together of ideas and events seemingly of wide disparity; the use of ironic puns as fundamental structural elements in arguing a serious thesis; and finally the attempt to get at not the mechanical but the symbolic reality underlying political events. Thus, Kenya's need for nationalistic heroes to cement her nationhood, it was stressed in "Heroes and Uhuru-Worship," would lead inevitably (and, it was implied, appropriately) to the deliberate distortion of the history of the "Mau Mau" insurrections. The reasons, typically, would be symbolic. Nations, new or old, must have heroes and must have "blood." Individual human agency and the palpable drama of violence were *symbolic* necessities that nevertheless defined practical political behavior. Thus, though "Mau Mau" had perhaps been no revolution at all, if one defined "revolution" strictly, it must paradoxically be construed as a revolution. Kenyatta must be not simply a powerful political leader, but "Mzee"—"old man," "parent"—"the hero who is a father-figure because he symbolizes the mother-country" (p. 24).

Thus, Carlyle's *On Heroes, Hero-Worship, and the Heroic in History* was drawn into what had started as a mere book review—partly as authority for such an extended analysis of the symbolism underlying political events, and partly, it seems, for the mere pleasure of transporting so distant and seemingly remote a figure into the contemporary African political fray. There was also, one suspects, the pleasure of finding an irreverent and incongruous pun, so ready to hand in Carlyle's title.

There were rejoinders. In *Transition* no. 13, Leonard H. Okola of Nairobi argued that Mau Mau had essentially been a Kikuyu uprising, and hence not nationalistic at all; and Gary Gappert of Tabora argued that the British revulsion at Mau Mau violence had proved their misunderstanding of the nature of "ideological" confrontations (pp. 5 and 6, respectively). But perhaps because "Uhuru-Worship" was so different in tone and style from earlier *Transition* articles, both Okola and Gappert seem to have missed the point of Mazrui's thesis—which was not that Mau Mau had been different as *fact* from the way it was now being pictured (even without hard evidence, he was willing to believe the stories about Mau Mau recruits drinking menstrual blood, he said), but that no one had yet considered its *symbolic* meaning, which was even then undergoing a process of transformation.

Transition had also by then come a long way graphically from its days of grubby matt paper, crude design, haphazard organization, and promiscuous typography. The cover art, by then an original and distinctive feature of each issue, had begun not only to serve as a lead-in to one or two key features but also to give the magazine continuity in the contents of each issue. Though the tie-in was frequently to a political article (as, for instance, in *Transition* no. 12, where a classified advertisement from a Paris newspaper for a James Baldwin lecture about that year's Washington civil rights march was used in the cover illustration as a lead-in to a Baldwin interview in that issue), the articles at first tended to be academic or to deal with distant problems. The first such feature to strike close to home was in *Transition* no. 16, whose theme, "Errors in Foreign Aid," was announced on the cover by a photograph of a galley proof for one of the two articles with hand-written editorial corrections.

The first issue devoted to a single extended theme and exhibiting *Transition*'s subsequent impudent and aggressive style, however, was probably *Transition* no. 21, which followed the expiration of Wali's and Achebe's literary controversy. The theme, following the lead of Mazrui's "Uhuru-Worship," was violence, with features by eight different contributors, including the former chairman of the political science department at Makerere, Colin Leys, and, once again, Mazrui. Leys's aim, essentially, was to apply the careful classificatory techniques of the social scientist to the question of whether the characterization of "troubled Africa" as an inherently violent place had any objective validity. Leys's method, however, pretty much abstracted itself out of existence. Once all border conflicts, internal political disputes, and struggles based on the presumed illegitimacy of various post-independence regimes had been omitted from consideration, there was not much left to say about levels of violence in Africa— nothing, certainly, for which there were reliable comparable data.

What was important about Leys's article, however, was not the validity or invalidity of his approach. Violence, like Mau Mau, was a symbolic issue. Africa was, in the West's collective mind, a continent where violence was a fact of everyday life, a defining social and cultural attribute. Unlike Mazrui, he had not found a style for considering symbolic issues without fettering them in a methodological straightjacket, but Leys's "Violence in Africa" did at least continue and extend the change in the *Transition* style away from a direct consideration of straightforward factual issues and toward consideration of largely symbolic ones. And in choosing "violence" as his point of departure, Neogy had chosen a negative stereotype that still stuck in the throat of educated Africans, still was a powerful element of the myth, not to speak of the reality, of Africa. Mazrui's article, "Sacred Suicide," moreover, ultimately turned the question of "violent Africa" on its head—examining "non-violence" rather than "violence," seeking to define in several cultural traditions (Christian, Buddhist, classical Greek and Roman), and in the career of Dag Hammarskjöld, the martyred UN secretary general, a collective longing for self-immolation that seemed to Mazrui perhaps the most insidious form of violence—and a form, moreover, totally alien to "violent Africa."

In issues like the special issue on violence, Neogy had begun to define for *Transition* a continuity and topical integration from article to article and issue to issue, using his editorial function to encourage contributors to define or sharpen particular ideas. He wrote:

> How does a magazine continue from one issue to another? Does it start all afresh with a new issue or carry strands from arguments raised in previous ones? Both. One of the functions of an alert editor is to have the ability to catch the tail of side-ideas and develop them. Side-ideas are ideas dropped inadvertently from the body of another, major, pursuit, which sometimes have enough germs in them to be developed and built up into something quite new and independent of their host. . . . Side-ideas are "just-born" in a fit of thoughtlessness, and the editor should here function like the obstetrician, if he thinks it is going to be a worthwhile gamble. Ideally, therefore, a well-edited magazine should, like sour milk, be capable of perpetuating itself.[29]

Thus in *Transition* no. 22, which followed the "violence" issue, for instance, the symbolic target shifted from the myth itself to the mythologizers—Westerners whose association with, or description of, Africa had permanently colored worldwide perceptions of the continent. The key feature essay, by Davidson Nicol, then principal of Fourah Bay College in Sierra Leone, called into question the attitudes, motives, and symbolic roles of three of Africa's "Lovers and Critics": Albert Schweitzer, Graham Greene, and Joyce Cary.

For Greene, Nicol mapped a mythic geography:

> Africa seems the most important territory of Greene-land—a territory of darkness and despair encompassing Mexico, Lithuania, Scandinavia, Brighton, Vienna, and Saigon; peopled by dangerously naive Americans, laughing African peasants and sad climacteric characters from an older civilization, for Greene, truly and historically based on the Roman Catholic Church.   (p. 35)

Nicol detailed what were then somewhat shocking revelations about Schweitzer. A doctor himself, Nicol averred that Schweitzer had set out for Africa without any notion at all of tropical medicine, picking up what he could from a French surgeon on the boat out; that Schweitzer's attitude toward Africans, long portrayed as saintly, had in fact ranged from patronizing to contemptuous.

More interesting yet was what Nicol saw as the underlying

meaning of these revelations: the Westerner's symbolic need to locate in Africa the nexus of "an established, important, and in some ways comforting" notion—his own cultural and social superiority (p. 32). This, then, was the reason for the Westerner's preference for the poor, ill-educated villager over the member of the urbanized African elite. Schweitzer pitied Africans, and doctored them, because of a "secret bond"—the fellowship of "all those who bear the mark of pain"—but basically he considered African lives as "worth no more than an insect's" (p. 34).

Nicol's context for judging these men, in contrast to that of Leys, or even Mazrui's, was purely subjective, imaginative. He placed his rejection of Greene, for instance, squarely in a personal context. Greene, whose famous *The Heart of the Matter* took place in Freetown, had seemed superficially cordial, unprejudiced; to an educated African, therefore, his reversion to distrust and incomprehension in his novel was a species of betrayal. The reason for Greene's incomprehension, Nicol speculated, was perhaps the colonial context itself, the feeling the educated African had of being "a citizen in an occupied country," vulnerable, guilt-ridden: "The educated African was insecure in the presence of Europeans and the latter made him more so. He reacted badly, as frightened people do. He showed either servility or brashness, mendacity or unctuousness" (p. 36).

That Nicol strongly identified with Africa's alien occupiers, however, was also sometimes unconsciously revealed in these three "reassessments." He confessed, for instance, to a lack of sympathy for the "nude Africans" of the up-country villages, though he felt equally comfortable with either his own English servant or a European professional equal (p. 36). The condescension, offensive to many other commentators, in Joyce Cary's caricatures of "semi-literate Africans" (p. 37) did not strike Nicol, nor did his sense of Greene's betrayal prevent him from a concluding gesture of amity:

> In the maturity of our independence we must now realize that foreign criticism does not necessarily mean neo-colonialism, hatred and prejudice.
> In its polished form of adult courtesy, combined as this is with ap-

preciation, admiration and understanding, our critics, white, yellow or black, can still be our best lovers. (p. 37)

This teasing, vaguely sexual allusion (of a type by then becoming typical of the *Transition* style) only slightly camouflaged an abiding need, in spite of embarrassment and discomfort (as Nicol had himself described it), to reconcile oneself to those Europeans who had created the African elites and remained their chief referents for purposes of self-definition. Thus, in a sense, though Nicol's was a notable attempt at making the sort of symbolic reevaluation that Mazrui had initiated in "Uhuru-Worship," and though he certainly scored some points in his deflation of the cult of the European mythologizers of Africa, in the end Nicol got not much further than Colin Leys had in reassessing the African image. The message—hadn't we better now take a hard look at the people responsible for our symbolic definition?—came through clearly, but in Nicol's article it had not yet found its full embodiment.

Reader reaction to Neogy's efforts to redirect *Transition*'s emphasis and remold its style was clamorous and absorbed. In *Transition* no. 24, for example, there was sharp comment ranging from the caustic to the merely sardonic about a number of pieces, fanciful or scholarly, argumentative or reflective, that had appeared in recent *Transitions*. One correspondent, James W. Fernandez of Dartmouth College in America, connected Nicol's essay with Mazrui's "Sacred Suicide" in *Transition* no. 21. Fernandez refused to accept Mazrui's seeming equation of self-sacrifice and suicide or his argument that direct violence was somehow healthier. By way of contrast Fernandez argued that Schweitzer's dislike for educated Africans came not from contempt for their intelligence but from a conviction that they were incapable of self-sacrifice. This concept belied Mazrui's depressing thesis:

> If sacrifice has always been understood as accomplishing increments of order and vitality in human affairs the essential point is that this can be better achieved if we move away from the barbarities implicit in the

sacrifice of the other to the atonement implicit in the sacrifice of the
self.   (p. 10)

Transition readers got most exercised, however, about an article
that had merely been reprinted from the American magazine *Commentary*, Leslie Farber's "I'm Sorry, Dear . . . ," a description of,
and reflection upon, Dr. William H. Masters' research into female
sexual response. What was particularly infuriating to some readers
was not so much what Farber wrote as the way that Neogy trum-
peted and illustrated it. In addition to a cameo portrait of Schweitzer
with the somewhat misleading caption "Did Schweitzer Like Africans?" there was on the cover, for instance, a picture of what one
correspondent (Audrey Wipper of Kampala) described as a "lan-
guorous brunette" (*Transition* no. 24, p. 5), captioned, "Is It Right
to Know What Happens When a Woman Has an Orgasm?" This was
not only misleading (since rightness or wrongness had not much to
do with Farber's article) but also seemed meant merely to titillate.

If the lead-in was far-fetched, the illustrations and their captions
were worse. One, for instance, showed Ingrid Thulin in Bergman's
film "The Silence," whose "self-gratification," the caption explained,
apropos of nothing in particular, "should be contrasted with the
filmed experiments described in this article" (p. 15). Wipper grasped
the point clearly enough—that Neogy would go far out of his way
to shock, astonish, or exasperate his readers. "No one would argue,"
she wrote, "that these subjects are not to be discussed . . . but it
is when the so-called avant garde has to resort to such gimmicks to display its 'progressiveness' that one begins to wonder whether it is not
as shibboleth-ridden as the middle class it so loves to criticize" (p. 5).

Neogy's best instrument for the kind of rethinking that he
sought—serious yet irreverent, imaginative yet pointed to harsh realities, eclectic yet tending toward unification—continued, however, to
be Mazrui. And Mazrui's efforts in this direction came to their most
characteristic and productive fruition in *Transition* no. 26 in an article entitled "Nkrumah: The Leninist Czar" that had as its lead-in
Neogy's most striking cover to date (designed by Michael Adams)—

a playing card (the king) motif in green, yellow, and black, with Nkrumah the superior face, Lenin the anterior, and for suit a star.

The article was, typically, an analysis of symbolic projection leading to paradox. Nkrumah had, Mazrui argued, set out rather deliberately to symbolically identify himself as Africa's Lenin: echoing from a new perspective Lenin's theory of imperialism; coining "Nkrumahism" as the African equivalent of "Leninism"; giving his own theoretical periodical a name (*The Spark*) that was a direct translation of the name of Lenin's theoretical paper (*Iskra*); borrowing from Lenin an emphasis on "organization" (though his was grassroots rather than elitist); and now copying the title of Lenin's *Imperialism: The Highest Stage of Capitalism* for his own *Neo-Colonialism: The Last Stage of Imperialism*. This, in turn, led to a sort of double paradox. Nkrumah, for reasons of national self-assertion that arose out of the humiliations of the colonial era, had become addicted to an opulent, regal style more reminiscent of the czar than of the Marxist revolution that had overthrown him. Mazrui added, "Nor is Nkrumah's Czarism necessarily 'the worst side' of his personality and behavior. On the contrary, his Czarism could—in moderation—have mitigated some of the harshness of his Leninism. . . . Nkrumah's tragedy was a tragedy of *excess*, rather than of contradiction" (p. 9).

Thus, Nkrumah's compulsive need to destroy all political opposition and to establish an opulent national style and a personality cult based around himself, the "Osagyefo," were produced by causes no less real for being symbolic. Nevertheless, though explicable, they were deplorable. Such ostentation, like the conspicuous consumption of consumer goods by lesser officials, was evil in both practical and symbolic terms, since it constituted both a severe drain on the country's foreign exchange, in a way that mere corruption did not, and a source of violent public disaffection and distrust (pp. 14–15).

Mazrui's article was remarkably timely (Nkrumah's overthrow took place after the magazine went to press, but before it appeared) [30] and insightful, in spite of its discursive style and what seemed occasionally to be mere asseveration. What was striking was its willful neglect of the standard conventions of academic organization and exposition. Mazrui was looking not for mechanical causation, but for striking parallels, symbolic correspondences, the texture of significant images and phrases. If, when his technique misfired, he could sometimes sound flippant or illogical, when it worked, as in "Leninist Czar," he could bring to his analysis a vivid sense of the incongruity, compulsiveness, and destructiveness of political events that was far more affecting than a mere academic exposition. So influential, in fact, was Mazrui's "Leninist Czar" piece that Neogy eventually had a special reprint published, bound in a reasonable facsimile of the original cover. That, too, eventually sold out.

In contrast, George Shepherd, founding editor of *Africa Today*, had covered the same ground in his "Socialism as Religion" in *Transition* no. 23 (pp. 11–14), but Shepherd circled ponderously around his thesis that Marxism suffered from its lack of some sort of spiritual dimension. There were none of Mazrui's acrobatics and flights of fancy, and as a result Shepherd's article attracted no special new attention to the issue. Shepherd touched many of the same points Mazrui had, but Mazrui's unpredictable eclecticism was missing, and therefore much of his force. Shepherd, like Mazrui, deplored the cult of personality that was asserting itself as a feature of African nationalism, but he did not venture onto the risky ground of the symbolic antecedents and consequences of that phenomenon.

This ground was trodden again in a companion article to Mazrui's, "Does African Socialism Make Economic Sense?" by Ralph Clark, an English economist who had worked in India, Australia, Pakistan, Nigeria, Uganda, and Kenya. Clark's was a purely literal analysis, along the variables of economic incentives, investment, and political constraints on economic decision making. It was a fitting foil for "Leninist Czar," balancing it with some rather hard facts— such as that Marxism tended to enforce mass sacrifices, financing development by depressing demand for consumer goods; and that if social factors remained unchanged, a 10 percent reinvestment level would be required simply to maintain the new African nations in their *present* economic position! (Clark foresaw that 20 percent would be required for any significant economic progress.) Clark's iconoclastic conclusions in a sense supported Mazrui's implied thesis—that symbolic necessity often obscured social, in this case economic, necessity. Facts, Clark maintained, made it clear that development would require either mass hardship or some radical, and unpopular, realignment of agricultural systems, but cultural factors, symbolic reasons, made either choice unlikely.

Transition no. 27 contained still another incursion into this same territory, Russell Warren Howe's "Did Nkrumah Favor Pan-Africanism?" (pp. 13–15), and *Transition* no. 28 capped the series when Neogy, on a visit to Accra, succeeded in interviewing Nkrumah's successor-apparent, Kofi Busia, then chairman of the Political Committee of the National Liberation Council (pp. 20–24). Busia's repeated references to the need for ethics and leaders whose heads are not turned by the "sweets of power" (p. 21) are ironic in retrospect in the light of the later persistent reports of corruption in his own regime.

Busia also, however, instituted with his own brief comment what were to be a storm of rebuttals, rebukes, and plaudits for Mazrui's "Leninist Czar." He simply said that it was a waste of time tracing Nkrumah's late Marxism, since it had been so completely obscured in the end by megalomania (p. 20).[31] A letter from Y. Tandon of Mazrui's own Makerere department of political science in the same issue soft-pedaled Mazrui's criticisms of Nkrumah but was savage in its denunciation of Howe, whom it accused of rearranging history in order to damn Nkrumah for alleged hypocrisy (pp. 5–6).[32] The other letter writers, too numerous to discuss, were often as inclined to assault Mazrui for alleged manipulation of history as Tandon had been with Howe.[33] In *Transition* no. 32, a full year after the original article, Mazrui was given room to respond in detail, and he did so point by point and at length, concluding by charging his critics in general with the very sort of blind hero-worship he had described in his earliest *Transition* essay, "On Heroes and Uhuru-Worship."

So much had happened in the year between the appearance of "Leninist Czar" and Mazrui's rebuttal to critics that it is necessary, at this point, to backtrack a bit. First, of course, there had been Nkrumah's overthrow in absentia while the "Osagyefo" was on a state visit to China. Then there were in the magazine itself a number of newer controversies issuing from Mazrui's pen and those of other writers. Last, but from Neogy's point of view hardly least, there was the controversy over CIA sponsorship that fatally threatened the hard-won success that had seemed, at last, to have come to *Transition*.

Transition no. 31, for instance, was notable both for another important article by Mazrui and for an extremely revealing and thoughtful assessment of the political role of the creative writer by no less a personage than Wole Soyinka. Mazrui's thesis, heralded by yet another Mazrui-logism, sought to explain the queer, almost personal attachment that Western intellectuals had to Julius Nyerere's Tanzanian government. Mazrui found the roots of this too-automatic approval in the chauvinism, elitism, masochism, and naive idealism of the Western liberal and Marxist communities. The Western perception of Nyerere, he broadly implied, bore only a tenuous relation to the real attributes of Nyerere's leadership. Again a conception of leadership—this time a Western one—was shown to have mythic proportions and political reality to be determined by symbol ("Tanzaphilia, a Diagnosis," pp. 20–26).

Soyinka's article, like Mazrui's, challenged an unexamined myth, held by its adherents for reasons of symbolic necessity—the prevalent notion of the political and social role of the African writer. The common conception of that role, Soyinka argued, led the writer only to betrayal of his distinct identity, and therefore of his artistic integrity:

> The writer must, for the moment at least (he persuades himself), postpone that unique reflection on experiences and events which is what makes a writer—and constitute himself into a part of that machinery that will actually shape events. . . . The African writer found that he could not deny his society; he could, however, temporarily at least, deny himself. (p. 11)

Such a betrayal was not isolated, or limited to Africa, but in Africa its effects had been fatal to much creativity:

> Cultural definitions became a new source of literature—not so new in fact, but these acquired a new significance in the context of political independence. The curiosity of the outside world far exceeded their criti-

cal faculties and publishers hovered like benevolent vultures on the still
foetus of the African Muse. (p. 12)

"The average published writer in the first few years of the post-
colonial era," he added, "was the most celebrated skin of inconsequence ever to obscure the true flesh of the African dilemma" (p. 12).
The article made teasing reference to writers, including Soyinka himself, who had flirted with political necessity, but it debunked prescribed social commitment and cultural unity (exemplified for Soyinka
by the *négritude* movement) and set before the African writer a more
subtle, more ambiguous, and more difficult task:

> We whose humanity the poets celebrated before the proof, whose lyric
> innocence was daily questioned by the very pages of newspapers[,] are
> now . . . [being] forced by disaster, not foresight[,] to a reconsideration
> of our relationship to the outer world[,] and it seems to me that the
> time is here now when the African writer must have the courage to de-
> termine what alone can be salvaged from the recurrent cycle of human
> stupidity. (p. 13)

The culmination of *Transition*'s irreverent, challenging style
came, ironically enough, in *Transition* no. 32 (August/September
1967), whose memorable cover announced an article by one of the
magazine's newer contributors, American expatriate Paul Theroux,
entitled "Tarzan Is an Expatriate." What was ironic about this issue
constituting the zenith, at least of one period, of *Transition*'s history,
was that it was also the issue in which Neogy was forced to defend
the magazine against the suddenly widespread perception that it had
been somehow tainted by CIA infiltration of its editorial offices. It
had, moreover, tucked into a modest corner of the front cover, an
announcement of another, Ugandan controversy that was eventually,
through the publication of a series of letters in succeeding issues, to
result in Neogy's and Abu Mayanja's arrest and in *Transition*'s virtual
suppression.

Theroux, whom the article on expatriates was to make as much
of a *Transition* stalwart as the article on Nkrumah had Mazrui, had
actually written for *Transition* before. His first *Transition* contribu-

tions, in fact, had been poems in *Transition* nos. 14, 17, 19, and 21, and a review of Christopher Okigbo's poetry in *Transition* no. 22. A former American Peace Corps worker in Malawi, Theroux was teaching English at Makerere. His review of Okigbo's poetry was later expanded into a treatment of five West African poets and published in *Black Orpheus*, where his own poetry also appeared.

It was the *Transition* "Tarzan" article, however, that made Theroux suddenly known and established his biting, cynical style. Again, as with Mazrui's articles, it was the symbol, the myth of Africa that was in question. In "Tanzaphilia," Mazrui had ruffled a lot of feathers, in the West as well as in Africa, by "de-mythologizing" the leadership of Julius Nyerere. Nyerere's ideology, Mazrui pointed out, was actually less original, less independent, than that of Hastings Banda of Malawi, whom Western liberals were in contrast inclined to anathematize. Nyerere's leadership, Mazrui added, had also had unfortunate practical effects, such as curtailing the movement toward East African political unification.

Theroux's approach, on the other hand, was to resurrect an anachronistic popular mythology about Africa and apply it not to the prejudices and emotional attachments of Westerners at home but to those of Westerners in Africa. Theroux's effort at *re*-mythologizing the white expatriate was aimed at revealing through ironic juxtaposition what Mazrui aimed at revealing through his style of eclectic analysis. Theroux's own style—cool, deprecating, yet free enough with its self-revelations—fit the tone of Neogy's *Transition* at that moment almost perfectly. And then, too, there was the cover to *Transition* no. 32, which almost matched the cover for the "Leninist Czar" issue—a three-box cartoon, beginning with a parody of the old Tarzan cartoon strip: Tarzan and Jane greeted by deferential natives, the balloon advertising Theroux's "Tarzan" article; then a playing card with the Nkrumah/Lenin motif, the balloon advertising "Mazrui Replies Critics"; then only a group of balloons, advertising several lesser topics, including, with accidental ironic prescience, "Uganda's Constitutional Proposals."[34]

The cover made immediately and graphically apparent the ludicrousness of the West's image of Africa—a ludicrousness beyond mere words. But the words of the title were also a challenge, a shock: Neogy and his new hatchet man meant not simply to analyze, but to ridicule the mannerisms, life-style, and convenient ideological evasions of the white expatriate in Africa. And for once the photographs and captions accompanying the essay did not belie its contents— here, in both photographs and text, were expatriates caught by one of their own with both their guard and their trousers down. Theroux quoted them (p. 19): "Frankly, I like the stupid Africans best" (white army officer in Malawi); "Oh, I know they're frightfully inefficient and hopeless at politics—but, you know, they're terribly sweet" (liberal Englishwoman). And sketched them in words:

> The mind dies and Tarzan discovers flesh. The suspicion about Africa . . . is confirmed in a Mombasa bar or a Lagos nightclub when three or four slim black girls begin fighting over him. They also fight for the fat bald man sitting in the corner (for the Italian merchant marine jigging in the centre of the floor, with his pants down). (p. 18)

There were also unflinching statements about the expatriate's political evasions—as tough and uncompromising as Neogy could have desired:

> He is the most fortunate liberal on earth. He makes a virtue of keeping silent while the jungle is splattered with gunfire. . . . He knows that certain topics are taboo; in Kenya he cannot defend the Asians when they are under attack; in Tanzania, Malawi, and a dozen other countries he cannot be critical of the one-party form of government; in Uganda, he cannot mention that, one year ago, there was a forcible and bloody suppression of the largest tribe. (p. 18)

This was strong stuff for a Ugandan magazine, but the government did not react, then or later (saving its resentment for another, more immediate topic, raised elsewhere in the issue).

Theroux's overall thesis also closely resembled Nicol's in "Our Lovers and Critics," although it was expressed both with more clarity and with colder disdain. It was his success in catching an elusive configuration of attitudes that made the article most controversial, not anything specific Theroux said about politics along the way. If the cartoon image—the white couple in their insipid racial isolation and thoughtless presumption of sovereignty—was absurd, so were its latter-day reflections among contemporary expatriates: the rules of conduct ("never be a loner or exclude other whites from your company," p. 15) and the standard advice, thoughtlessly replicated ("if you run over an African on the road you must drive away as fast as you can or you'll be killed by the murderous mob that gathers," p. 15). These new Tarzans were, most of all, willing to capitalize on their easy, racial, predominance, even if it meant that in doing so they must acquiesce in a parody of self, a ludicrous burlesque:

> He may even decide to fortify his uniqueness by carefully choosing af-
> fectations: odd clothes, a walking stick, a lisp, a different accent; he may
> develop a penchant for shouting at his servants, losing his temper or
> drinking a quart of whiskey a day; he may take to avocados, afternoon
> siestas or small boys.   (p. 15)

If the portrait stung, it was perhaps because it was so recogniz-able, even in its occasional exaggeration and extravagance. Despite all the other matters occupying, or soon to occupy, the intense attention of *Transition* readers—the CIA revelations, the constitutional contro-versy, the Asian controversy, the arrest of Neogy, Abu Mayanja, and later "Steve Lino" (Davis Sebukima)—there was a storm of protest-ing letters from expatriate readers, which Neogy, with great apparent delight, printed in a special section sarcastically entitled "Letters From the Tarzans" (*Transition* no. 33). Theroux was accused there of "hip liberal" self-flagellation, unfair exaggeration, cynical manipula-tion of racial prejudices, and, most often, an admission of *his own* "Tarzanism" (he had, he replied, not pretended to exclude himself).

As if in exculpation from the latter charge, the same issue of *Transition*, however, offered Theroux's third *Transition* feature, on the thorniest of the issues that he had accused the expatriate Tarzans of covering with their conspiracy of silence—the Asian issue, then becoming more controversial because of Jomo Kenyatta's policies in Kenya. Theroux's "Hating the Asians" was, moreover, as sweeping an indictment of indigenous East African prejudice as his earlier condemnation had been of expatriate prejudices. Again the cover design (by Byron Birdsall) contributed to the article's powerful impact, displaying, without comment, a jumbled array of inflammatory reports from the East African press, most prominent being a headline from Kenya's *Daily Nation*: "Kenya Deports Six Asians," with the subhead, "Government Levels Charge of Being 'Disloyal and Disaffected.'" This time, moreover, there was nothing ambiguous or indirect about Theroux's approach. His absolutely straightforward thesis must have appealed to *Transition*'s editor, who was, after all, not only committed to individual freedoms, but himself of Indian descent. Theroux wrote:

> I believe the Asians to be the most lied-about race in Africa, and I also believe that after I have left Africa I will remember these lies better than my cerebral snapshots of what American political scientists like to call "the drama of your Old and your New." These lies, and the hatred the lies have made, illustrate the failure of liberal thinking, of good-will, and of politics in East Africa. (p. 47)

He recounted a particularly ugly dispute that had played itself out in the pages of the *Daily Nation*, involving himself and a series of other correspondents, including Tom Mboya, on the subject. Theroux quoted from a number of sources—letters (from the *Daily Nation* and other publications), articles, editorials—offering ample evidence of precisely the illogical, hysterical prejudice that he had charged.

Theroux's disinclination to blame race hatreds merely on indigenous prejudices must also have appealed to Neogy. The colonialists, Theroux averred, had begun the anti-Asian prejudice, had inculcated it, and were now perpetuating it. There was "almost a conspiracy of Africans and their European apologists, who would very much like to see Africa succeed, even at the expense of a pogrom, a thorough purge of these immigrant peoples" (p. 47). The letters about Theroux's article, printed in *Transition* no. 34, only confirmed its controversiality and demonstrated, as Theroux had maintained, that these were indeed illogical, virulent hatreds, not mere prejudices. A fair example of their intemperate style was one from a postgraduate student in politics at Makerere, Jeremiah Muthoni:

> It is true that nasty statements are occasionally issued against the Asian community, but these statements on a majority of cases are not made with racial motives, but as a measure of correction or retaliation against their failure to integrate with the indigenous population. We shall never tolerate blood-sucking, lascivious bigots. These semi-colonials cannot be let free to exploit the indigenous masses at the expense of our being non-racial. (p. 6)

It was a risky and difficult subject that made *Transition* a lot of enemies and did not win it many friends. That Neogy persevered in tackling difficult topics testifies to the high-mindedness of his motives. He did not touch every hot political problem, but those that he featured were pursued without fear or favor and with remarkable even-handedness.

The CIA and a Crisis of Integrity

Looking back on those super-heated times, one is surprised both at Neogy's temerity, his willingness to take risks as the self-appointed scourge of communities of not particularly willing penitents, and at the length of time for which the Ugandan authorities tolerated such irreverences. This is especially so in light of the widespread employ-ment at that time of the preventive detention powers constitutionally available to the government as a result of the declaration of a state of emergency following the overthrow of the *kabaka* of Buganda in 1966.[35] There was also the contributing factor of the magazine's own growing vulnerability, assaulted as it was by angry disputants from all sides of the political free-for-all and at the same time tainted from afar by a scandal in which it had no direct part: that is, the revelation of clandestine CIA funding.

Why the CIA would have wanted to support *Transition* is still not entirely clear, but as Thomas Powers has pointed out it was not in those days a particularly tightly organized agency. Much that went on was neither closely controlled nor logically justified as part of a larger scheme. The man behind the Congress for Cultural Freedom, the Farfield Foundation, and the related efforts to infiltrate liberal in-tellectual circles, Cord Meyer, was perhaps the least disciplined and least consistent of the agency's deputies. Hardly anyone in the CIA knew exactly what Meyer was up to, and with no check to his pro-grams, they grew to have only a tenuous relationship to the osten-sible objectives of his division. Eventually, this lack of programmatic control led to the unraveling of the whole skein of his activities:

> One of [William] Colby's first acts as Deputy Director for Opera-tions was to form a special study committee for reorganization of the D.D.O. under the chairmanship of Cord Meyer, Colby's deputy, a man with something of a public reputation but never considered an opera-tional professional within the C.I.A. As Head of the International Or-ganizations Division, for example, Meyer had established a web of

funding groups so intimately interconnected that a single compromise—the discovery of C.I.A. funding of the National Student Association in 1967—exposed the whole network within a period of days. The
identities of scores of dummy foundations, and the groups subsidized
by them, were revealed in the press. This is not exactly covering your
tracks.[36]

One of the foundations exposed was the Farfield Foundation, and
among the groups subsidized by it were the Congress for Cultural
Freedom and a bewildering network of cultural and intellectual
magazines around the world, from every part of the political and cultural spectrum—including the English *Encounter* and its brash small
brother in Kampala, *Transition*.

The executive director of the Farfield Foundation, funding agency
for the Congress for Cultural Freedom, was John Thompson—a poet,
critic, and university professor who had caught on pretty quickly
after taking his first job with Farfield that it was CIA-funded and
CIA-controlled. Thompson nevertheless stayed on as executive director, without ever quite becoming an insider, an operational professional. He recalls the flexibility, the casualness of those programs:

> Well, in those days, we wanted to aid and support the intellectuals of
> what were then the only independent classes [in Africa]. In those days,
> 1960 or so, Ghana was independent, Nigeria was independent, Kenya
> was about to become independent. There was a small number of in-
> tellectuals and writers and our particular interest was in the literary
> people. . . . Our interest was in establishing an independent publishing
> program based on Africa and aiding African intellectuals to find their
> own feet on the ground. . . . We didn't know—nobody knew—a per-
> son's political affiliation.[37]

There was, Thompson says, a certain naivete in this, a belief that
writers and intellectuals were "the good guys" who could be counted
on to oppose corruption and political instability. In countries where
Western-style political institutions were almost everywhere still in
place, stability and economic integrity would keep Africa in the non-
communist camp. There was, moreover, an idealistic belief in the
universalism of art and literature if only it could be given free reign—

in its ability to serve as the foundation for a cultural unity that would also perpetuate democratic institutions. It was, perhaps, merely a "historical coincidence," Thompson reflects, but "our national interests happened at that point to coincide with what I thought and still think important, with freedom of speech and freedom of writing."

Here was this young fellow Neogy, who was "independent and running an excellent literary magazine, which in those days we thought was a good thing in itself"; who was "trying to do something very sophisticated, totally, you would say, European, bringing together politics, literature, art, from an international perspective"; who shared with other literary intellectuals, including Thompson, the belief that "there was some common foundation, that we could understand one another, and that it wasn't as complicated as politicians made it seem." The decision to support Neogy's *Transition* was taken largely by Thompson himself, on the recommendation of Mphahlele, simply on the grounds that Neogy was a capable editor who stood for ideals that Thompson in particular (but also Cord Meyer and, more vaguely, others in the CIA hierarchy) wanted to see strengthened in Africa—that is, multi-party democracy; freedom of speech; the predominance of intellectual over bureaucratic, political, military, and traditional tribal elites; and a continued cultural interchange with, and allegiance to, the West. Working as he did within Cord Meyer's International Organizations Division, Thompson could make such a decision somewhat informally, without overwhelming pressure to justify it to higher-ups. When it came right down to it, he recalls, Africa was still looked upon as so backward and remote, and the amounts actually needed were so small, that discussion was often shelved and he was given wide discretion.[38]

Thompson met Neogy in 1962 on his first visit to Kampala, and he felt immediately that Neogy was "the only person who had anything going" there, the only person producing something unique in literature and the arts. Mphahlele, then working for the Congress for Cultural Freedom out of Nairobi, agreed with him. Thompson saw also that Neogy was a first-rate editor, producing a creditable magazine "on a shoestring." When Neogy, soon thereafter, asked Mphahlele for support from the Congress for Cultural Freedom,

Thompson, who controlled that purse string, was receptive: "At that time he [Neogy] had been backing the magazine entirely on his own," Thompson recalls. "He had a certain amount of money from his family, and he had just about blown that, so I recommended that he be backed."[39] Mphahlele also organized the Kampala writers' conference, reported in *Transition* no. 5, as a further stimulus to the magazine's growth. "For a long time," Neogy later recalled, there had been no financial backing for *Transition* at all: "I can't really say that I backed it myself, but it was my debts that subsidized the magazine for a long time. . . . It was very tough."[40] When help offered itself, Neogy jumped at the chance.

Neither Neogy nor Mphahlele later mentioned Thompson's part in these events. Under the pressure of the revelations of CIA funding, Mphahlele himself shouldered the blame. Thompson, at any rate, had by then left the Farfield Foundation to return to teaching and writing. Neogy reported that Mphahlele was his contact with the Congress for Cultural Freedom, which was true enough. He had merely asked Mphahlele for support and had gotten it, with no stipulations or conditions.[41] Mphahlele himself said that he had never known of the Congress's CIA connection and had, in fact, insisted, as a condition to his taking the job of director of the Congress's African programs, that it be understood that he would never back any program that was committed to a particular ideology (p. 5). He later raised doubts very similar to Thomas Powers's regarding the logic behind these CIA programs. Why had the CIA wanted to secretly fund African intellectuals, musicians, actors, and writers?

> One reason must be that the Agency does not know some of the activities it sponsors; another must be the fact that capitalism does go out of hand often. It has a way of proliferating beyond control. It has to keep breeding, spreading, spilling over. It is conceivable that in the process it can quite easily sow the seeds of revulsion or suspicion against itself. (*Transition* no. 34, p. 5)

For Neogy, revulsion was precisely the seed sown, as he said again and again in an interview with Tony Hall for the Nairobi *Sunday Nation*. What was his immediate reaction on learning the news?

"Helpless resentment," Neogy answered. "Shock, later turning into a massive two-month-long depression." What depressed him, he said, was "a feeling of being smeared by something one neither knew about nor was prepared for" (*Transition* no. 32, p. 45).

Since the money had come, as Thompson puts it, with "absolutely no strings attached" (a point that both Neogy and Mphahlele confirmed), Neogy never had the least suspicion of CIA connivance. He later commented, "Had there been any pressure from any source whatsoever we would have exposed it. And of all the magazines aided by the CCF, *Transition* is perhaps the most Left-wing oriented" (ibid.). In fact, Neogy emphasized, *prior* CIA machinations were hard to credit, since *he* had approached the Congress for Cultural Freedom to ask for support, as part of a deliberate effort after the third issue to find some other method than his own private debt-absorption to underwrite *Transition*. The Congress had not approached him. A number of respected private foundations, Neogy added, including Carnegie and Rockefeller, had likewise been taken in by the CIA masquerade, to the extent of using the Congress for Cultural Freedom as a sort of "clearing agent" for international funding projects—a "clearing agent," however, that had "much more flexibility of approach, both in the projects it chose to support and the immediacy with which assistance could be made" (ibid.). Even though outside support then had to match circulation receipts at roughly a five-to-one ratio,[42] the support given to *Transition* by the Congress, though sufficient to prevent further debt from accumulating, was very small, according to both Thompson and Neogy.

To Hall's pointed question, "What makes the integrity of your operation exploitable by American interests, however subtle the exploitation might be?" Neogy answered, "Because, quite frankly, we do belong to the Western tradition of liberal inquiry. This tradition is tempered and qualified by the African experience. . . . If open-mindedness, a lack of ideological bias and a willingness to discuss different points of view are 'exploitable,' then magazines like *Transition* could be . . . victims" (*Transition* no. 32, p. 46). However, Neogy pointed out, *Transition* had often carried articles harshly critical of American policy and American interests, and though intellectuals might be naive, starry-eyed at times, they were "beginning to play a much more real role in governmental affairs." He added, "The trouble in Africa is that we have too few intellectuals—those that will not put their personal interests before intellectual honesty" (ibid.).

Both ends of the political spectrum, left and right, seem then to have accepted the idea that a liberal intellectual elite would, by its nature, be inclined to support those Western democratic institutions that had nurtured and favored it. With such intellectuals, as Thompson said, it would only be necessary to set their feet on the ground. No penetration or manipulation, covert or overt, would be necessary. The perplexity of the world at large stemmed from the assumption that only sanctioned political ideology could be useful to U.S. interests. From his equally perplexed vantage point, Mphahlele wrote,

> One finds oneself asking why the CIA would be interested in helping intellectuals, musicians, actors, writers and so on in Africa—people who must eventually recognize the emptiness of the American dream, the naivete in so much of the "Great Society," some of the cruel realities of private enterprise. (*Transition* no. 34, p. 5)

Neogy added,

> So many people have been affected by the CIA infiltrations that there comes a point when the whole thing becomes a farce. . . . The daily disclosures in the newspapers staggered one for the way an American organization had succeeded in subverting the very tenets of American beliefs, freedom of the individual and democracy. It was like watching a snake eat its tail. (*Transition* no. 32, p. 45)

The CIA, Neogy ventured, was exploiting *Transition*'s very integrity. Hall pushed him with a pointed statement:

> Nevertheless, the CIA is not in the game for fun. It has helped overthrow governments and would surely not for long support any publication which even occasionally went against the fundamental interests of the United States as the CIA sees them.

Neogy's response makes it clear that he did not know how to answer Hall's statement. "*Transition*," he said, "exists as a forum of free discussion. The very nature of free discussion is that it can be used by interested parties when it suits them" (p. 46). If the reasons for CIA support were mystifying to the recipients of that support, the after-effects of the revelations of clandestine support were immediate and obvious. Neogy described the reaction to Hall:

> Most of our contributors in Kampala are aware of exactly how the magazine began and what difficulties it went through to survive. The recent news has caused them concern for what damage it might do to the future existence of the magazine.
>
> Of course, there are some people for whom the news is godsent: a long-awaited stick with which to beat the magazine. Some of this senti-ment showed up in our current Nkrumah debate.
>
> Letters appeared in a local newspaper equating our "anti-Nkru-mahism" with evidence of CIA infiltration. We have received letters our-selves . . . saying the same thing. (p. 45)

One of the first to join the stick-wielders lining up to beat the magazine that had given common currency to the phrase "Uhuru-worship" was none other than early literary protégé James Ngugi (now Ngugi wa Thiong'o), who wrote from Leeds in England to question *Transition*'s credibility in printing analyses of the CIA con-troversies in which it was itself embroiled. Neogy's editorial response simply referred readers to the *Sunday Nation* interview reprinted in the same issue.

Even if it was true, as Ngugi charged, that *Transition* was not unbiased, it was nevertheless true that Neogy had always made room for opposing viewpoints in *Transition* (particularly in the Letters sec-tion). As he himself commented: "A good magazine editor must be neutral, allowing participants to travel the lengths of their arguments. But he mustn't be a neuter. He cannot be mindless with no views of his own, or no beliefs he holds strongly" (*Transition* no. 32, p. 46). In fact, one of the first articles in *Transition* to examine the CIA reve-lations was by Robert McDonald, an Australian who had once been active in international student organizations and whose politics were far different from Neogy's own. For instance, McDonald asserted the need for students in developing countries to sacrifice the "sacred trust of intellectual independence" when it conflicted with the demands of "national development"—as, indeed, it had in Nyerere's Tanzania (p. 18). The purpose of his article, however, was to expose the techniques used by the National Student Association to direct, manipulate, and control the international student movement and to use it, correlatively, as a source of intelligence about nascent political movements. ("NSA/CIA: The Kiddies and Their Playmates," *Transition* no. 31, pp. 14–19). Nor was such a critical perspective on U.S. transgressions without precedents in *Transition* before the CIA revelations.

Although Ngugi and other critics of the magazine chose to view the revelation of *Transition*'s CIA funding in isolation from the other CIA revelations around the world, another letter writer pointed out in *Transition* no. 33 that a larger view of the CIA revelations made clear to disinterested observers what Neogy was otherwise at pains to establish by printing arguments from all sides—that the magazine's CIA support had not made it a mouthpiece for the CIA. The very extent of the revelations said something about them. The correspondent, Pierre L. van den Berghe, an American professor of sociology at University College, Nairobi, wrote:

> A substantial proportion of the academic establishment, both in the United States and overseas, and a great many "intellectual" periodicals have been manipulated and utilized in ways which are often extremely devious and seemingly contradictory. So complex is this intellectual infiltration . . . that there is no readily perceptible logic to the scheme. The CIA has given financial support to virtually the whole ideological spectrum. For all we know, *Pravda* may be CIA supported.

The CIA obsession with Africa, said van den Berghe, who had been approached (and had refused) to do studies for that agency, was not precisely a function of capitalistic hegemony or cold-war paranoia, but "if communism no longer scares many people, the Yellow or Black peril will. The United States is casting itself in the role of neo-colonialist guardian of stability, prosperity, law and order."[43] Thus, from their very different perspectives, both Thompson and van den Berghe stressed that a desire for political stability, not anti-communism per se, was behind CIA operations in Africa.

Taken together, Mphahlele's, Neogy's, and Thompson's statements, more recent revelations summarized in Thomas Powers's book, and van den Berghe's theories seem to add up to a few key conclusions: first, that the reasons for supporting *Transition* were never rigorously analyzed by those within the agency who backed the decision to support the magazine; second, that a desire to guarantee political stability, rather than cold-war allegiance or ideology, essentially accounted for the support; third, that the support was given because of the notion that an established intellectual elite, with its own independent vehicle of expression (*Transition*), would prevent a social, tribal, or merely military cataclysm in Africa that might open the way to political instability, and hence to externally defined ideological polarization; and fourth, that neither Neogy nor anyone else at *Transition* knew about or was directly influenced by the CIA support.

As Neogy sensed right away, however, the tragedy was that *Transition* would never again be entirely free from the charge of CIA complicity.[44] Even if most readers continued to believe in the magazine and to support it with subscriptions, Neogy said, there would still always now be this constraint on its flexibility and spontaneity—that if it stepped on toes, it was now vulnerable to the knowing sneer, the cynical innuendo. Even after Neogy left the magazine, handing over the editorial direction to Wole Soyinka, it was necessary for Soyinka to cope with the aftereffects of this stigma, which he ultimately did by seeking an outside commercial publisher for the magazine. It was indirectly the CIA stigma that eventually killed *Transition*, therefore, when Soyinka's efforts to divorce the magazine from the sponsorship of the reorganized "International Association for Cultural Freedom" led him to hand the editorial management over to *Africa Magazine*, which oversaw the suspension of its publication.

The year between the CIA disclosures in mid-1967 and Neogy's arrest (which constituted a virtual suppression of the magazine) in mid-1968 was nevertheless probably *Transition*'s commercial zenith, and also began a curious transformation of its influence. More and more vulnerable to criticism within Africa, *Transition* was becoming better known and more influential abroad. Neogy's special issue on the Biafran War (*Transition* no. 36) both attracted international attention and had the distinction of being banned—though only in Nigeria itself, and only through the agency of its distributor there. (Christopher Okigbo, who had been killed fighting on the Biafran side, had won *Transition* a modest Nigerian circulation.)

Transition no. 36, appearing when the war was nearly over, featured gruesome photographs of Biafran bombing victims and contained a bitter interview with Chinua Achebe, Biafra's best-known intellectual, who denounced the British for supplying the Federalists with arms and the Federalists (whom he called "barbarians") for terror bombings and for the anti-Ibo hysteria that had been the sole cause of the conflict. The interview and the photographs graphically evoked the cruelty and futility of the war. Achebe described bombings and starvation and gave a glimpse of the incomprehension and helplessness of even such influential figures as himself and Christopher Okigbo. The two of them, Achebe recalled, had been sharing an office and a project to publish children's books when the first bombs fell in Lagos:

> So we made fun of it, we went to the floor, then got up and continued our work. Then, after that, he said he had to leave, and I went to check on something that was already in the press—the first booklet that we were publishing for children, and while I was there somebody was talking about a house that had been hit, and as they described this house, the area, I thought it might be my house, so I went back to the place and found that it was indeed. The whole town came to see, and Chris came in again saying this was terrible, and that was the last I saw of him. Five days later I heard over the Nigerian radio that he had been killed.   (*Transition* no. 36, p. 33)

Transition no. 36 represented Neogy the journalist at his best—if also at his most deliberately provocative. He was widely accused, especially in the Nigerian Federalist press, of cheap sensationalism. Nevertheless, *Transition* no. 36 succeeded well in conveying the shock, the terror, and the poignancy of the war. Moreover, it inspired an appreciative feature article in the *New York Times*, whose correspondent ventured that it was "the only apparent common ground between Nigerians and Biafrans" at the Addis Ababa peace conference—everyone wanted a copy of the issue that had been banned in Lagos. *Transition* was, the correspondent (Alfred Friendly, Jr.) said, "Africa's slickest, sprightliest, and occasionally sexiest magazine." "A questing irreverence," he continued, "breathes out of the pages of every issue since Number 26, published in mid-1966, featured a still-controversial dissection of the career of the Ghanaian dictator Kwame Nkrumah, shortly after he was overthrown." Special reprints of both Mazrui's "Leninist Czar" article, Friendly noted, and Theroux's equally famous "Tarzan" article in *Transition* no. 32 (an issue that Friendly had also mentioned enthusiastically) had been sold out. A few weeks before the *New York Times* plaudit, another approving notice, in the London *Observer*, had described *Transition* as "something like a slim illustrated version of *Encounter*."[45]

Neogy and his editorial associates were aware of, but inclined to scant, the magazine's growing alienation from its immediate environment. Paul Theroux, in his gleeful report on these far-flung appreciations of the magazine, commented:

> What is most interesting about reactions is that invariably the good ones come from afar. The *New York Times* says yes, the *Kenya Weekly News*, the Nigerian distributor and the local expatriate yahoos say no. *Transition* has been accused of taking things too seriously, not taking things seriously enough, being political, puritanical, unnecessarily licentious, demented, childish, pro-Indian, Afrophile, anti-African, CIA-inspired, left-wing, erotic, anti-white, anti-black, hippy, honkey, trendy, academic, mealymouthed, *au courant*, dirty-minded, immodest, and just plain boring. Arthur Schlesinger, Jr. takes special pains to renew his subscription and add his new address; Rudolf Augstein begins a new one; the weirdo bull-dyke headmistress in Chad cancels hers when she sees the word orgasm staring out at her from the pages of issue 22.

Theroux, who became with that issue an associate editor, was inclined to crow about *Transition*'s success. "It was started on a shoestring by a young Ugandan Indian, Rajat Neogy, in 1961 and now sells about 12,000 copies an issue," he quoted *The Observer* as saying, adding, "What *The Observer* failed to mention is that in a country like Uganda where 90% of the population is barefoot, even shoestrings are hard to come by."[46]

Neogy had, the *New York Times* article said, succeeded over a five-year period in reducing *Transition*'s deficit-ratio (the degree to which it had to attract outside support as against its subscription receipts) from roughly five-to-one to one-to-one.[47] Neogy himself was a bit inclined to brag. *Transition* had started as a fairly parochial regional magazine, he told the *Times* correspondent, but it had become "the single most important magazine on the continent" (ibid.). Friendly was moved to agree: *Transition*, he said, was "imaginatively designed, provocative," and Neogy had "a great deal to be immodest about."

Neogy's success, moreover, was different in kind from that of *Transition*'s rival and predecessor, Ulli Beier's *Black Orpheus* (by then reorganized under the editorship of Abiola Irele and J. P. Clark). First, after a period of imitation, he had struck out in a different field, emphasizing intellectual controversy rather than literary innovation and promotion, and feature essays rather than poetry, fiction, and art. Neogy had also rejected *Black Orpheus*'s unexpressed formula of using literature as a vehicle for cultural awareness of, and among, black people all over the world. As Okigbo commented, *Transition* was not interested in fostering what he called "the black mystique," in promoting "blackness for its own sake," and it would not, as he thought *Black Orpheus* would, publish a writer merely because he was black.[48] In a 1964 panel discussion about the magazine in Kampala, Alan Ogot, Erisa Kironde, and Ali Mazrui again discussed the issue of "blackness" as an editorial consideration. Mazrui and John Nagenda, the moderator, agreed that there seemed not to have been much consideration of a contributor's color at *Transition*. Nevertheless, Mazrui reflected, *Transition* was, after all, an African magazine. Perhaps, he suggested, a simple editorial criterion might be either that the nationality of each contributor ought to be African or that the "subject itself ought to be of interest to Africans."[49]

In fact, of course, Neogy's sole criterion had always been the latter, as Mazrui no doubt realized, since he added that among "straight articles" there had been "an encouragement of the non-African writing on African themes." The "special virtue" of *Transition*, Nagenda added, was that in this regard it had no policy, since it had not gotten to the point where it could afford to discriminate—it had so few contributors that it had to print whatever would work, would have appeal for its audience—and therefore it was always fresh and unpredictable: "You don't know what you're going to get next time."

Transition's circulation had not yet expanded significantly abroad. Its audience was only, Kironde estimated, about three-eighths African, the bulk of its readers being made up of East Africa's expatriate Europeans—the very community that Theroux's "Tarzan" article had so successfully satirized. Nevertheless, Nagenda and Mazrui agreed that the imbalance in *Transition*'s audience was due largely to the relatively small size of East Africa's indigenous intellectual elites. *Transition*'s imbalanced readership was not because of an editorial approach or style pitched toward Europeans, but simply because the magazine was too difficult, too sophisticated, for any but an elite audience, and the indigenous East African elite, though growing rapidly, was still quite small. This situation, Mazrui felt, was nevertheless bound to change, since "the kind of fairly serious readership in East Africa is going to grow all the time." *Transition*, Kironde thought, therefore had a special responsibility to its growing public—not "to lead," or to "pull its audience up," or "instruct," but to "reflect opinion" without seeking to "form opinion." Kironde's theory is most interesting, of course, in its divergence from Neogy's own stated editorial aims— which, though they were not precisely to "pull [*Transition*'s] . . . audience up," were certainly more than to merely "reflect opinion." Neogy's notion of free intellectual exchange was, in fact, something closer to the way Alan Ogot had put it in responding to Nagenda: "All we can hope to do is to expose as many of our readers as possible to many of these ideas, and it is up to our readers to absorb what they want, and reject what they are not interested in."

Not only did Neogy define his editorial role differently, but he was also at odds with Nagenda's estimation of his audience, feeling strongly that it was *not* made up primarily of expatriates, even though they may have been providing the bulk of circulation receipts. School library copies, he comments, were shared by secondary school students, "averaging ten to a copy."[50] Neogy was thinking along lines different from Nagenda's in other ways as well. In fact, rather than focusing on providing a mere editorial blackboard for passive lessons in intellectual development, Neogy was thinking beyond his immediate, East African environment, and toward opening routes of cultural commerce with the outside world—as, in fact, Beier had done in his different way with *Black Orpheus*.

The difference, however, as Thompson has pointed out, was that Neogy was interested in doing something more reciprocal and more sophisticated. In an interview with Dennis Duerden around 1965, Neogy affirmed *Transition*'s commitment not solely to cultural development, but to the other half of the reciprocal relationship—to breaking down "the self-centeredness of European writers," as Duerden put it. Neogy elaborated, "You have this tremendous kind of lack of real knowledge on who are the real people working in Africa, who are the people writing and thinking new things, [taking] new directions—in political thought, poetry. . . . I do think that *Transition* is helping to dispel some of these cozy tendencies that—'Oh, well. Nothing important is really going to come out of Africa.' I say that as an editor, not as a publicist."[51]

Black Orpheus's own associate editor, Abiola Irele, moreover, wrote of *Transition*:

> What is really gratifying is the amount of discussion in its columns provoked by theories about Africa. They are analyzed, commented upon—turned inside out, as it were—and sometimes more closely scrutinized in the correspondence section than in the main columns. In short, an animated debate on Africa is being carried on regularly in *Transition*: a debate that has its ponderous and irritating moments, but which hardly strays from the center of interest. . . . By force of circumstances resulting from the fact that more western commentators on African affairs are at hand than Africans willing to give expression to the ideas and preoccupations of the continent, the magazine has been preserved from being a medium of mere self-reflection and self-contemplation for the African intellectual.[52]

Irele's comment, of course, gave credit to the "force of circumstances" for what had actually been a deliberate choice on Neogy's part—the choice of active intercultural engagement over "mere . . . self-contemplation." If Neogy did not deliberately favor Western contributors, he did favor writers who took tough stands, who were ready to help make the "contribution in iron and steel" that he had in mind.

In a little over seven years of publication, *Transition* had developed an important following around the world. It had added West African editors as well (first Christopher Okigbo in Nigeria and then Kofi Awoonor in Ghana) in an effort to broaden its appeal, influence, and circulation within Africa. The creation of a special Ghanaian edition, Awoonor recalls, had been on Neogy's mind ever since he and Awoonor had met in 1963.[53] Neogy was soon to get his wish in a way he had not intended, for the Ghanaian edition of *Transition* was soon to be the only edition.

Transition's circulation figures had risen by 1968 from a low of eight hundred (for *Transition* no. 2) to eleven thousand (for *Transition* no. 37, the last published in Uganda). Its second-year resubscription rate, Neogy recalls, was an unheard-of 80 percent.[54] In Ghana later, with the publicity surrounding Neogy's arrest and the campaign for his release, the pressrun rose to seventeen thousand. Nevertheless, in *Transition*'s case success was expensive—both because of what it cost Neogy in personal suffering and because, publication costs being what they were in Uganda, he was actually losing money on each new subscription. Even though they lowered the publication cost per copy, increased pressruns continued to mean increased deficits that had to be matched by increased outside subsidies. *Transition* sold single issues for U.S. $.75 per copy, but each copy cost more than that to produce. The printing cost alone for each copy, Neogy writes, probably averaged U.S. $1.00, and the editorial cost probably averaged another $.50.

Neogy continued, nevertheless, to hold fast to his principle that *Transition* must pay fair rates to its contributors, and in achieving "editorial mobility," he developed a more sophisticated editorial regimen, involving a number of associate editors in the planning of each new issue through consultations that were "involved but not binding."[55] The growing office staff had more work than it could handle. Mazrui's recollections confirm Neogy's:

> On those special magazine issues like the one[s] on "love" or "violence," Rajat used to seek suggestions from me in advance. He was also keen to know what I would like to contribute to those special themes. I believe that the Guest Editor of the issue on "violence," Henry Beinen, was most unhappy about my article on "Sacred Suicide." Beinen would not have published it! Rajat over-ruled him![56]

Neogy's associate editors as announced in *Transition* no. 37 were Mazrui, Raymond Apthorpe, Paul Theroux, George Awoonor-Williams (Kofi Awoonor), and John Goldblatt, but those resident in Uganda, especially Mazrui and Theroux, had far more direct impact on future issues than someone such as Awoonor, who could only communicate infrequently, after frustrating delays, through the post. It was, however, Neogy's own editorial ideal—his conception of *Transition* as a vehicle for cultural and intellectual debate—that continued to set policy, as Mazrui's anecdote about the special issue on violence illustrates.

Nevertheless, by the time *Transition* no. 37 appeared in 1968 a discussion of the magazine's success, prospects, or editorial aims inevitably necessitated a corollary statement about its sources of overseas subsidy. The smoke of Theroux's high-spirited editorial vaunting in *Transition* no. 37 did not obscure the announcement that necessarily followed it in the same issue, flatly stating, at length and without apology or equivocation, the goals and structure of the organization that had taken over sponsorship of *Transition*. The successor to the discredited Congress for Cultural Freedom, *Transition*'s editors announced, would be the International Association for Cultural Freedom, which had been "completely reorganized with Mr. Alan Bullock, Vice Chancellor of Oxford University, as Chairman of the Board, which includes among its members John Kenneth Galbraith (the American economist), Dr. Alexander Kwapong (Vice-

Chancellor of the University of Ghana), Professor Edward Shils and Ignazio Silone (the distinguished Italian author and novelist)." The announcement also gave a lengthy profile of Shepard Stone, the association's president, and described with careful thoroughness its relationship with its chief sponsor, the Ford Foundation, whose International Affairs program Stone had previously directed. There was an even more scrupulous definition of the association's aims, which were a close reflection of *Transition*'s own:

> The Association seeks to provide a bridge beween the international intellectual community and men engaged in social, political and economic action. It defends intellectual, academic and cultural freedom against infringement from whatever source, while aiming at the promotion of the non-partisan critical spirit essential to the exercise of these liberties. . . .
>
> Two of the Association's main concerns in coming years . . . [are] the contemporary crisis of rationality, of which the cult of violence and the revolt against industrial society are some aspects, and the dialogue between intellectuals from highly developed industrial societies and of societies in the process of development—between intellectual communities of societies following liberal and democratic patterns and of societies emerging from totalitarian rule or engaging in new experiences of the authoritarian type. *(Transition* no. 37, p. 42)

Neogy's editorial aims had remained constant, in spite of risks and unmerited recriminations, and it is a tribute to his perseverance that his editorial policies continued to bear fruit in 1968. A crisis that was to overshadow even the CIA crisis of 1967 loomed, however. As he commented somewhat wistfully when *Transition* no. 38 finally appeared in 1971, nearly three years overdue:

> The magazine in its eighth year was just beginning to get into its stride—both financially through its rapidly rising circulation figures and in the editorial mobility it had begun to achieve. Just when we were about to enter our more mature years, our plans and innovations for future issues had to be abruptly put aside.
>
> (Editorial, *Transition* no. 38, p. 5)

Men in "Immaculate Black Suits": Neogy's Arrest

It was at this moment both of dramatic success as a vehicle forged in "iron and steel" for controversy and debate and of unexpected vulnerability as the discredited agent—witting or unwitting—of a foreign power that Neogy and his associates launched *Transition* no. 37, which was projected to be the most ambitious yet of the magazine's single-theme issues. Focusing on "Students Around the World," it featured a survey of East African university students by Joel D. Barkun, a doctoral student in political science at the University of California at Los Angeles who had done research in Uganda, Kenya, and Tanzania under Ford Foundation sponsorship. However, *Transition* no. 37 was not really a controversial issue by *Transition* standards. Barkun's survey, though hardly uncovering hopeful signs of progress, was not immediately provocative from a political standpoint. East African students, Barkun concluded from his survey of attitudes, saw themselves not as an elite in the making, but rather as a sort of professionally trained middle class. They were more interested in financial and social stability, in promotion and security, than in moral leadership of their societies. Barkun commented:

> In an area of the world which needs not only highly trained people, but people who are interested in formulating new solutions to the countless problems of underdevelopment, the fact that the most knowledgeable people in society are merely content to reliably follow the routine of their jobs is not very encouraging. (p. 31)

Again *Transition* was questioning a myth about the new Africa—that its universities served national development by building a cultural, intellectual, and political avant-garde. Neogy might reasonably have expected a furious reaction from the African universities themselves, but Barkun's survey could not have seemed a politically sensitive issue to other, more dangerous groups—certainly not in comparison to the more risky topics that had been cover features to the issues immediately preceding *Transition* no. 37.

Nevertheless, it was *Transition* no. 37 that finally led Milton Obote to send his secret police after *Transition*'s young editor-in-chief. Six thousand copies of *Transition* no. 37 were stacked on the floor of the magazine's crowded editorial office in Kampala ready for posting to subscribers and distributors abroad, and more copies were already on the street in Kampala, when a half-dozen men in "immaculate black suits"—Ugandan Criminal Investigation Department agents—suddenly entered and announced Neogy's arrest under the Emergency Powers Act. It was October 18, 1968, a Friday. What about the magazines on the floor? someone asked. Did this mean that they couldn't be sent out? No, the senior CID officer said. The government had "nothing against that issue."[57]

There was much confusion at first on both sides. It was soon learned that two other men had been arrested as well sometime before dawn on the same day. The first, Abubakar Mayanja, an opposition politician and barrister, had for months been hotly engaged, partly through the medium of *Transition*'s Letters column, in the debate over Uganda's proposed new constitution. *Transition* no. 37, which the magazine's office staff had just been told was *not* proscribed, contained yet another exchange of volleys in this skirmish, conducted primarily between Mayanja and Picho Ali, a Moscow-educated lawyer on the executive staff of Ugandan President Milton Obote.[58] Ali had argued on the government's behalf that judges ought to be required to profess specific allegiance to the policies and ideologies of the government in power, and Neogy had devoted a special section of the expanded Letters column in *Transition* no. 37 to the resulting debate, reserving space for Abu Mayanja, whose letter appeared with a number of others. Hours before the CID came looking for Neogy, the army had arrested Mayanja in his home at gunpoint.

Adding to the confusion, the third man arrested had been the British editor of the government's own weekly, *The People*, Daniel Nelson. Nelson had sometimes been controversial, but what was his connection with Mayanja and Neogy? The answer, which did not surface for several days, was that Nelson had apparently been arrested by mistake. Illiterate soldiers had simply been told to bring in that editor fellow. They had picked the wrong editor and also roughed him up a bit into the bargain. The whole maneuver, *Transition*'s by then substantial staff conjectured, must be a delayed and somewhat illogical response to Mayanja's article analyzing the new constitution.

Mayanja's article had been published nearly a year before, but unmistakable signs of trouble were recalled. During the months from August 1967 to January 1968 there had been hints by government officials to Mazrui and others that the government was "'disturbed' by the critical articles appearing in a journal as 'prestigious and internationally read' as *Transition*."[59] In an editorial entitled "Indigenous Ills" (*Transition* no. 32, p. 62), Okot p'Bitek had written that "the most striking and frightening characteristic of all African governments is this, that without exception all of them are dictatorships and practice such ruthless discriminations as make the South African *apartheid* look tame." He was soon dismissed from his post as director of Uganda's National Cultural Center, ostensibly for other reasons (*Transition* no. 38, p. 43). At a panel discussion on Ugandan National Television about press freedom in January 1968, Neogy had privately been told by Uganda's defense minister, Felix Onama, also appearing on the program, that "*Transition* was subversive and would soon be dealt with by the Government" (*Transition* no. 38, p. 43). There were other confused fears that suppression, if that was what these arrests meant, might really be owing to the recent revelations of CIA support. There were even those who continued to look for secret sins in Barkun's survey of Ugandan students.

The truth was much simpler. Milton Obote, Uganda's president, had been growing more and more uncomfortable with *Transition*'s participation in, and analysis of, the debate over the new constitution. The proximate reason for the arrest of Mayanja and Neogy was not, however, the constitutional debate (in *Transition* nos. 32 and 34) or the exchange between Mayanja and Picho Ali that followed (culminating in *Transition* no. 37) on the question of whether there should be an ideologically committed judiciary in Uganda; rather, it could be found in an offhand addendum to Mayanja's argument. Mayanja's sin ultimately lay in *agreeing* with Ali. In his letter to the editor in *Transition* no. 37, he noted that, as Ali had observed in a corollary to his own thesis, Uganda's High Court was not even Ugandan. It still employed exclusively non-Ugandan judges—primarily European expatriates. No "dialectical materialism" was therefore necessary to prove that the High Court was alienated, Mayanja jibed, and neither could there be any defensible reason for this state of affairs.

He then borrowed a familiar Ciceronian rhetorical device to cast aspersion without seeming to. "I do not believe the rumour circulating in legal circles for the past year or so that the Judicial Service Commission has made a number of recommendations in this direction, but that the appointments have for one reason or another, mostly tribal considerations, not been confirmed," he wrote. "But what *is* holding up the appointment of Ugandan Africans to the High Court?" (*Transition* no. 37, p. 15). Milton Obote was not to be diverted by rhetorical evasions, however, and it was, Ali Mazrui later learned, an advance copy of Mayanja's letter, with its thinly veiled charge of tribalism (coming so soon after the Buganda emergency) that caused the virtual, if not the actual, suppression of *Transition*.[60]

The controversy that eventually resulted in Neogy's arrest had begun in a neglected corner of the famous 1967 "Tarzan" issue (no. 32). A pair of articles in that issue sought to analyze Uganda's proposed constitutional "reforms."[61] The first, by A. W. Bradley, was a scrupulous, dispassionate academic study, restrained in the extreme when it touched on several immediate Ugandan political controversies. (Bradley contented himself, for instance, with the mild observation that the deposition and banishment of the *kabaka* of Buganda might have "cultural and psychological effects" that he could "in no way" estimate.) Bradley's statement about the new Emergency Detention powers, however, was surprisingly direct: "The range of controls over the new pattern of the Executive has been less carefully considered than the need for strong presidential powers, and . . . the framers of the proposals seem impatient of almost any form of constitutional restraint" ("Constitution-Making in Uganda," pp. 27–28).

The contentiousness of Abu Mayanja's article must have stood out all the more in contrast. A Ugandan nationalist leader since 1958 (when he had returned from Cambridge University) and minister of education in the *kabaka*'s government until 1964, he did not mince words or equivocate. Though he praised Obote's government for framing a new constitution at all, for publishing the proposals in advance, and for inviting public comment, he condemned in absolute terms the new constitution's tendency to concentrate unchecked powers in the president's hands, including even the power in some circumstances to deny Ugandan citizens their civil and judicial rights and equal protection under the law. Obote, Mayanja pointed out, would be able to appoint up to one-third of the members of the national assembly; would no longer have strong local governments to contend with; would for the first time absolutely dominate his cabinet (under the 1962 constitution, Uganda's president was to be strictly accountable to his cabinet); and would be enabled, under the threat of unspecified emergencies, to arrest dissidents nearly at will, denying them "fundamental rights and freedoms" of the judicial process. Mayanja's final summary of the government constitutional proposals was even more aggressively negative:

> In many respects they are illiberal, authoritarian, and dictatorial. They make serious inroads in the concept of the rule of law as accepted by most jurists and civilised nations. They provide for the concentration of excessive, autocratic, and dangerous powers in the hands of one man. They are even repugnant to the concept of the African personality in so far as they provide for a wholesale abolition of all the traditional institutions. (p. 25)

There was certainly plenty of material in Mayanja's article for severe alienation of affection between Mayanja and his own political party (he had joined the ruling Uganda People's Congress in 1964, but had remained an independent voice and had not hesitated to criticize UPC policies from his parliamentary back bench). It was to the government's credit, however, that it contented itself with a mild rebuke, in the form of an article in *Transition* no. 33 by Akena Adoko[62] merely defending the constitution as reflecting a consensus of the will of the Ugandan peoples, arrived at through democratic means. It was probably, in fact, Neogy himself who unintentionally precipitated the acrimony that soon entered what until then had been a reasonable enough debate, though an impassioned one, when he allowed a student at Makerere named Davis Sebukima to respond to Akena Adoko's article pseudonymously.

He may simply have felt that Sebukima, dependent on a government scholarship, needed the protection of anonymity. However, Sebukima's assumed name, "Steve Lino," allowed him to adopt a tone of contemptuous dismissal that was a new note in a debate whose participants, including Mayanja, had until then carefully avoided personal derogation. The government, Sebukima asserted, might have been better served if Adoko had, instead of attempting to vindicate the new constitution, "kept silent and not written such a lame defense of it." Sebukima's sarcasm became harsh and personal. Of Adoko, he wrote:

> He begins his article with the wild assertion that "there is a consensus of opinion that the way the Constitution of the Republic of Uganda was introduced, and passed, with most of its provisions, deserve[s] the highest praise." I don't know how Mr. Adoko obtained his "consensus of opinion," but I do know, as all the honest citizens of his country know, that the Uganda constitution was introduced in the worst possible way. It was proposed and introduced by a government which had outlived its legal life; it was introduced to a Parliament about ten percent of whose members were either in detention or otherwise politically incapacitated; it was introduced at a time when the most important single unit of the country, and the capital, were (and still are) under a state of emergency. If Mr. Adoko thinks this was the best way of introducing the constitution, his standards must be very low indeed. No doubt the constitution and the manner of its introduction have received praise from the ministers and many U.P.C. members of Parliament, from men like Adoko and sycophants in general. And perhaps this constitutes his "consensus of opinion." (*Transition* no. 34, p. 9)

At this point, Neogy, whose iconoclasm seems always to have increased in direct proportion to the degree of angry opposition it provoked,[63] had gone too far by the government's standards. In printing Sebukima's anonymous abuse, he had upset what had been the tenuous balance between *Transition* and a grudgingly tolerant regime. The government's response, in a letter published in the same issue, signed on Akena Adoko's behalf by a UPC Parliamentarian named Odur-Aper,[64] clearly exposed its exasperation with Neogy and his associates. In fact, Obote and his advisors seem strongly to have suspected that "Steve Lino" was Mayanja, Neogy himself, or perhaps both of them or one of Neogy's other editorial associates, such as Theroux or Mazrui.

"Who is Steve Lino?" Odur-Aper wrote,

> I have never met nor heard of the person and, however insignificant that may be, it is probably true that many persons in Uganda are in my position. This leads to the assumption that Steve Lino is a fictitious name—what cowardice! I have no means of knowing whether Steve Lino is a Uganda citizen or an expatriate "Tarzan." The trash and ignorance displayed in the letter could indicate that Steve Lino is not a resident of Uganda and that he may be living either in Salisbury or Cape Town or Washington or Moscow or London. (p. 10)

Odur-Aper went on to defend both the legitimacy of the constitutional process and the nature of the "consensus" that it represented. He answered Sebukima's sneer with one of his own: "I challenge Steve Lino to say when he carried out a referendum of 'all the honest citizens of this Country' and what was the standard of honesty" (p. 10). The remainder of Odur-Aper's rebuttal, however, might have merited the charge of lameness that Sebukima had leveled at Adoko. Although Odur-Aper's defense of the process of indirect presidential election was cogent enough, his argument that Obote had not in the *past* broken his oath to "maintain the dignity" of the *kabaka* because there *was now* no *kabaka* was clearly specious. On the issue of constitutional checks and balances, Odur-Aper merely counseled patient insouciance: "Give Uganda time: precedents and practices limiting the President's power will evolve" (p. 11).

The first of Picho Ali's contributions to this extended debate, which also appeared in *Transition* no. 34, took a similar tack. Like Odur-Aper, Ali denied Sebukima's contention that the constitution-making process had been illegitimate or had functioned in an atmosphere of constraint, citing Mayanja's original article as supporting him on this point. Like Odur-Aper, moreover, he advised incuriousness. The process of constitution making, he said, need not be analyzed. A successful revolution alone legitimized a new order and truly expressed the public will. It made moot the question of whether the constitutional debates had been truly representative: "This argument adds and subtracts nothing, for the events of 1966 which the High Court found as a fact as constituting a revolution, had the same effect of ensuring their absence from the debates" (p. 13). This shift in the terminology of debate, toward Marxism, Neogy would later reflect, had been merely a species of opportunism. "In Uganda," he wrote, "the immediate reason for a move in this direction was an urgent need to replenish [the government's] political vocabulary and not because cabinet ministers discovered Marx or knew anything about him."[65]

When Picho Ali next entered the fray, in *Transition* no. 36, it was to take the offensive, not to rebut criticisms. In a lengthy letter headed "Ideological Commitment and the Judiciary," Ali made the largely theoretical argument that law in a new "revolutionary" society such as Uganda's should base itself not upon the ideal that there was some dispassionate, "pure" legal norm, irrelative to sociopolitical allegiance, but upon "the principle of ideological parity." The traditional notion of a dispassionate judiciary unaffected by political realities was a fantasy, he argued, and since Uganda's judiciary would always be politically aligned, why should it not be required to be ideologically committed at least to the broad revolutionary goals of the new Uganda? The practical implications of Ali's theory were left somewhat vague, however, and his examples of cases in which "ideological commitment" ought to have figured in the judge's decision were, as it afterwards turned out, rather disquieting to many readers. That disquiet made itself apparent in the next issue of the magazine.

The final installment of the constitutional debate, in the special Letters section of *Transition* no. 37, reached the streets of Kampala in spite of the arrest of Neogy and Mayanja. There was, however, nothing especially remarkable about Mayanja's new thrust therein. He stuck pretty much to defining the legal process and questioning matters of fact in rebutting Picho Ali's vision of Uganda's brave new judicial future. Both Mayanja, writing from his perspective as a trial lawyer, and another Kampalan barrister, John W. R. Kazzora, past president of the Uganda bar association, stressed what seemed to them obvious errors of fact or interpretation in Ali's use of recent cases as examples. Both Kazzora and Mayanja pointed out, for instance, that in a recent treason trial cited by Ali, involving an alleged conspiracy to overthrow the Ugandan government, the presiding judge had not said, as Ali had implied, that twenty-two defendants were too many because twenty-two persons were too many to have attempted to overthrow the state, but only that twenty-two defendants were too many to be tried together in a single trial.

Both Kazzora and Mayanja took exception, moreover, to Ali's contention that the expatriate judge in a recent immigration case involving two mercenaries who had fled the Republic of the Congo (Zaire) would have given a much stiffer sentence had he been "ideologically committed." The judge had no right, under the existing laws of Uganda, Kazzora and Mayanja maintained, to make any events that had taken place in the Congo a factor in passing sentence in Uganda, since engaging in mercenary activity elsewhere was not specifically prohibited under Ugandan law. The Uganda People's Congress had a comfortable majority in Parliament, Mayanja further argued; if it wanted to make such activities illegal under Ugandan law, it could therefore do so. But, "it is unfair to expect the Judiciary to correct the situation by acting contrary to its professional traditions, and also usurping functions which properly belong to the Legislature" (p. 15). Kazzora added the further criticism that Ali had misrepresented the theoretical underpinnings of the law, particularly in his reference to Hans Kelsen's *Pure Theory of Law*. Kelsen had never denied, Kazzora corrected, that law bore a relation to sociopolitical factors.

Insofar as their letters rebutted or criticized Picho Ali, Kazzora and Mayanja ran about dead even. In fact, if anything, Kazzora's letter was the harsher in tone—more belligerent and personally stinging. In one place he called Ali "presumptuous and confused." In another he suggested that Ali was "grossly ignorant of the British judicial system" and perhaps "should never have displayed his ignorance in print" (p. 13). Kazzora concluded with the conditional suggestion that Ali "not make statements containing libellous innuendos which might, inter alia, bring him perilously within the ambit of the law of contempt of Court" (p. 14).

Why, then, if it was the response in *Transition* no. 37 to Ali's ideas that had angered Obote, was it Mayanja, and not Kazzora, who was the object of Obote's ire? Why was it Mayanja who was arrested the day that *Transition* no. 37 appeared? Was the issue of an "ideologically committed judiciary" really the underlying root of the arrests?

Probably not. It seems, rather, to have been a pair of offhand asides that Mayanja had directed not at Picho Ali but at the Obote government as a whole that caused the government's harsh reaction. First, there was the implication, already cited, of tribalism as a cause for delay in appointing Africans to the Ugandan High Court. Second, there was also, in the letter's concluding paragraph, a direct suggestion that the government's use of emergency powers for the curtailment of dissent equated it with the former colonial regime. The delay in repealing colonial statutes, Mayanja speculated, was deliberate—a cynical perpetuation of injustice for indefensible concealed purposes. Mayanja wrote,

> The interesting point . . . is that far from wanting to change the outmoded colonial laws, the Government of Uganda seems to be quite happy in retaining them and utilising them, especially those laws designed by the Colonial Regime to suppress freedom of association and expression. . . . If, therefore, it be true, as Picho Ali argues, that "the aims and objectives of the British Colonial regime in Uganda and those of the new Republic of Uganda . . . run diametrically counter to one another," the Uganda Government seems to be doing singularly little in repealing and modifying the laws of the country and mak[ing] them more attuned to the requirements of the Republic.   (p. 15)

Taken in themselves, these two insinuations were bad enough, but the damage that they did was compounded by the fact that Obote and his associates were inclined to see Mayanja, Neogy, and "Steve Lino," whoever he was, as being in collusion. It is also clear that the government's feelings had already been hurt by Mayanja's earlier article and by the letter from "Steve Lino" a few months before. Mayanja's letter in *Transition* no. 37 may just have been the last straw.

Moreover, as Ali Mazrui has recently pointed out, Davis Sebukima's subsequent arrest was "no afterthought"; the government had apparently hoped all along to unearth "Steve Lino's" identity and had searched the *Transition* office files following Neogy's and Mayanja's arrest for that specific purpose.[66] In the absence of information to the contrary, they may have assumed that Neogy, Mayanja, and perhaps others, under Mayanja's name and the pseudonym "Steve Lino," were setting out to wage a campaign to discredit them, using means—pseudonymous ridicule, invocation of tribal prejudices, and the imputation of unscrupulous motives—that Obote and his advisors saw as unfair. After his arrest, Davis Sebukima, under interrogation by CID Chief Mohammed Hassan, would repeatedly be asked, "Did you really write this letter yourself?"[67]

Whatever their motives, the result of the government's action was that *Transition* saw itself—and was seen by the world at large—as virtually suppressed, for reasons that could only be related to the government's desire to stop the press from criticizing its actions. In *Transition* nos. 35 and 36, ironically enough, Neogy had printed articles on the freedom and viability of the Ugandan press, followed in *Transition* no. 37 itself by letters commenting on the earlier articles, including one by Salvatore Yoanna Olwoc of Kampala, under the heading "The Press in Uganda," which opined that the test of Uganda's press freedom, and with it of its democracy itself, was yet to come; and another by George Kaggwa of Entebbe, under the heading "A True Democracy Means a Free Press," which hinted that democracy was under notice of dismissal in Uganda. Nearly as ironic even as the fact that *Transition* no. 37 precipitated this test of freedom was the fact that the man who had broached the subject with the publication of a thoughtful, mildly stated article in *Transition* no. 35 had been none other than Daniel Nelson, the editor of *The*

People who was mistakenly arrested with Mayanja and Neogy on October 18.[68]

There had, by all accounts, been as much miscalculation and confusion on the government's side before the arrests as there would be on *Transition*'s afterwards. Obote's government had, in fact, itself precipitated both the constitutional and the free-press debates. In the summer of 1967, Obote had made an effort to win support for his new constitution by calling for an open debate on its merits. In her recollection of these events, published four years later from *Transition*'s new editorial address in Accra, Barbara Neogy (whose husband, though released from prison, had not yet sufficiently recovered to return to his duties) impugned Obote's motives. Though he had called for a "free voice" and "fearlessness" in discussions of national affairs, what Obote really wanted, she said, had been merely a semblance of debate to camouflage its actual suppression. Neogy, in answering the Uganda president's call for a "free voice," had in a sense been set up by a government that had misjudged the "fearlessness" of which he and his correspondents and contributors were capable. As Barbara Neogy was later to put it:

> Given the perspective of events that took place since, it can be supposed that in opening the debate to the public, the Government had simply miscalculated. It assumed that the citizenry and the Parliament, intimidated by the violence of 1966, would acquiesce. Far from intending as a matter of policy to set a unique example of tolerance for itself and the rest of the continent, the Government had merely been unprepared for the strenuous attack that ensued from all quarters. That these attacks set some Ministerial noses out of joint is obvious: a part of their large ambitions focused on eventually avenging the damage.
>
> (*Transition* no. 38, "A Matter of Transition," p. 43)

The debate over the role of the press, in *Transition* and elsewhere, had in fact inspired a response from Obote himself, delivered before Parliament two weeks to the day before the arrest of Neogy and Mayanja. While seeming to encourage free discussion, Obote had hinted ominously of limits on press freedom in a way that was later to seem portentous. Barbara Neogy later paraphrased Obote's argument:

Since the constitution purposely provided for press freedom—in order that this freedom could serve the interests of the people as a whole, if any newspaper adopted an anti-Ugandan attitude, created division—all in the name of press freedom—such publications were unconstitutional.   (Ibid., p. 44)

Obote's hint was, however, misleading. Neogy and Mayanja (and later Davis Sebukima) were not arrested through any invocation of constitutional provisions, old or new, against "anti-Ugandan" publications; were not, at first, charged with a crime relating to Mayanja's writings or Neogy's editorship; were not, in fact, for a long time charged at all. Their initial arrest was unexplained, carried out under the summary powers of the Emergency Acts, executed under provisions that made due process unnecessary. No warrant was sought. No charges were filed. Neogy and Mayanja were simply taken to Luzira Prison and placed in solitary confinement, without being allowed either to communicate with their families or to consult a lawyer.

"*Transition* Is Not Neogy, and Neogy Is Not *Transition*"

Having no legal recourse, Neogy's wife, Barbara, and Ali Mazrui discussed instead seeking a hearing for Neogy and Mayanja through the international press. *Transition*'s recent notoriety, they felt, would make its editor good copy. Barbara Neogy would handle this angle herself, she said, through her connections with journalists in London and New York. Mazrui was to concentrate his energies on raising some sort of protest within East Africa, especially in Uganda itself. Though Mazrui felt that he, too, might do something abroad, through his academic connections (he had, for example, just returned from a prolonged speaking tour in Europe and America), he agreed to concentrate for the time being on local activities.[69]

It was, in fact, Mazrui who provoked the first skirmish in what was to become a war of wills and words. He circulated a petition among intellectual circles in Kampala, particularly among the faculty and staff of Makerere College, where he was then professor of political science. His letter was moderately worded, expressing concern that such prominent intellectuals as Neogy and Mayanja should be detained without explanation and urging that they be explicitly charged and speedily brought to trial, but it provoked an immediate and forceful response that emphasized the seriousness with which Neogy's "little" magazine was taken. Obote's own private secretary promptly phoned Mazrui with the mysterious suggestion that he attend a special session of Parliament scheduled for October 21, three days after Neogy's arrest. At that parliamentary session, Obote denounced "the professor of political science" and called on him to "go and teach elsewhere."[70]

That evening, as Obote's denunciation of Mazrui was being excitedly discussed over Radio Uganda—and, one supposes, speculated about in thousands of private conversations in Kampala—

190

Mazrui himself was talking the speech over with Sir Udo Udoma, Uganda's chief justice and a personal friend. Udoma suggested that Mazrui now take the initiative and seek a direct audience with President Obote. Mazrui recalls what then transpired:

> The next morning I phoned the President's office. I was granted an audience the same day. I spent five hours with President Obote. During those five hours I discovered that the really offensive part of *Transition*'s latest issue was Abu Mayanja's letter about the judiciary. I also found out during those five hours that Obote recognized *Transition* as a "potential" asset of Uganda. I remain convinced that Obote valued *Transition* and would have preferred to see it saved under what he regarded as a more dependable editorship. He kept on emphasizing to me: "*Transition* is not Neogy, and Neogy is not *Transition*!"[71]

Obote also made it clear to Mazrui, as he would later to journalists at the Commonwealth Conference in London, that he had no desire to destroy or suppress *Transition*. He hoped that it would survive Neogy's incarceration, and even suggested that Mazrui might take over the editorship himself in Neogy's absence. Obote's characterization of Mazrui as "a more dependable editor," Mazrui reflects, seems, if anything, an unintentional credit to Neogy's independence and determination. Mazrui respectfully declined, however, to usurp the editorship.

Obote seemed, Mazrui observed, to have read *Transition* no. 37 very carefully indeed.[72] He had even noticed a parody of Mazrui by Theroux in that issue and hastened to deplore it (Mazrui, he suggested, had good grounds there for a libel suit against Theroux). Far from wanting to kill *Transition*, Obote in fact seemed at that time to have hoped rather for a surgical removal . . . of its head. If only another head could be quickly grafted onto the corpse's still quivering shoulders, perhaps the resultant anomaly might be docile. Mazrui writes:

> I do not believe that Obote wanted to kill *Transition*. That was our weapon against him, and not his weapon against us. Obote wanted to

save *Transition* (if only it would behave), but we were prepared to kill it (if the price of survival was what he regarded as "good behavior"!).[73]

Once Mazrui had had his talk with Obote, the *Transition* staff scrapped plans for new editions in order to make clear to Obote their non-compliance with his suggestions.

The next step was Barbara Neogy's. She circulated copies of Mazrui's letter of protest among the London and New York press corps, thereby attracting the first press coverage abroad of her husband's arrest. Under the heading "Speaking Up for Neogy," the "Times Diary" column in *The Times* of London was the first to pick up the story, two weeks after the arrests. "A leading intellectual in Uganda, Professor Ali Mazrui, has bravely spoken up against the arrests under emergency powers two weeks ago of Rajat Neogy, the editor of the bi-monthly magazine *Transition*, and Abu Mayanja, the Opposition M.P. and leading Muslim," the piece declared. Following the tack of Mazrui's protest letter, it quoted "the outspoken and popular professor of political science at Makerere University College" and "television pundit" Mazrui as asserting that Mayanja and Neogy had been arrested "for being intellectually honest" (p. 10).

Less than a month before, Mazrui had written an article for a special Uganda supplement of *The Times* (October 9, 1968) that had concluded that in Ugandan politics "frank controversy on various issues continues to be a major aspect of intellectual life." In his new letter about the arrests, however, Mazrui added a rueful postscript to his earlier statement: "Today I am groping for reassurance that I was not wrong."

The Times's piece concluded with a report of a telephone interview with Barbara Neogy, initiated, so the writer said (under the subhead "A Model Wife," punning on her former career), to investigate reports that Mayanja had been severely beaten when he was arrested and "has since had a head operation." Mayanja's life was in no danger, Barbara Neogy reported, and her husband was bearing up well. *Transition* had not been explicitly banned, she admitted, and she meant to bring out a new edition herself (this even though Mazrui's conversation with Obote had taken place a week earlier). Beyond the Ugandan protest engineered by Mazrui's letter, however, the only other stirring of protest that she could definitely report was a cable of concern from eight American university professors. Although the rumors she passed on to *The Times* of his needing surgery turned out to be false, Mayanja had indeed, as Barbara Neogy reported, been severely beaten. "Have you had breakfast yet?" Mayanja recalls a Special Force sergeant asking him the morning of his arrest. "No," he had replied, surprised at this kindness. "Give him some breakfast—outside in the courtyard," the sergeant had instructed several other officers. Mayanja was taken outside then and beaten.[74]

In Kampala, meanwhile, the police stepped up their pressure on *Transition*. There were repeated searches of its editorial offices, as well as of Neogy's home. Cartons full of material were packed up and carried off—editorial files, correspondence, photographs, personal documents, tapes, tape recorders.[75] Protests paid off in at least one respect, however: though Neogy continued to be held in solitary confinement under a harsh and restrictive regimen, he was at last formally charged a few weeks after *The Times* had given its coverage to Mazrui's protest letter.

The formal charges followed a curious effort on the government's part to set afloat various rationalizations for the arrests on the waters of public opinion, both in public and in private. "One of the charges raised informally against Neogy by government sources," Henry Beinen reported a few months later in an article for *Africa Report*, "was that he had deceived the country by 'posing' as a Ugandan editor when in fact he had failed to take the step of renouncing his British citizenship with the British High Commission in Kampala."[76] In anticipation of its own strategy, apparently, the government had quietly taken the step of stripping Neogy of his Ugandan citizenship a few days after his arrest. Though Neogy's improperly registered citizenship had been an accidental oversight, and, as Beinen pointed out, applied to "many other Asians who held British passports prior to independence and missed this technicality in the process of adopting Ugandan citizenship in the early 1960s" (p. 14), it was to be one justification for an eventual charge of sedition. Beinen concluded:

> What President Obote and Foreign Minister Odaka appeared to be try-
> ing to support by indirection was a thesis that *Transition*, financed by
> foreign money, staffed by several non-Ugandan associate editors, and
> widely-circulated outside the country, was a "foreign body" operating in
> Uganda. (ibid.)

Other efforts to discredit the magazine ranged from the more or less direct (implications, based on the CIA revelations of the previous year, of tainted contents) to broad hints. In the November 21 issue of the Kampalan periodical the *Uganda Argus*, for instance, Obote, un-happy with the picture of Uganda beginning to form abroad as a re-pressive and anti-democratic nation, was once again quoted as main-taining that *Transition* itself had not been suppressed. Obote was himself, he said again at length, in favor of a free press and a free ex-change of ideas. The *Uganda Argus* paraphrased him, however, as adding:

> *Transition* was being debated these days as if it were bigger than
> Uganda, although Uganda was not all that small. No action had been
> taken against the magazine, although action had been taken against its
> editor. . . . Some people have said that the editor should be prosecuted.
> [But] a state of emergency prevails in Buganda, and those arrested
> under the Emergency Regulations [all] had to be treated in the same
> way.[77]

The following day, Neogy and Mayanja, brought to court in handcuffs, were formally charged with sedition. Released on bail bond by Uganda's chief magistrate, who pointed out that the sedi-tion charge, since it was a separate matter, did not justify detainment under the emergency regulations, they were immediately rearrested under these regulations in a curious distortion of the chief magis-trate's ruling. They were returned immediately to Luzira Prison, but the chief magistrate's bail ruling had, in a breath, taken away what the trial had been precipitated in order to provide—justification for Neogy's and Mayanja's continued detention.[78] The specific charges, which had been filed on three counts, alleged that Mayanja's animadversions on the president's failure to Africanize the Ugandan High Court "were intended to bring the President into disrepute."[79]

Meanwhile, conditions for Neogy in his tiny cell in Luzira Prison remained as before. It was not actually the physical suffering and deprivation that bothered him most, but the anxiety and sense of isolation. He had, he wrote in an article for the *New York Times* a year later, been completely unprepared for his arrest. Although politicians had sometimes been jailed for being on the wrong side of an issue, in Uganda as elsewhere in Africa, "editors, writers, and intellectuals have been subject to banning orders only in South Africa." Neogy had spent the first night, a "cooling off" period in a police cell, in a near state of shock. The questioning that he was first subjected to— so formal and perfunctory—made everything all the more unreal. Who was he? What was his address? The police, of course, knew quite well who he was. Neogy even recognized some of them as "'regulars' of the city's more popular beer-drinking hangouts." Even a year later, his strongest recollection was of a sense of the scene's futile illogic: "Detention is gratuitous and the chilling fact is that there has to be no reason for it other than somebody, up there, got suddenly frightened." Even more so than his wife and his associates on the outside, Neogy found the government's actions bizarre and inexplicable. Why had he been arrested? How was the outside world reacting to his arrrest? He had no way of knowing. At first severely censored, his reading materials were eventually taken away altogether. Enforced silence made a mystery of the simplest occurrences, and constant surprise searches left Neogy always in a state of apprehension and uncertainty. Even the logic of the censorship of reading materials was mysterious. Solzhenitsyn's dissident prison memoir, *The First Circle*, was allowed Neogy—perhaps because the warders had never heard of it—but Norman Mailer's *The Armies of the Night* was proscribed—perhaps, Neogy reflected later, "because of the title." The political prisoners were segregated and constantly scrutinized, their isolation made evident by the "ill-fitting grey uniform" that they were issued to distinguish them from mere criminals, who wore white uniforms. Helplessness, isolation, and incomprehension, moreover, bred an obsessive desire for news from the outside, and an obsessive fear of abandonment or betrayal:

> The political prisoner's greatest fear is of being forgotten. His gratitude to anybody or any organization that keeps him alive in the outside world is humble and boundless. When Amnesty International in Britain declared me a "prisoner of conscience," our underground grapevine was seething with excitement. It meant Uganda's detention laws had been brought to world attention and for some detainees who have been imprisoned for over three years it was like breathing new air.[80]

By then Barbara Neogy and Ali Mazrui had gotten their publicity machine into full gear. With Mazrui now concentrating on "the international academic lobby" and Barbara Neogy on the international press, more and more reaction was generated in the form of letters of protest and formal inquiries, as well as press reports. Mazrui writes, "When we combined the forces of the press and the forces of academia, international protest became quite formidable."[81]

So formidable was the protest, in fact, that even the international question of the rights of Asians resident in East Africa, threatened as they were by recent developments in Kenya, was partially and temporarily overshadowed at the Commonwealth prime ministers' meeting in London in January, where Obote was surprised into his impromptu justification of Neogy's arrest (see p. 101, above). There was, moreover, a tie-in between the issue of press freedom and racial and ethnic antagonisms, as the press was quick to note. Obote's first statement on his arrival at the Commonwealth Conference had, in fact, been an announcement that Uganda's forty thousand Asians would at some unspecified future date be summarily required to leave Uganda, "and they will just leave."[82]

Under pressure from Neogy's and Mayanja's supporters in London, and made uneasy by the growing climate of antagonism against resident Asians, the British High Commission in Kampala had even attempted to counter the Obote government's action in stripping Neogy of Ugandan citizenship. It declared that Neogy's ambiguous citizenship entitled him to "the full consular protection and assistance of the British government."[83] The Ugandan government, however, countered quite ingeniously by merely accepting with gratitude the High Commission's declaration of foster-nationality for Neogy, on condition that a similar offer forthwith be extended as well to the other forty thousand Asians in Uganda holding similar anachronistic British credentials. This the British declined to do, and there the matter rested, the Obote government having at last won a round.

Perhaps their adroitness in dealing with the High Commission emboldened Neogy's government adversaries. Perhaps the government began to feel the pressure of the private campaign by Barbara Neogy and Ali Mazrui to force formal charges and a trial. At any rate, government prosecutors did at last in early January bring Neogy and Mayanja to trial. They were also apparently making an effort to comply with the provision of the emergency regulations that detained persons be formally furnished with a statement of the grounds for their detention within ninety days, since separate grounds under those regulations justifying the two detentions were also proffered *in camera*. Government prosecutors thus hedged their bets, justifying the detentions with both public criminal charges and *in camera* proceedings under the emergency regulations. The closed criminal arraignment took place on November 21; the statements of grounds under the emergency regulations were delayed until mid-January, however, the last possible moment before the expiration of the specified ninety-day period under the emergency acts. In the meantime, in the interim between the arraignment on November 21 and the first day of the trial on January 9, the government also worked assiduously at promoting its case and discrediting those of Neogy and Mayanja through its own communications media.

Daniel Nelson had abandoned his editorship of *The People* and had returned to England, after his mistaken arrest and maltreatment in October.[84] He had been replaced by an editor from the president's own staff, and *The People* thereafter became, along with the government radio and television stations, Neogy's chief calumniator. There was much confusion in the direction of these attacks and justifications, owing apparently to the fact that the government had never really fixed squarely upon one of its two possible strategies—detention and trial on criminal charges of subversion, which would have the advantage of offering the outside world a justification for the detentions; or summary arrest without trial under the executive powers of the emergency regulations, which would have the advantage of being without risks, and the disadvantage of justifying nothing. There was also confusion and contradiction regarding the justification to be employed for the sedition charge and the detention under the emergency acts. Were Mayanja and Neogy guilty of having written and published seditious articles? Or of belonging to seditious organizations? The trouble was, apparently, either that no firm decision was taken between these separate strategies, or that Obote, Odaka, and their chief lieutenants simply got their signals crossed.

At the public criminal trial, beginning on January 9, the accused were charged with seditious writings under Uganda's civil statutes. The prosecutor, later to play a major part in Uganda's destiny following the overthrow of Idi Amin, was Godfrey Binaisa. At the separate *in camera* tribunal presided over by a High Court judge in Luzira Prison a week later, Neogy was presented with formal justifications for his detention under the emergency acts.[85] The prosecutor in that instance was not Binaisa but the CID head, Mohammed Hassan. Though somewhat different, the charges again hinged on articles printed in *Transition*.

What Hassan did not know, however, was that Obote, speaking to journalists at his own press luncheon at the Commonwealth Conference in London a few days before, had flatly contradicted the charges that Hassan was now putting forward on his government's behalf. Why was he stifling free debate in the press? Obote was asked. He was not suppressing *Transition* at all, he answered, resorting to the hopeful response that he had first broached in his long private chat with Mazrui in October—*Transition* was free to continue publication under a new editor. This time, in his enthusiasm, Obote went further, as the *Uganda Argus* itself reported on January 18:

> Speaking to a hushed silence, he said: "I have always read *Transition* very, very religiously and there is not a single criticism of the Government of the nature reported in the British press." Not one issue of the magazine had challenged the legitimacy of the Constitution, he said, and he had brought a bundle of the magazines with him to London to prove it. (Quoted in *Transition* no. 38, p. 45)

Neogy, Obote further asserted, was not being held for anything that he had published or written in *Transition* at all, but for his involvement with "certain organizations." Were it not for these unsuitable allegiances, "he would be sitting in the editor's chair today."[86]

Hassan, apparently, had not yet seen the January 18 edition of the *Uganda Argus*. Unfortunately for him, however, Neogy's lawyer, Byron Georgiades, whom the *New York Times* described as "one of the most successful lawyers in East Africa" (January 10, 1969, p. 12), had read the *Uganda Argus* account of Obote's London press sideshow and had given it to Neogy. Standing alone, without counsel, before the judge presiding over the secret tribunal, Neogy adroitly countered Hassan's statement by reading aloud Obote's London statement. He then pointed out that Hassan's representations were contradicted by President Obote himself. *Transition* had not unduly criticized the government, as Obote himself had said, and Neogy was only charged by Uganda's chief executive with belonging to these mysterious unnamed organizations. Moreover, Neogy argued, *Transition* had always given the government prior notice of criticisms and ample space to reply to them. The government had frequently taken advantage of these opportunities to respond to its critics in the magazine's pages—which indicated, did it not, that the government was satisfied with *Transition*'s even-handedness.[87]

Hassan was thunderstruck. He fumbled with his papers and hastily announced that there had been a "typographical error" in the statement of grounds for detention—Neogy really should have been charged with belonging to "certain organizations." (Hassan was handicapped, of course, by not yet knowing what organizations to specify.) The judge refused to accept Hassan's amendment, however, pointing out that Hassan had already certified his statement as complete. Nevertheless, later that afternoon, back in his cell, Neogy was visited by a courier bearing an amended and redated statement of grounds, which he was admonished to sign. He refused to do so.

At the public trial, in the interim, the government had suffered worse reversals. From the first, the trial became the public spectacle that the government had no doubt intended, but a spectacle that threatened to make heroes of the defendants rather than to justify the government's actions. The courtroom was packed with spectators, even to the steps of the building. Others crowded around the windows.[88] Though restrained by the presence of police, the sympathies of the huge crowds seemed to be with the defendants. After each session, the crowd surged forward for a look at the prisoners as they were led to police vans: "As they drove off, . . cries of good wishes went out to them. It was the only public evidence, and courageous at that, that it was not a popular trial" (*Transition* no. 38, p. 45).

The foreign newspapers, largely unsympathetic to the government's representations of sedition and treasonous conspiracy, ticketed the trial from the first as a public showdown on the issue of free speech. "The uncertain new concept of a free press in black Africa is at stake," wrote Lawrence Fellows in the *New York Times*, adding: "There is no way of telling what effect the trial will have on the press in Africa, only that it will have an effect, whether the defendants are found guilty or not." *The Times* of London, in its bare report of the facts, merely quoted Mayanja's declaration at the trial: "The state is much more on trial than I am."[89]

In the court sessions themselves, meanwhile, the government prosecutor, Binaisa, hampered by his lack of a credible case, was outmaneuvered from the first by the defense attorneys. Binaisa's first thrust raised the issue of tribalism, an especially pernicious evil in East Africa, and therefore, he implied, so deleterious in its effects as to merit special rules when it was discussed in print. "Tribalism as we know it," the *New York Times* quoted him as saying, "is a running sore."[90]

Byron Georgiades, however, rebutted by coolly reiterating and seconding Mayanja's initial criticism of Obote for not appointing Ugandans to the High Court bench. It was, he emphasized, a fact that such appointments had not been made and were long overdue. One might indeed ask, as Mayanja had, what, if not tribal considerations, was causing the delay. The charges against Neogy and Mayanja were "absurd," he said; "manifestly they lack a sense of proportion." Mayanja's criticisms had been eminently reasonable and appropriate: "If there is a free press in Uganda within the recognized limits of the law, neither the President, nor Ministers, nor Government are immune from constructive criticism."[91]

Mayanja's own lawyer, flown out from London especially to represent him, was Sir Dingle Foot, an Englishman who had made his reputation in East Africa during the colonial era by defending nationalists accused by the colonial government of sedition. There was, therefore, a special irony, which the English press was quick to underline, in his returning to defend a new generation of dissidents against excesses stemming from the same set of laws—now employed, however, by an independent African nation against its own citizens. Sir Dingle, moreover, did not allow the irony of his return to pass without comment. He recalled in court, the *Guardian* reported, the criticisms that once had been made—in courts of law, in the press, even in the British Houses of Parliament—of colonial Kenya's detention camps and other repressive measures. It was "very strange," the *Guardian* quoted him as adding, with reference to one of the dangerous allusions in Mayanja's letter, if similar measures could not "any longer be criticized in an independent African country." To Georgiades's arguments, Sir Dingle added the simple observation that Mayanja could not have brought Milton Obote "into contempt," since he had not mentioned Obote by name. Moreover, that Mayanja's objections to Picho Ali's ideas were reasonable was emphasized by the fact that Mayanja's had been only one of five letters in *Transition* no. 37 that took strong exception to Ali's call for a "committed judiciary."[92]

When the proceedings had come to an end, it was apparent, though the actual judgment was to be delayed for several weeks, that Georgiades and Sir Dingle had had the legal arguments pretty much their own way. At this juncture, the government began again to apply pressure in other areas. There were, first of all, the *in camera* representations before a separate tribunal within prison walls, and there were also the private and public campaigns of hints and allusions. On January 8, the very day before the criminal trial was to begin, an official government press release attempted to turn even the hue and cry abroad about the detentions to the government's account. Obote had received a cable from Syracuse University in New York, signed by "some members of the East African Studies Program" (*Transition* no. 38, p. 44), suggesting, in a mild enough way, that the trial might well have an adverse effect on Uganda's image abroad and might, therefore, eventually cost Uganda money in the form of institutional academic aid. The cable, which Georgiades read aloud a few days later at the trial itself, merely said, "Concerned lest unfavorable outcome threaten our own effort to channel academic assistance into Uganda" (ibid., p. 45). It was a bald attempt to apply financial pressure, but hardly qualified as what the government's press release called it (without quoting the cable itself)—an "outrageous attempt" by foreign influences at "mortgaging the interests of eight million people for that of a couple of individuals."[93]

On January 9, the first day of the trial, there was yet more palpable evidence of the government's determination, one way or another, to communicate its intolerance of dissent. Davis Sebukima, who must have been known to the government for some time as the author of the "Steve Lino" letter, was arrested at Makerere and taken to Luzira Prison. A letter implicating Sebukima, *Transition*'s editorial staff surmised, must have been discovered in the final search of the magazine's files in mid-November. The timing of the arrest seemed to *Transition*'s editors a particularly sinister announcement to the

Makerere student body that they were "to restrain any undue interest in the sedition case" (*Transition* no. 38, p. 45).

With the adjournment of the criminal proceedings, the government's campaign to discredit *Transition* broadened at last—reluctantly, one supposes—to include the associate editor, and reluctant candidate for the job of editor-in-chief, Ali Mazrui. Again at the Commonwealth Conference in London, Foreign Minister Sam Odaka, who continued to be questioned about Neogy and Mayanja, hinted at enigmatic American subterfuge. The *Uganda Argus* quoted him as saying that Uganda "was crying out for help and cooperation," but received instead only foreign interference.[94] For instance, he said, with eight million Ugandans to choose from, the American Parvin Foundation had awarded fellowships to Neogy and Mazrui. In fact, however, Neogy and Mazrui had not *received* fellowships, but had only been asked to nominate others. The Parvin Foundation's query may, of course, have been intended to exert subtle pressure on the government by reminding it that *Transition* had attained international stature, but even so, its request for nominations could not really be called subterfuge or direct interference.

Tremendous pressure, direct and indirect, was being put on Obote and Odaka to release Neogy, Mayanja, and now Sebukima. As is often the case in such campaigns for political amnesty, much of the pressure, though superficially official or institutional, had actually been generated through personal contacts and friendships and had taken whatever institutional channel had been at hand. Bombarded inexplicably from odd and unexpected directions, Obote and Odaka may have begun to believe their own allegations that they were victims of something underhanded, some sort of conspiracy—or at least of a furtive private campaign whose real springs and cogs were being concealed.

In later reflections on these events, Neogy himself acknowledged the subtlety of the government's relations with its intellectual critics. Africa's first leaders, he pointed out, had themselves come into power as young, half-formed intellectuals. At the turn of independence, "sought after and paid court to, their every word noted down by outside visitors," these young lions had quickly acquired a sense of inviolability and an inability even to understand, much less tolerate, criticism. They retained, however, Neogy thought, an "involuntary respect," a "reverence for learning," a reliance on the discretion of the intellectuals whose advice they were learning to disregard. When they attained full power, their office corridors were open to their former colleagues for a while. Their attention could be had for a quiet word in the ear. That that relationship had ended, Neogy thought, was a minor tragedy. "The relationship that had ended," he offered, "could have been said to have been that of 'intellectual as collaborator.' From now on they would be out in the cold—or they would be straight government hacks; the period of ambiguous roles would no longer sustain either side." [95]

Freedom and Its Consequences:
Transition and Its Editor Cut Adrift

That Obote's government did not win its campaign of justification and discreditation was attested to by the public response on February 1, when the magistrate's judgment of acquittal was read to the reconvened court. Barbara Neogy had been silent throughout the proceedings against her husband, the *New York Times* reported, but now she, too, "was smiling and crying," repeating "I feel so good, I feel so good!"[96] Though the judgment by Magistrate M. Saied vindicated Neogy and Mayanja on all counts, they were both immediately rearrested, the police taking their cue from Saied himself, who had rejected out of hand the arguments of Sir Dingle Foot and Byron Georgiades that the impropriety and injustice of their clients' detention under the emergency regulations invalidated the criminal sedition proceedings. "The legality or otherwise of the detention(s) [is] in no way material . . . to the present charges of sedition," Saied declared.[97]

Ironically, Saied's judgment on the substance of the sedition charges turned, at least in part, on a presupposition that seems invalid in light of the public's response to the acquittals. *Transition*, Saied surmised, would be an unlikely vehicle for someone intending subversion, since it "had a limited appeal and would be read by relatively few people in the country."[98] That *Transition*'s influence was, on the contrary, enormous both in Uganda and abroad, in spite of its modest circulation, was demonstrated both by the intense public interest in the case and by the lengths to which the government was willing to go in order to muzzle, muffle, or discredit it.

As to the precise culpability of Mayanja's two statements (see above, pp. 186–87), Saied was more equivocal. The rule of law, he maintained, placed rather strict limits on what might be labeled a "seditious" statement, purposely excluding criticism of existing laws and institutions that might, looked at in the most broad-minded and constructive light, be construed to have as its purpose convincing the public to seek legitimately to change those laws or institutions by democratic means. This was manifestly what Mayanja had done, Saied said, even if one viewed his allegedly "tribalistic" suggestion in the worst light. Like Georgiades, Saied flatly declared that he shared Mayanja's incredulity as to the lack of Ugandans qualified for appointment to the High Court. Thus, the larger context of Mayanja's admittedly "intemperate, reckless, and defamatory language" was its purpose of suggesting an obviously desirable change in the national makeup of the judiciary, to take place through legitimate means (p. 49).

The same was true of Mayanja's criticisms of the use of the emergency regulations. The only construction one could put on that passage in Mayanja's letter, Saied felt, was that it showed "his disapproval in his capacity as a citizen . . . [of] certain laws with an obvious view at obtaining their alteration or amendment by lawful means" (ibid.). This did not constitute sedition, even if it were unintentionally to tend "to create a discontent which may be seditious" (*Transition* no. 38, p. 48). The context of Mayanja's criticisms made it clear that the means sought for redress were to be merely the people's exercise of their legal right to seek political or constitutional change.

It was almost what the *New York Times* correspondent called it, a "sweeping judgment," that "struck a blow for the continued independence of the judiciary in Uganda as well as for freedom of the press."[99] Saied delivered a salvo in passing against Picho Ali's original article proposing a "committed judiciary," a suggestion he called "repugnant in the extreme" (*Transition* no. 38, p. 47). The effect of his decision had been to turn aside, in principle, this first assault on the dignity of the Ugandan press. However, Saied's interpretation left ample room for the government in the future to behave toward the press in general, and *Transition* in particular, just as it saw fit, since detentions that failed to satisfy the strictures of the sedition laws could always thereafter be rescued by recourse to the extraordinary powers of the emergency regulations.

Although Neogy's partisans in Uganda and abroad celebrated,

and although *The Times* of London and the *New York Times* awarded the free press a moral victory, the fact was that Neogy and Mayanja were promptly and directly returned to separate wings of Luzira Prison, where Davis Sebukima also continued to be held without even the publicity of a trial. Having won the legal proceedings, Sir Dingle Foot and Byron Georgiades were nevertheless left with no recourse except to wait. Uganda insisted, wrote *The Times* of London (as Saied himself had explicitly agreed), "that the trial had no bearing on [Neogy's and Mayanja's] detention. . . . However, the Ugandan authorities have never given any other reason for the detention." [100] The Ugandan authorities, unfortunately, were not required by the provisions of the emergency regulations to give reasons publicly for a detention under their invocation. That they had done so before, in fact, had only been a sop to public opinion. It remained to be seen how much Obote would continue to care about public opinion. The government could legally hold the detainees for six months without public explanation or recourse to the courts. It might then even conceivably rearrest them for another six-month period.

Barbara Neogy and Ali Mazrui had no choice but to return to the publicity and letter-writing campaign. However, as anyone who has been involved in such an effort knows, the most difficult governmental response to deal with is silent intransigence, which is deadly both to press coverage and public interest. As a story of political detention fades to the back pages of the newspapers, it becomes more difficult to generate pressure of other kinds. Obote and Odaka had clearly, in bringing Neogy and Mayanja to trial, chosen a poor strategy. Though it waned and its effect was delayed, pressure from abroad continued, and ultimately it bore fruit.

More than three weeks after the sentencing, on February 26, Obote advised Barbara Neogy of his intention to bring her husband to trial once again, this time on the grounds of his pseudonymous publication of the "Steve Lino" letter in *Transition* no. 34. This time, moreover, there was to be an added wrinkle: Neogy would be tried as an alien, under a sedition law that applied only to aliens and brought with it a sentence of ten years' imprisonment, Obote informed her. Perhaps, he mused, Neogy would be prosecuted in prison, perhaps upon his release—perhaps soon after his release. "And we will win," Obote added, "this time."[101]

Though Obote's motive for the telephone call may have seemed mysterious at the time, in hindsight one can see that it was actually tantamount to capitulation. Faced with the pressure, however diminished, of international opinion, and confronted with a six-month limit to summary detentions under the emergency regulations, he needed to salvage the situation. He had decided to release one of the detainees, Neogy, in hopes that international opinion would forget about the other, Mayanja. In hinting to Barbara Neogy that her husband might thereafter be rearrested and retried at any time and that the consequences of conviction might be as much as ten years in prison, Obote probably meant to enforce Neogy's silence and thus finally to put a lid on an embarrassing and potentially dangerous situation.

Barbara Neogy was to take the hint that her husband must either muffle *Transition* or leave Uganda. Though Georgiades's and Sir Dingle's "victory" in court could not be won back, Neogy's release might be less damaging to the government if it were followed by *Transition*'s silence or its young editor's quick withdrawal from the scene. Having made his threat, however, Obote could then risk relenting. When he got in touch with Barbara Neogy again, a month later (on March 26), to say that Rajat Neogy would be released the following day, he coolly suggested that *Transition* again begin publication, "for a while" (*Transition* no. 38, p. 46). His point, that a weapon of retribution remained in his hand, had been made. On March 27, without ceremony or more formal notification, Neogy and Davis Sebukima, along with twenty-four other detainees, suddenly found themselves on the street, free. Abu Mayanja, who was retained in custody, would not be released until August 1970, when Idi Amin freed him along with other political detainees following the coup that overthrew Obote.

No longer a Ugandan citizen; under explicit threat of arrest, with or without trial; and warned that an outspoken press would not be tolerated any longer in Uganda, Neogy decided almost immediately to emigrate. He left within a few weeks, flying directly to India and giving as his purpose a visit to his parents in Bangalore. Air India helpfully left his name off the passenger manifest. Barbara Neogy and the couple's two children stayed on for a while in Kampala, while she settled the family's affairs, and then met Neogy in Paris, from where they traveled via London to New York.[102] In London he complained bitterly to reporters about the indignities of his second-class British passport; "I had to show that I already had a ticket on to America even to get into Britain," he said. His arrest, Neogy added, had not been for specific sins, but because of "a built-up resentment; one made enemies in government circles simply by existing." "Honest voices," he declared, "are a threat to government."

This was not the old Neogy, his friends soon realized. Prison had injured and demoralized him. He complained of the contradictions and paradoxes of his case and of the "politicization" of the Ugandan penal system—of warders and guards who were becoming political flunkies. He seemed adrift, unwilling to think about when or where he and his magazine might now ultimately come to shore. Nevertheless, he had already decided a few things about himself and about the magazine. He intended, he said, to take six months off from his editorship. He had no intention of returning to Uganda. Nor did he intend to establish *Transition* as an expatriate journal like the Paris-based *Présence Africaine*. He had, he said, been "having intensive and serious discussions about the magazine" (with Shepard Stone of the International Association for Cultural Freedom in Paris), and he hoped "to restart *Transition* on an African base." During his six-month retreat, he added, he meant to work on a book of essays about freedom of the press in Africa.[103]

A few weeks later Neogy arrived in New York and began a brief lecture tour of college campuses, meeting first with members of the African American Institute at the Time-Life building in Manhattan.[104] For the next four months Neogy remained at the home of his wife's parents in Yonkers, New York—writing, negotiating a new site and a new publishing arrangement for *Transition*, and, primarily, resting and regaining his equilibrium. Shepard Stone continued to encourage him to reestablish *Transition*, but though Neogy hoped to do so, the task seemed mammoth in light of the vicissitudes that were coming to characterize the political life of much of independent Africa, and the equally complicated problems of finance, communication, and organization—all of which had to be settled at long range.

In October Neogy finally composed a letter to *Transition*'s subscribers explaining the circumstances of his, Abu Mayanja's, and Davis Sebukima's arrests; describing the trial and its aftermath; and promising, somewhat uncertainly, that *Transition* was nevertheless not quite dead. Addressed from the office of the International Association for Cultural Freedom in Paris and mailed through its resources, Neogy's letter apologized for the delay in communication, explaining that "it has taken me until now to find my bearings," but promised no immediate permanent solution to the problem of the magazine's suspension. "Obviously," Neogy wrote, "I cannot, for the present, return to Uganda—the country of my birth and ex-citizenship. . . . It is difficult to operate as an alien in your own country." He added, "To have continued publishing *Transition* in Uganda under these circumstances would have been a betrayal of the principles that it stands for."

Nevertheless, Neogy could not yet, after a year's suspension of publication, give readers a clear signal of his intentions. Though he said, "*Transition*'s home is . . . all Africa," he added, "And it was at home in the world outside." Though he said, "If the magazine can continue to perform usefully from elsewhere, we will resume publication," he also said, "I do not know as yet whether magazines can survive transplant." In the meantime, though he meant to sort out these several contradictions, Neogy also made it clear that most of his time would continue to be devoted to his own recuperation: "For the immediate present, I am taking my first time-off from *Transition* in seven years. For the next six months I have no desire other than to live a normal life with my family and write a long overdue book."

Neogy never did finish that book, although part of it, or at any rate a reflection on the same materials, appeared in the Autumn 1970 issue of *Survey*. Its chief note was of betrayal, failed idealism, and anger. He saw his tormentors in government office and his readers and intellectual colleagues as equally sullied by events, equally contemptible. Of the former, he wrote: "These first 'intellectuals' of East Africa still hold power now. Intellectually most of them are adolescents—and some delinquent at that." He assessed the latter even more harshly: "With a handful of exceptions, the intellectual in Africa has failed both as an intellectual and as a man," he wrote.[105]

In spite of doubts about himself, and about the future of intellectual discourse in Africa, however, Neogy announced that there would probably be an interim issue of *Transition*, brought out by "close friends and associates" during the editor-in-chief's "self-imposed absence." Thus, he said, *Transition* would "keep in touch" with readers while its editor figured out how to revive the periodical. "Close friends and associates" seems to have meant primarily Mazrui and Theroux—one still in Uganda, the other transplanted to the University of Singapore—and they seem to have contemplated an issue of *Transition* courting yet more controversy and possible confrontation. What was contemplated, in fact, was a special issue evoking the period of the Buganda emergency, beginning with the attack on the *kabaka*'s palace at Mmengo in May 1966. *Transition* had not directly confronted the events in Buganda when they had occurred (although Neogy had printed a small, black-bordered memorial notice in no. 25 [1966]), but Buganda remained an incredibly sensitive topic in Obote's Uganda even in 1969. Ali Mazrui's staunchness was remarkable. Were the special Buganda issue of *Transition* to precipitate another free-press crisis in Uganda, as it seemed it well might, Mazrui would be *Transition*'s visible representative on the spot in Kampala, and the person therefore most likely to suffer any government retribution.

Moreover, Mazrui was himself planning to contribute to the special interim issue, submitting a partially autobiographical, partially biographical memoir of himself and Sir Edward Mutesa, the former *kabaka* of Buganda, late in 1969. Curiously enough, Mazrui had gotten the idea from a rough note left surreptitiously and anonymously on his office desk at Makerere, suggested perhaps by his earlier semi-autobiographical reflection on the career of Tom Mboya (delivered as a lecture following Mboya's assassination and later published in the

East African Journal of September 1969 as "Tom Mboya, Under-development, and I"). Though the few friends to whom he broached the idea of a lecture about the *kabaka* were unanimous in discouraging it, Mazrui determined to write and deliver such a speech.

In fact, it was only because Neogy, favored by Mazrui with a fragment of his work in progress, wrote from New York to claim it for the interim issue of *Transition* that Mazrui refrained from delivering his thunderbolt in the main hall at Makerere University as he had originally planned to do. "Given the apparent imminence of the appearance of *Transition* at that time," he later wrote in a preface, upon the belated publication of the article in *Transition* no. 38, "I decided not to steal the thunder of the magazine by anticipating its appearance with a lecture" (p. 56). To Mazrui, from his vantage point in Kampala, it seemed at least as appropriate that the article on the *kabaka* should appear in this special "ad hoc" *Transition*, arriving in Kampala, via the overseas mails, as if from out of the grave.

This gesture of defiance and continued commitment, moreover, would convey the serious reminder that Neogy's arrest and *Transition*'s consequent disappearance from the scene were products of larger, equally unpleasant political realities. The emergency regulations under which Neogy and Mayanja had been arrested and detained, after all, had owed their initial invocation to the Buganda crisis of the previous year. The emergency declaration had been scheduled by law for extension or termination only a few days after Neogy's and Mayanja's arrest, and the chief purport of Milton Obote's speech before Parliament in which, in passing, he had also denounced "the professor of political science" had been to request an extension of the Buganda emergency decree. Finally, it seemed to Mazrui no innocent coincidence that Abu Mayanja's original hint at tribalism, via his letter in *Transition* no. 37, had left unsaid precisely the implication that Obote had delayed Africanizing the High Court bench because the appointees nominated to him had been Bagandas (*Transition* no. 38, pp. 55–56).

Along with Mazrui's essay on the *kabaka*, there was also to have been another, by Paul Theroux, recalling the repressive atmosphere of the curfew imposed in the wake of the *kabaka*'s deposition. All in all, this was intended to be *Transition*'s most controversial issue yet— a provocation, evenly yet deliberately offered, which would have seemed almost an open insult in that superheated atmosphere. Ali Mazrui later wrote,

> If the magazine had come out in time, this very non-provocative essay on Mutesa and myself—entering Uganda within the covers of a distrusted magazine—might have precipitated yet another crisis between myself and the authorities in Uganda's regime.
>
> *(Transition* no. 38, p. 56)

That this did not happen was due to two separate accidents. First, Neogy, seemingly close to a deal through Shepard Stone that would enable him to relocate *Transition* in Ghana, decided to put off publication of *Transition* no. 38 until it could come out from its new home. The magazine was nearly ready for press, but its editorial transplantation seemed even closer at hand. Neogy himself was, in fact, in Accra in January 1970 to make definite arrangements. A notice in the "Times Diary" reported the visit with the assertion that Neogy meant to revive *Transition* there "before midsummer" and an explanation for previous delays: "The main stumbling block is cost— prices in Ghana are about three times as high as in Uganda." [106] Neogy was not, however, able finally to confirm the arrangements and announce them to the Ghanaian press until November of that year.

Even after the press announcement, yet more delays followed, and the first Ghanaian issue of *Transition* did not actually appear until mid-1971. By then, Milton Obote had himself been deposed, while absent from the country, in a military coup led by General Idi Amin, who had also led the army in its attack on the *kabaka*'s palace in 1967. Amin's latest coup had been consummated nearly two years to the day after Neogy's acquittal.

Neogy, *Transition,* and Amin's "New Dawn for Uganda"

When *Transition* no. 38, the first from Accra, finally appeared, it had about it a curious combination of consequence and irrelevance. The pieces on Uganda, including an anonymous "Letter from Uganda" composed in the heat of Amin's February coup, had been made almost innocuous by succeeding events. What might a few months or a year earlier have been telling, even dangerous, copy now had an air of gloating. Mazrui's "The King, the King's English, and I," for instance, seemed now rather unconsciously to emphasize the first-person pronoun of the title and to leave the dead *kabaka* in its wake.

Now that his subject had been defused, Mazrui's delight in coincidences and his offhanded expository development lost their ironic circumflexion and seemed to leave the *kabaka's* story unanalyzed. Most of the essay recalled the schooling, at the Muslim Technical Institute in Mombasa and elsewhere, of the young Ali Mazrui—his early deficiencies as a scholar, his love of the English language and of public speaking, his discovery of sympathetic patrons within the British colonial administration.

Mazrui's mirrored portrait of the *kabaka* as an equally earnest, equally anglophile young man—polite, condescending, urbane, yet with the iron commitment to traditional Bugandan autonomy that had been a complicating factor in Uganda's first stirrings of nationalism—which would have seemed slyly provocative in the atmosphere of Obote's Uganda, now almost seemed merely nostalgic. An intended comparison between the *kabaka's* first exile, which grew out of his opposition to a colonial governor, and his second, which grew out of an equally stubborn defiance of Obote's efforts at national unification, retained its circumspect irony, but lost its more pointed relevance in the aftermath of Amin's putsch.

One sure stroke retained its edge in what circumstances had otherwise transformed into a sub-standard effort on Mazrui's part—

the coolly ironic ending of his leisurely memoir, invoking, with seeming inadvertence, the new atmosphere of racial antagonism and bigotry that had characterized Obote's Uganda after the deposition of the *kabaka*. Mazrui, his wife and child, and a colleague from University College, Nairobi, had made an unauthorized visit to the *kabaka*'s deserted palace some time after the "insurrection" had been quelled. Arrested suddenly and unexpectedly for trespassing, Mazrui and his friend were forced to prove that they could speak Swahili (as most Bagandas could not), it being made clear to them that they would be treated very roughly if they failed this impromptu language examination. Mazrui's colleague had indeed not understood the first shouted command to halt, since it was in Swahili, which he did not speak, and they had both almost been shot. What made the incident doubly ironic was that Swahili had, in fact, been Mazrui's first language.

There was also, for Mazrui, a third, crowning irony to the elliptical connection of this unlikely event with the deposed *kabaka*. Here they were, he and the *kabaka*, made in a sense to take the same degrading language test—schooled in, lovers of, the English language, yet helpless inheritors of a world in which African languages had been stripped of their dignity and made to serve as tests of tribal identity for the sake of mindless repression. "I looked at the Palace and its scars once again," Mazrui wrote. "The voice of the soldier commanded 'Njoo Hapa!' We drew near in obedience" (*Transition* no. 38, p. 66).

Theroux's piece on the curfew following the *kabaka*'s overthrow also partially misfired. Like Mazrui's it seemed now to manifest a fundamental self-absorption—in Theroux's case joyless and abstracted—that made one somehow distrust its subtle irony. Unlike Mazrui's, Theroux's narrative was from the outside, and not the least polite. Once again, the subject was the European expatriate—his greed, his hostility, his debasement in an environment suddenly gone completely sour—an environment that had in any case always been alien. This was, in effect, a reversion to the earlier "Tarzan" essay, except that in this instance Theroux's subject was himself and the setting was one of absolute stress, overlying the boredom and snobbery he had described in "Tarzan Is an Expatriate."

As if in answer to the critics of "Tarzan," who had complained of his telling tales out of school on everyone but himself, Theroux now confessed his own drunken afternoons, his own loneliness, his own meaningless encounters with whores, his own silent acquiescence in bigotry:

> Jean was waiting in the hallway when I walked out an hour later. He was helpless with suppressed giggling. We stood there in the darkness, our clothes slung over our shoulders, not speaking but communicating somehow in wordless giddiness which might have been shame. At the time I thought it was a monstrous game, like a child's, but hardly even erotic, played to kill time and defeat fear and loneliness, something the curfew demanded. ("Curfew," *Transition* no. 38, p. 53)

There was something unattractive and disquieting about this—self-pitying, as the more temperate contra-"Tarzan" letter writers had said four years before. Nevertheless, the portrait was at least honest, if no longer politically controversial, and in a different way it illustrated Mazrui's point about bigotry and prejudice in this new black-on-black context.

Like Mazrui, Theroux saw the irony of Kampala's switch from its former lingua franca, Luganda, to "bad Swahili," now suddenly the politically fashionable substitute. He noticed, too, the coldly unreflective nature of this new—or, rather, old—racism:

> Once we turned on the radio and got Radio Rwanda. Jean insisted on switching it off because the commentator was speaking the language of the Bahutu who were formerly the slaves of Jean's tribe [the Batutsi]. That tribal war, that massacre, that curfew had been in 1963.
> Jean told me what ugly swine the Bahutu were and how he could not stand any Bantu tribe. He squashed his nose with his palm and imitated what I presumed to be a Hutu speaking. He said, "But these girls—very *Hamite*." He traced the profile of a sharp nose on his face. (ibid.)

Another ironic stab that might have retained some sting had *Transition* no. 38 appeared anywhere near on time touched the issue of press freedom. There had been no need, Theroux reported, for the

Kampala newsboys to hawk their wares, particularly if their wares were Kenyan or Tanzanian papers ("since they were printing all the facts and even some of the rumors"). On the other hand, those local papers that had "showed some courage during the first weeks were banned or their reporters beaten up." After that, Theroux commented wryly, an insidious change took place. "They now began all their curfew stories, 'Things are now almost back to normal'" (*Transition* no. 38, p. 52).

In September 1971, however, when the new Accra *Transition* finally appeared, Theroux's hints of censorship four years before under another regime were hardly news. And their appearance in the absence of anything timely or tough-spirited on the subject of the new Amin government was odd and disquieting, as one reader, Wyn Williams of the School of Education, University of Nottingham, pointed out in the Letters column of *Transition* no. 39 (1971). "Where is the attempt to analyse the contribution and the weaknesses of Obote's regime?" Williams asked. "There were remarkable achievements as well as failures which surely ought to be examined by some of the excellent contributors to *Transition*." Mazrui, Williams suggested, might work up such an article. He added,

> Where is the attempt to look at the current situation in Uganda? We have the usual adulatory, and completely understandable, personal letter from Uganda dated 5th February, 1971. But since then much has happened within the Army which suggests to outsiders a repetition of events which overtook the Nigerian Army in 1966 between January and September. . . . Surely it is unwise for *Transition* to offer us a "current" comment for February, 1971, and nothing thereafter.   (p. 7)

What had happened was that Neogy, still suffering, as he had himself admitted, from the aftereffects of prison, continued to feel and to manifest a hostility to the regime that had put him there. Still prey to the feelings of victimization produced by his prison experience, Neogy felt unrestrained elation at the news of Amin's first bloodless coup. In some symbolic fashion, he saw Amin's victory as a vindication and a negation of his own lingering emotional malaise, and Amin as Uganda's savior. In company with many African political leaders, Neogy for a long time resisted giving credence to the growing number of reports of ruthlessness and abuse of power. Such reports merely misunderstood a simple soldier's decisiveness and strength.

Neogy had himself returned to Uganda during the first two weeks of August 1971 and had been given a hero's welcome, as one whose freedom and safety had been at forfeit through his opposition to the deposed tyrant.[107] In Kampala, Neogy was enthusiastic in his support of Uganda's new strongman, who was already secretly suppressing political rivals, particularly within the army, with a cool ruthlessness that Obote's arrest of Neogy, Mayanja, and Davis Sebukima had in no way matched. Mayanja, who had not finally been released from detention until months after Obote was deposed, was now minister of education in Amin's government, acting at the time of Neogy's visit as nominal president in Amin's temporary system of rotating authority. Their reunion was emotional.

Another Baganda who extended a warm welcome was Robert Serumaga, a young playwright whom Neogy convinced to join *Transition* as associate editor. Serumaga's traditional ceremony of welcome was shown in a photograph in *Transition* no. 39 (p. 35). Neogy called this return visit to Uganda "one of the most exhilarating experiences in my life, both intellectually and symbolically." He had found "an openness in relations between civil servants and ministers that he had not seen elsewhere in Africa," he told *The Times* of London. "He was aware of disturbances within the Army, admitted by the Government, but believed that if Amin were to go, 'all chaos' would follow in Uganda."[108]

For a time, Neogy was incapable emotionally of the hard look at the new Ugandan regime that Wyn Williams was soon to feel the lack of—he was too much swept away with the throngs hailing Amin in the wake of his very popular coup. For that matter, it is to Neogy's credit, under the circumstances, that he didn't go to the other extreme. If there were no skeptical scrutinies, neither were there the blind encomiums that he may have felt more inclined to write. And disillusionment followed soon enough: within a year Neogy was devoting much space in the magazine to criticism of Amin's arbitrary and illiberal measures, particularly his expulsion of the Ugandan Asian population.

Another odd by-product of Neogy's emotional disequilibrium was his conversion, upon his return to Kampala, to Islam. His personal mullah was Ali Mazrui, and Neogy's primary motivation for conversion may have been the "humble and boundless" gratitude he had himself acknowledged in another context (see above, p. 196). Mazrui, Neogy's staunch friend while he was in prison, was after all a Muslim. Neogy may also, Mazrui himself speculates, have been influenced by two more abstruse motives. "Amin's assumption of power in Uganda," Mazrui writes, "did for a while look like a new dawn for Uganda—and Amin was a Muslim." Moreover, though born a Hindu, Neogy was horrified by contemporary events in what had been his home region of India and was sympathetic to the plight of Muslim Indians. As Mazrui puts it in his inimitable style, "The martyrdom of Bangladesh coincided with the martyrdom of Rajat Neogy. (Rajat was a Bengali.)"[109]

His conversion was also, in a way, a rejection of what he had called in his first *Transition* essay his special "condition"—his status as "outsider" (*Transition* no. 1, p. 49). Britain, in a sense, had rejected him, had in his distress been willing to grant him no more than second-class status. America, in a sense, had betrayed him, had permanently and clandestinely tainted the magazine whose integrity he had labored to establish and had had to go to jail to validate. And yet England and America had also been his salvation, had applied much of the pressure responsible for his release from prison. Neogy had long outgrown his youthful bohemianism. Though he found himself suddenly a famous crusading editor, with influential friends to whom he owed, and wished to feel, gratitude, nevertheless he now found his allegiances—political, national, personal—to be suddenly contradictory and unsatisfying. And now suddenly he needed very much to understand and define those allegiances. However one reads Neogy's conflicts during that difficult period, their personal urgency to him is evidenced in his conversion both to Islam and to what

Mazrui has described as the apparent "new dawn for Uganda."
Mazrui writes,

> A fusion of Bangladesh, Idi Amin, and Ali Mazrui brought Rajat
> Neogy to the Kibuli congregation on Friday, seeking a public conver-
> sion to the message of Allah. Briefly Rajat found peace—and subse-
> quently moved on to new torments in the world abroad.[110]

"Born Again": Neogy's Accra *Transition*

Neogy was also treated, at least at first, as a conquering hero in Accra. Although he had already come to be known to a circumscribed intellectual audience both within Africa and abroad, his arrest had made him ordinary "news," and therefore suddenly a public figure. In Accra, he was noticed everywhere, and a public ceremony was scheduled so that the first issue of the new *Transition* could be formally presented to Ghanaian Prime Minister Dr. K. A. Busia (see *Transition* no. 39, p. 35). Among other formal welcomes was one at the University of Legon, Dr. Busia's former institution, under whose official auspices *Transition* was to function in Ghana.

Along with fame came also a different style of life. The lengthy negotiations involving Neogy and Shepard Stone (and their Ghanaian counterparts) had won the magazine more comfortable editorial arrangements, and an annual subsidy of over $40,000 from the International Association for Cultural Freedom.[111] *Transition* moved into spanking new quarters—an entire floor of the (by African standards) ultramodern Dakmak House on Kojo Thompson Road—and Neogy suddenly had enough funding almost to go first class. The new arrangements and accommodations were a major change for a journal that had had as its first "office," according to Soyinka's recollection (*Transition* no. 45, p. 4), only its proprietor's own makeshift desktop. Even during its first period of international recognition, *Transition*'s Kampala offices had always been cramped and modest. Now, there were the new office, the administrative affiliation with Legon, and the renewed and expanded support from the International Association for Cultural Freedom (IACF). Moreover, aided by the reams of free publicity that Neogy's arrest and trial had generated, circulation continued also to show encouraging growth. Eventually it reached seventeen thousand in Accra.[112]

Both Prime Minister Busia and Dr. Alex Kwapong, then vice-chancellor of the University of Ghana, had worked with Shepard

221

Stone and been funded by the IACF. This time, Neogy had prior government assurances of press freedom. He also had every prospect of working within a university and press community that were delighted with *Transition*'s migration to Ghana. J. Oppong-Agyare of the Kumasi *Pioneer* was one of the first to trumpet Neogy's coming. He wrote in his periodical:

> It is with extreme joy that I have learnt of the arrival of Mr. Rajat Neogy in the country to resume the publication of *Transition*, a magazine which is claimed to be "perhaps the best African-produced there has ever been" and "one of the six best in the world." . . . It should be a matter of pride to all Ghanaians that the Busia administration, in consonance with its declared policy of practising true democracy in Africa, has found it right to allow Rajat Neogy to come to Ghana to resume the publication of *Transition*.   (rpt. in *Transition* no. 39, pp. 35–36)

To John Thompson, who had long since left *Transition*'s former funding source, the Farfield Foundation, and was now teaching and writing in New York, Neogy seemed to be in a paradoxical position: he had to publish the same sort of tough, thoughtful material about Ghana that he had once published about Uganda or else he would lose his credibility; and yet if in Ghana he started right in where he had left off in Uganda, he once again risked estrangement from his host government, if not outright suppression.[113] Though his point of view was now absolutely from the sidelines, Thompson's assessment was seconded in Ghana. Oppong-Agyare, for instance, writing in the Kumasi *Pioneer*, was equally sensitive to this danger:

> In allowing Neogy to publish *Transition* here, surely, the Government knows what it has taken on. The whole world will be watching with keen interest the fortunes of the paper and its courageous Editor.
>
> I am sure that a time may come when the Government will have reason to disagree completely with what *Transition* publishes. But when that time does come, may our enlightened Government never resort to undemocratic action.
>
> Journalism has its own risks: the laws of libel, of defamation and of sedition. As long as the Courts remain open, let these laws deal with offending journalists, including Rajat Neogy, if he comes within that category.   (rpt. in *Transition* no. 39, p. 36)

This was not exactly an expression of absolute confidence either in Neogy or in the government's tolerance of dissent!

That Neogy reprinted Oppong-Agyare's article might imply that he was more conscious of the excitement over his arrival in Accra than of the tenuousness of his relationship with the government. But Neogy, though hopeful, was also realistic. In the editorial that re-inaugurated *Transition* he wrote simply:

> It is a sad commentary on the state of affairs today that when faced with such a situation [the need to find a "new home" for *Transition*], the list of countries in Africa with democratic governments and constitutions that can play host to an international journal of opinion . . . becomes depressingly small. (*Transition* no. 38, p. 5)

Even Neogy's expectations of Ghana itself were somewhat qualified. Why, Oppong-Agyare had asked him, had he chosen Ghana? "Because Ghana, of all African countries, offers the nearest to a government that is committed to freedom of expression, and which seems to regard press freedom as [being as] important as free elections," he replied.[114]

If this new relationship remained untested, Neogy nevertheless pointedly reiterated *Transition*'s ideal of serving as a vehicle, open to all, for the free exchange of ideas. Even the cover of the first Accra issue (*Transition* no. 38) seemed a wry reminder—a photomontage of a "mammy-wagon," Ghana's colorful catch-as-catch-can local private means of motorized mass transportation. The cover was both a graphic gesture of allegiance to *Transition*'s new Ghanaian setting and an announcement that, though it meant to fit into its new milieu, *Transition* still intended to be a vehicle on which the collective intellect of Africa might "travel for certain distances." Neogy still intended to make his "contribution in iron and steel." On the back of the pictured lorry, a crudely painted motto expressed his exuberance: "Born Again"!

If Neogy's relationship with, and feelings about, Amin's new Kampala regime remained nebulous, he soon enough tested his relationship with the new Accra regime, blithely resurrecting in the first new *Transition* a controversy that the magazine's suspension in 1968 had left half-explored. This Ghanaian controversy bore remarkable similarities to the one in Kampala that had ultimately led to Neogy's arrest, and in taking it up again in 1971 where he had left it in 1968, Neogy might have been taking a similar risk. Ghana, like Uganda, had recently been in the heat of drawing up a new constitution, which *Transition* no. 37, winding down the debate on the Ugandan constitution, had begun to investigate. Like Uganda's, Ghana's proposed constitution had been promulgated after an enforced (and therefore, of course, unconstitutional) political change. Like Uganda's, Ghana's proposed constitution had faced strong objections that it sought to concentrate power in the wrong places—including potentially repressive emergency powers. In this case, however, judicial power was thought to overbalance executive power.

Like Mayanja, moreover, the two men whom Neogy commissioned to analyze Ghana's new constitution, E. Yaw Twumasi and B. G. Folson, were committed to an independent outlook. Twumasi, a founding editor of the Legon *Observer*, and Folson, a National Liberation Council insider and a participant in the constitution-making process, both thought that the process had gone wrong at some point and to some degree. Ironically enough, Twumasi's article in *Transition* no. 37 ("Ghana's Draft Constitution Proposals") had criticized the new constitution as placing *too many* restraints upon the executive branch of government. Moreover, the legislative branch would be both hamstrung and insulated from the pressure of public opinion. This eccentric modification of the balance of political power, Twumasi thought, had been caused by overreaction:

> It was only the judiciary, the assumption seems inexorably to be, that stood up to Nkrumah; it is wise therefore, if a dictatorship is to be avoided in the future, to make the criteria of judicial decision-making relevant and crucial in assessing political and legislative acts, short of saying that the judiciary is a super-legislature in the constitutional system. (p. 48)

Folson's response two years later had the benefit of hindsight. Like Akena Adoko in his response to Mayanja in *Transition* no. 33,

Folson defended not the product but the process. By then, influenced partly by Twumasi's and others' criticisms, Folson said, Ghana's constituent assembly had struck down some salient features of the original proposal, including features that had been meant to discourage tribalism, executive usurpation of power, and multi-party instability (among them, a partially nonpartisan cabinet, greater independence for tribal chiefs, judicial review of legislation, and a bicephalous executive branch). Twumasi had argued for the direct sovereignty of the people, through Parliament, and had derogated American-style judicial review. Folson now responded in *Transition* no. 38 that the British system depended, more than the American, on traditional parliamentary self-restraint and on the people's internalization of "the values of the system":

> By ignoring this vital point the critics failed to ask themselves whether any legislature on the African continent . . . could be *trusted of its own volition* to keep open those democratic institutions and practices which make possible the co-existence of . . . the sovereignty of the people and the sovereignty of Parliament. (p. 23)

Without checks, including judicial review, Folson argued, Parliament could suspend elections; ban individuals, parties, and labor unions; institute emergency regulations; and suspend individual liberties.

In commissioning Folson to respond to Twumasi, Neogy had returned to the original debate from an opposing viewpoint quite distinct from what had since become the government position. Though Folson had been named executive director of the newly formed Centre for Civic Education (a public civic awareness scheme), he was by no means satisfied with the constitution that had ultimately ensued from his own efforts of three years previously. Neogy's troubles over the Ugandan constitutional debate, it should be remembered, had begun in just such an atmosphere of moderation and evenhandedness.

Perhaps the long lapse in its resumption prevented the debate from once again catching fire. Perhaps (as a correspondent in *Transition* no. 39 was to suggest) Folson's somewhat academic tone rendered his criticisms innocuous. Perhaps (as Neogy himself believed) Ghana's peculiar atmosphere of tolerance made any debate in Ghana less volatile than it might have been elsewhere in Africa. Neogy later commented with specific reference to press freedom: "Ghana was essentially the friendliest country I have been in . . . [in Africa]." [115]

Periodicals from throughout the world—the Kumasi *Pioneer*, the Accra *Daily Graphic*, the Kenyan daily and Sunday *Nations*, the London *Times*, *Observer*, and *Guardian*, the British magazine *Encounter*, the New York *Post*, and the *Uganda Argus* and *The People* in Kampala—hailed *Transition*'s reappearance with pleasure or relief. *Encounter* commented, "It is to be hoped that in future Rajat Neogy will be left to exercise his considerable editorial gifts in peace" (September 1971, p. 82). The Kenyan *Sunday Nation* called Mazrui's article "a banquet of food for thought," and added that if "The King, the King's English, and I" were "the only article in the magazine, [it] would still make *Transition* worth very much more than its retail price" (1 August 1971).

Nevertheless, in spite of the readiness of scattered fans and readers to receive *Transition* again, and in spite of Ghana's favorable climate, *Transition*, reborn in Accra, struggled a bit to find itself at first. If there was continuity in style, in purpose, in layout and design (one way to assure patient readers that this was indeed the same lost magazine), there was also some misdirection, and an odd, ill-defined harping on what had befallen the magazine and its editor three years before and 2,300 miles away. If there were new contributions by Mazrui, Theroux, and others of the old *Transition* school, there was also, as one reader commented, something missing—a lapse from the magazine's old style of cocky exuberance and tough irreverence. A correspondent, Aaron Segal, editor of *Africa Report*, found the new *Transition*'s "excess of first-person reminiscence at the expense of intelligent analysis" particularly odd (*Transition* no. 39, p. 6). Though an expatriate news reporter, John de St. Jorre, had provided "snatches from his notebooks" about the Nigerian civil war, though Theroux had recalled the curfew, and Mazrui the *kabaka*, there was, Segal thought, a failure of incisiveness, of point:

Ali Mazrui goes into considerable length to discuss his brief encounter with the late Kabaka and other personages but makes scant effort to evaluate the role that these individuals played in the history of East Africa. Granted that Freddie was kind, generous, magnanimous et al. when he met Mazrui but was he foolish, predestined, inept or right in playing the role that he did in the political evolution of Uganda?[116] The lack of such analysis was accentuated by the amount of space devoted to the demise of *Transition* in Uganda at the hands of the Obote government. Instead of a thoughtful evaluation of what Obote meant for Uganda we are given a first-person account by Paul Theroux of the effects of the curfew on his sex-life in Kampala. Who cares?

The only article with real point, Segal thought, in the first Ghanaian issue, was Lewis Nkosi's "On South Africa," and he found Nkosi's message (that resistance or sanctions from outside South Africa were probably futile, since only internal violence would overthrow apartheid) inimical and irresponsible. Though Segal was willing, he implied, to listen to theories about organized, directed violence, Nkosi's version of the coming apocalypse offended by its randomness and illogic. Nkosi had written:

> When the oil tanks go up in flames down Eloff Street; when it is no longer safe for white South Africans to go to their all-white cinemas at night; when the suburbs are no longer safe for walks and the bombs start going off in the Johannesburg stock exchange and C. to C. Bazaar, it will no longer be necessary to convince an organization like the United Nations Security Council that the pursuance of apartheid policies by the South African Government is an immediate threat to peace and the peaceful coexistence of black and white people in Southern Africa. (*Transition* no. 38, p. 34)

For another correspondent, however, the new *Transition*'s awkward tone of emotional recapitulation struck a sympathetic chord. Peter Rigby, professor of sociology at Makerere University, wrote a rambling, appreciative comment on the three Ugandan pieces in *Transition* no. 38. The chief purport of his comment, however, was personal. For him, Rigby wrote, as apparently for Neogy, the events of those few years had left an indelible sense of failure and incapacity. Rigby, too, had been involved in a case of political detention under the emergency acts. Though a friend had been detained, rather than Rigby himself, he felt a similar sense of "anguish" and failure at having neither anticipated events nor entirely coped with them when they came. He wrote of his own futile efforts to help his friend: "I felt like a trapped animal, trying to get out of a cage" (*Transition* no. 39, p. 9).

That Neogy, too, was still turning over his role in Uganda's troubles was attested to by the focus of the second Accra issue, *Transition* no. 39. The cover feature, for instance, was "A Letter From Prison" by Greek political dissident George Mangakis, and there was an essay as well about the press in the new Uganda by Ugandan Attorney General P. J. Nkambo Mugwera ("On Press Freedom," pp. 29–31). Mugwera seemed, however, to place the blame for the "insignificant role" played by the Ugandan press in Uganda's public life on the press itself. Newspapers in Uganda were "dull and uninteresting," he implied, because the journalists were groundlessly gun-shy, even though "His Excellency the President has said on many occasions . . . that 'a government that fears opposition is a weak government'" (p. 30).

Two articles about the military elite ("Officers and Gentlemen of the Nigerian Army," by Robin Luckham, pp. 38–55; and "The Law of Military Plumage," by Bernard James and Roger Beaumont, pp. 24–27) bore a more subtle relationship to Neogy's lingering fixation on Idi Amin. Both articles defined a dichotomy between the simple virtues of traditional soldiers and the distortion of those virtues when political power, egotism, or greed come into play. It is significant that Amin was at first seen as just such a simple, honest military man, with neither pretences to grandeur nor overweening ambitions. Nevertheless, the late 1960s had seen military revolts, temporary or permanent, in Burundi, Upper Volta, the Central African Republic, Togo, Nigeria, Sierra Leone, Mali, Libya, and Somalia,[117] and if these articles on the military continued an unhealthy trend in the magazine's scope and focus, they did at least recall some of the punch and relevance of the old, pre-Luzira *Transition*.

James and Beaumont's piece on "Military Plumage" even had

about it something of the magazine's old cheeky eclecticism, claim-
ing, as it did, to have invented a system for predicting winners of
wars based solely on the relative elaborateness of the costumes of the
opposing sides, and committing the further outrage of extending the
argument even to the animal kingdom. Other pieces were in keeping
with the spirit of the old *Transition* as well. There was, for instance, a
delightful interview with an Accra "tro-tro" driver, who dilated,
from his idiosyncratic point of view, upon morality, Christianity,
wealth, and other topics. His disbelief in Ghana's new "democracy"
cast an appropriate sidelight on the two articles about the military,
defining the popular context in which authoritarianism was beginning to seem inevitable. "Now people dey say we dey practice something called democracy," he was reported to have said, "and so every-
body fit talk nonsense to the Prime Minister. If it be Nkrumah, who
go fit talk nonsense?"[118]

Transition no. 39 also maintained continuity with the magazine's
former literary emphasis, publishing important new poems by Chinua
Achebe and Wole Soyinka. Achebe's poem ("Their Idiot Song") bore
an interesting accidental synonymy to the tro-tro driver's remarks,
purporting to give an "old pagan's" response to another imported
notion, the Christian message of the resurrection. In contradistinc-
tion the persona of the poem speaks of death as a mocking being
from the traditional pantheon of the Ibo:

> . . . Sing on, good fellows, sing
> on! Someday when it is you
> he decks out on his great
> iron-bed with cotton-wool
> for your breath, his massing odours
> mocking your pitiful makeshift defences
> of face powder and township ladies' lascivious
> scent, these others roaming
> yet his roomy chicken-coop will
> be singing and asking still
> but YOU by then
> no longer will be
> in doubt!
>
> (p. 55)

Soyinka's series of poems, in contrast, were political—"Poems of Bread and Earth," couching in related images a pointed vision of Africa's future that Soyinka was later to express more directly in the pages of *Transition*, first as contributor and then as editor. The vision was pan-African and revolutionary, but based on a personal sense of betrayal and disillusion. One poem, "Après La Guerre," for example, called on Nigerians not to invalidate their own sufferings in the civil war by forgetting them:

> Do not cover up the scars.
> In the quick distillery of blood
> I have smelt
> Seepage from familiar opiates.
> Do not cover up the scars.
>
> (p. 21)

In the other three poems, however, decay was followed by fecundity that gave promise of generation. The pollen—the "rust" of the "wilted corn-plume"—gave way to "the germ's decay," figured both in the "laden stalks" of the burdened, dying plant, and also in the germ of life within both the seed and the yeast that would eventually help transform it into bread ("Season," ibid.). The images were thus of mixed "promise" and deterioration, as well as of betrayal—and that betrayal political:

> It cannot be
> That policy, deliberation
> Turns these embers of my life
> To ashes, and in polluted seas
> Lay sad beds of yeast to raise
> Dough
> On the world market.
>
> ("Capital," ibid.)

The personal context of these poems was unmistakable. Soyinka's imprisonment during the Nigerian civil war had hardened and angered him. Like Neogy, he did not intend to forget or to let bygones be bygones. However, he differed from Neogy in that prison, far from leaving him rudderless, had given him an even stronger sense of identity and determination. Soyinka's prison diaries, published soon thereafter by Rex Collings in London as *The Man Died*, struck a sympathetic chord in Neogy (who printed a lengthy extract in *Transition* no. 42, pp. 37–61) because of their evocation of the prisoner's sense of helplessness and defilement. The two men moreover shared the additional similarity of having been lionized in the press after their release, and both had enjoyed a sudden access of attention in Paris, London, and New York. Nevertheless, Soyinka's adjustment to events took a very different form. He seems to have regarded his celebrity with a cynicism and distrust that Neogy did not muster. Upon his release, Neogy had looked for a hero and a conversion—and he had temporarily found both. Soyinka had maintained an absolute skepticism about both heroes and conventional certitudes. Both men cultivated bitterness at the kind of repression they had suffered, but Soyinka saw in his experience merely a pattern repeated in human history—always and everywhere content to descend without protest back into the barbarism from which all human societies had emerged. Cynicism leavened his bitterness.

Prison had given Soyinka as much reason to be bitter and cynical as it had given Neogy to be bitter and disoriented. Like Neogy's, Soyinka's incarceration and release had been sudden, unexplained, and arbitrary. For him, too, prison had been characterized by isolation and silence. Afterwards, Neogy had been forced to flee Uganda; Soyinka had remained in Nigeria, but the alienation of prison and what he saw as his betrayal by friends and fellow writers made him thereafter progressively estranged. Neogy's estrangement was more subtle, but both men ultimately faced a crescendo of vitriolic criticism. Though produced by analogous circumstances, the two separate series of attacks were on grounds and along lines that were quite distinct, but both the assaults on Soyinka, *Transition*'s last editor, and Neogy, its first, were to bear upon the magazine's fortunes.

A Convenient "Stick with Which to Beat"

The attacks on Neogy and his new Accra *Transition* seem to have had several sources—some new, some left over from the old *Transition*. There were, first of all, wounds that still festered, inflicted by controversial articles in the old *Transition*. Mazrui's essays, particularly "On Heroes and Uhuru-Worship," "Tanzaphilia: A Diagnosis," and "Nkrumah: The Leninist Czar," especially continued to rankle, and *Transition* was still seen in some quarters as having chosen to make itself a stumbling block in the path of Africa's best-known nationalist leaders. There were also many who had remained—or at least professed to have remained—skeptical about Neogy's complicity in the magazine's former CIA funding. Though some critics seemed sincere, there were undeniably others, as Neogy once commented, who cherished this "stick with which to beat the magazine" (see above, pp. 166–67). Nearly everyone had been willing to forget about the intellectuals that the Congress for Cultural Freedom had directly funded throughout Africa, and about its funding of *Black Orpheus*, *The Classic*, and other periodicals, but *Transition*'s provocativeness either made it more suspect or its enemies inveterate.

With the reestablishment of *Transition* on more liberal terms in Accra after his release from Luzira Prison, Neogy himself seemed inclined to forget past recrimination and to expect his readers to forget as well. That some chose not to do so began immediately to be apparent with the first new issues. The initial hint of trouble was a letter (*Transition* no. 39, p. 10) from Mauri Yambo of the University of Dar es Salaam. Yambo attacked on the most fundamental grounds, though what precipitated his response was topical.

As we have seen, Neogy had dedicated his editorial in *Transition* no. 38 to a reaffirmation of his, and the magazine's, commitment to press freedom. Yambo's letter quite simply threw Neogy's dedication back in his face. Neogy's very ideal, Yambo argued, was grounds for suspicion of disaffection. He wrote:

It is infinitely more desirable that what the people should read is determined, not by some pretentious benefactor (internal or external), but by the people themselves (through a machinery they themselves have established). Granted, it is not always that a people is under a government it could, in liberty, call its own—and is this not the precise cause of revolutions? (p. 10)

Transition's commitment to "press freedom," he implied, was determined not by some phantom nonpartisanship, but by its illicit funding from abroad. The magazine was actually, therefore, committed solely to neocolonialist counterrevolutionary reaction. Yambo added:

How we criticize (or even attack) those whom we must criticize—this is a good pointer to where our sympathies or preferences lie. It goes without saying that the way we point out the weaknesses of our allies must differ, in a subtle kind of way, from the way we exploit those of our foes. (p. 10)

All the hints, all the subtle suggestions, Yambo concluded, pointed to *Transition*'s being, beneath its "nonpartisan" surface, very partisan indeed. The "people of East Africa," he declared, were engaged in "a bitter struggle—against neocolonialism, against international monopoly capitalism." *Transition* must define itself within the context of this "African struggle": "You have implicitly resolved to take a stand," Yambo challenged, "—there are only two choices: you are either for or against the revolution of the African peoples." Neogy, Yambo implied, had already taken his stand against the "African revolution," otherwise he would not have leaped so wholeheartedly onto the Amin bandwagon; would not, in spite of his own suffering, have so readily forgotten Obote's stature (with Nyerere and Kenyatta) as one of East Africa's premier nationalist leaders; would not have made such a (to Yambo) fatuous pretense of an implausible nonpartisanship.

Beyond a facetious superscription ("Ah Well, Back to the Drawing Board"), Neogy did not reply to Yambo's allegations until *Transition* no. 41, by which time they had been sympathetically chorused by other letter writers. As the superscription indicates, he did not take Yambo very seriously, and at any rate his mind was focused elsewhere. Wole Soyinka, in contrast, who would also later be criticized in the pages of *Transition* as a pro-Western reactionary, was nevertheless on something like Yambo's wavelength. He was also, at the same time, irreconcilably antagonistic to Yambo's style of tunnel vision. His series of poems in that same issue, after all, simultaneously celebrated the African revolution (though in the future tense and in terms uniquely Soyinkan) and criticized the corruption and hypocrisy of Africa's first generation of political leadership. If this was Yambo's partisanship, it repudiated his know-nothing stand.

Whether one was inclined to approve or discredit Soyinka's position, it stood in sharp contrast to Neogy's. Neogy also needed to take a new stance at that point (undoubtedly it would have differed from Soyinka's), to make *Transition* a vehicle for a redefinition of the terms in these new debates. Something stopped him, however. He remained temporarily displaced, unfocused—as, for the most part, did *Transition*.

A new setting, separation from old associates such as Theroux and Mazrui, even new fame and success, brought special difficulties, following as they did in the wake of the shattering ordeal of two years before. Africa, meanwhile, had hardly stood still, and changed debates brought a need for originality in editorial response. Neogy now needed to find what it had always before been his special gift to find—new editorial approaches, new themes, new focuses for debate, new contributors, new cross-relevances. If *Transition* was to retain its impetus and originality, it needed a good dose of what he had once called its "sour milk" of editorial creativity. Instead, his mind seemed to be spinning around in the same rut— . . . around himself . . . around Obote's Uganda . . . and around similar stories of political detention, press suppression, and official tyranny and corruption elsewhere.

That Neogy was having some difficulty in putting *Transition* back on its "pair of rails" is attested to both by the growing virulence of his critics and by the political analyses he was now inclined to print. In *Transition* no. 41, for instance, P-Kiven Tunteng, a young

Cameroonian working on a doctoral thesis at the Graduate Institute of International Studies of the University of Geneva, contributed an article entitled "Pseudo-Politics and Pseudo-Scholarship (in Africa)" that seemed to owe something of its style and contentiousness to one of *Transition*'s best-known contributors, Ali Mazrui.

Like Mazrui, Tunteng was interested in overlooked subtleties underlying the great upheavals of post-independence politics. Like Mazrui's thesis in "Uhuru-Worship" and "Leninist Czar," Tunteng's thesis tended toward a demythologization of the great nationalist heroes. Like Mazrui (and, for that matter, Theroux), Tunteng seemed to harbor an emperor's-new-clothes delight in saying what one was not supposed to say. For Tunteng, the progressive degeneration of African political leadership showed, as it had always shown, the limitations and consequences of the system of popular agitation that alone had legitimized and created the nationalist leaders. Many of the founding fathers of nationhood remained politically naive, Tunteng argued, having won power in the first place merely through "vernacular persuasiveness" and an ability to build personal loyalty at the grassroots level. "It was one thing," Tunteng concluded, "to win votes from an illiterate electorate but it was quite another to govern, let alone participate meaningfully in international conferences and intricate trade negotiations" (p. 27). Such leaders had no tolerance for any independent intellectual outlook, and their insistence on loyalty superseding intellectual integrity was eagerly accepted by African academics whose selfish opportunism outweighed their professional standards. What resulted was a system where politicians and intellectuals worked assiduously from their separate ends to keep unpleasant truths from reaching public view, and where "personal insecurities are expressed as ministerial pronouncements and rumours as national policies, and personal cleavages are the parameters of political competition" (p. 30)

However cogent and convincing Tunteng's initial description of the grassroots basis and ultimate consequence of political power in newly independent Africa, there was something disturbing about the way his essay's overall thesis swung off at last onto the bypath that was becoming Neogy's, and therefore *Transition*'s, special fixation. Tunteng wrote:

> The suppression of dissent, the ostracization of opposition groups and the identification of any resistance with subversion, and all these in the name of nation-building, have dangerously jeopardized the creative contribution which African scholars could make in the interest of national development.   (p. 30)

The reference to Neogy's own arrest in Uganda seemed unmistakable. Equally unmistakable were references to Africa's dominant political personalities and their one-party democracies. "Nation-building," Tunteng argued, had become simply a justification for "leadership failures, hastily conceived policies, corruption, and political irresponsibility" (p. 30). Self-absorbed, placing a premium only on "political reliability," Africa's political leaders stood accused by Tunteng equally of incompetence and selfish myopia. To further sour the picture, Tunteng's counter-example of fruitful collaboration between intellectuals and politicians was the involvement in America of Henry Kissinger in Richard M. Nixon's administration, then engaged in "winding down" the war in Vietnam and seeking "détente" with the People's Republic of China.

For Mauri Yambo and the other "partisan" correspondents, of course, Kissinger was anything but a hero, and the Letters column of *Transition* no. 41 inevitably manifested the increasing polarization that threatened to overbalance *Transition*'s putative nonpartisanship. A letter from C. Kallu-Kalumiya, the president of the African Students Society at Cambridge University, for example, seconded the earlier obloquy of "Comrade Yambo" and added that Neogy's characterization of Africa as a place where the list of democratic countries capable of hosting an "international journal of opinion" was "lamentably small" was an indication of the editor's pro-Western bias. Neogy had implied that such freedom of opinion was available in Western Europe. "That means," the correspondent concluded, "that *Transition* is a partisan, and committed to the 'liberal bourgeois democracy' of the West" (p. 8). It was no less revealing, the letter writer gloated, that Neogy's earlier editorial had praised the idealism of the Busia government, since revealed to have been extraordinarily corrupt.[119]

Along with another correspondent, Thandika Mkandawire, Kallu-Kalumiya drew what began to seem the inevitable conclusions: that liberal democracy on the Western model went hand in hand with foreign subversion, official corruption, and demands for press inviolability; and that *Transition*'s "nonpartisan" support for liberal democracy and press freedom was merely surface evidence of underlying infiltration. To Mkandawire, in fact, even Neogy's protestations that he was innocent of complicity in *Transition*'s CIA support were irrelevant; the big corporations that supported the new IACF were *at least as insidious* as the CIA, which had supported the old CCF:

> Your paper was once supported by the Central Intelligence Agency (through the Congress for Cultural Freedom now refurbished with new sheep's clothing) and now by big business and both these sources of finance are an indication of the extent of your non-partisanship.

It was "no mere accident," Mkandawire observed, that directors of major American foundations could "shuttle back and forth" from philanthropic board rooms to "Presidential councils." He concluded with a bit of condescending advice:

> If you really wish to be honest to yourselves, you have to grasp the fact that Ford Foundation, the CIA and the International Congress [*sic*] for Cultural Freedom are not "non-partisan" and disinterested lovers of culture. Once you . . . [comprehend] this elementary fact, then you have to ask your good-selves what forces these agencies support in Africa and what cultural policies they seek to promote in . . . [pursuit] of their objectives in Africa. . . . You may then choose to go along with the Fords or fight them and you are free to choose sides, but don't continue this nonsense about "non-partisanship." (p. 10)

Neogy responded explicitly in an editorial as well, but *Transition* no. 41 itself in its entirety was essentially his response to these new detractors. Tunteng's article, "Pseudo-Politics and Pseudo-Scholarship (in Africa)," was the central feature, keyed by a cover illustration of an African man holding before his face two masks with realistic features. Identical, except for accouterments, to the man's own visage, the masks were of a military officer and, behind that, a bespectacled intellectual. The cover also bore the motto that Neogy advanced in his editorial as summing up his response to Yambo, Mkandawire, Kallu-Kalumiya et al.: "Vox Populi Vox Dei" ("The voice of the people is the voice of God"). The graphic gesture seemed deliberately directed at his critics, most of them fledgling academics, and at the ultimate authority (as Neogy believed) of the regimes they championed—military power. In response to the continued charges of CIA complicity, Neogy also reprinted the interview on the subject, originally published in the Kenyan *Sunday Nation* on June 11, 1967, in which he had been hotly questioned by journalist Tony Hall about his funding through the Congress for Cultural Freedom.[120]

Neogy's editorial hastened to deny allegiance to either side of the old cold-war confrontation. He found "bourgeois democracies" and Marxist systems equally "habit-bound," he declared. "And the similarity between bourgeois and Marxist thinking . . . [is] uncomfortably close—they are both rooted in a fundamental orthodoxy; both require a subservience of the mind to dictums, whether these are social or intellectual is irrelevant" (p. 5). Nevertheless, he featured in *Transition* no. 41 articles that chiefly served to wave a red flag before the magazine's partisan critics. In addition to Tunteng's provocative article, there was another by Pierre L. van den Berghe (professor of sociology at the University of Washington, Seattle) on "Neo-Racism in the United States of America," which denounced the black power movement as inegalitarian in its premises and counterproductive in its results. What van den Berghe favored instead was the abandonment of confrontation in favor of black/white cooperation. This was also the position taken by James Baldwin, albeit with many more reservations, in an interview in the same issue. Van den Berghe was, however, most incensed about the various "affirmative action" and black studies programs that had followed in the wake of the black power movement.

Neogy's publication of Tunteng's and van den Berghe's articles was not in itself remarkable. *Transition* had often in the past printed articles with which it did not entirely agree—so long as they seemed to bring some new point of issue to the debate. What seemed new and provocative about Tunteng's article, for instance, was probably its stinging portrait of the power syndrome in emerging Africa and the complicity of the academic elite. Neogy doubtless felt no particular sympathy with the assertion that Africa needed its own home-grown Henry Kissingers, any more than he was sympathetic to Obi Wali's demand ("The Dead End of African Literature," *Transition* no. 10) that African literature be written exclusively in African languages. The effect of *Transition* no. 41, however, was to overbalance the debate on one side, and thus to place *Transition* on the far side of an ideological barrier from its critics. If contributors were citing the example of Henry Kissinger, critics were citing Frantz Fanon. That left little room for calm debate. In the storm of controversy that ensued, Neogy's "vehicle upon which the wagon of culture may travel for certain distances" would have need of all the "iron and steel" it could find in itself if it were not to end up utterly derailed.

Meanwhile, on top of a growing political polarization, there were also immediate practical difficulties suddenly facing the new Accra *Transition*. For one thing, Neogy's comfortable deal with the civilian government came to an abrupt end after barely three issues of the new *Transition* had gone to press, with the overthrow of the Busia government by a military coup while Neogy was out of the country on a visit to Uganda. The establishment of a military government by a Supreme Military Council under the chairmanship of Colonel (later General) Ignatius Kutu Acheampong brought with it first a suspension of publication, pending the lifting of yet another emergency declaration, and then a few months later "a new publishing license ritual." *Transition* no. 41, all printed, "just sat there for eight months," while Neogy petitioned for the issuance of the license number that must be superimposed on each cover. The delay on the government's part, he always felt, was "deliberate," though perhaps compounded by the confusion of sudden political change.[121]

Neogy spoke hopefully about the new government in his edi-

torial reply to Mkandawire and Kallu-Kalumiya and (perhaps mindful of Obote's overthrow in Uganda) hesitated to criticize this usurpation of power by the military. "When a civilian regime gets carried
away with its own self-importance," he wrote, "then a surgical operation is necessary to remove it from power" (*Transition* no. 41, p. 5).
Transition no. 41 also carried a brief interview with Colonel Acheampong that sought to pin him down to some sort of distinct program or ideology (he was not easily pinned down, and at any rate the
Transition interviewer did not press him very vigorously).

Hopeful comments apart, however, these new difficulties tipped
the balance for Neogy personally. With only three new issues to his
credit as editor, and with a storm of new critics in Africa and abroad,
the possibility of continued government disaffection or intransigence
did not at all appeal to Neogy. He has since commented: "I waited
[for a new license to publish] for nine months, got it, and then
quit."[122] Neogy's chief reason for turning over the editorship, according to a retrospective editorial farewell in *Transition* no. 44, was progressive disenchantment with Africa's political climate. Neogy's "personality," the editorial writer, Associate Editor Adu Boahen, averred,
made him "a passionate believer in the freedom of *all* men, in individual liberty, dignity, and the rule of law." His shift toward politics
ten years before, "with independence and the beginnings of arbitrary
rule and threats to those principles he held so dear," had been almost
a personal matter, as had his growing sense of estrangement as editor
of Africa's one successful magazine dedicated to "providing a forum
for the discussion of opinion, any opinion, on a continent where
such an opportunity was becoming increasingly curtailed." The three
most telling blows to Neogy personally, and therefore to the magazine that he had led with such imagination and vigor, had been the
CIA revelations of 1967; then, in 1968, Neogy's arrest and the long
interruption of publication; and now, in 1973, Ghana's discouraging
and potentially threatening political changes. Boahen alluded to the
viper's nest of critics stirred up by the recent *Transition*s only vaguely,
choosing instead to dwell, as had most of the new "partisan" critics
themselves, on what had seemed to Neogy when he arrived in Accra

two years before to be distant, no longer relevant events—the CIA disclosures of 1967. These, said Boahen, had been "a particularly nasty blow to Rajat, indeed a cruel irony," since they most of all had threatened the magazine's ideals and independence (p. 4).

It was true, nevertheless, that the CIA disclosures had begun a process of destabilization and polarization to which, ultimately, Neogy's editorship would succumb. Coming hard on the heels of this CIA stigmatization, the magazine's suppression in Obote's Uganda then threatened to turn a symbolic loss of identity into an actual one. Had Mazrui or Neogy allowed themselves to be bullied by Obote's hints about "good behavior," *Transition*, as Neogy himself later observed, would indeed have ceased to be *Transition*. In resisting such a violation, however, Neogy had risked the magazine's silent expiration in exile.

The political polarization between the new Accra *Transition* and its vocal critics was also indirectly a product of the events in Uganda—occurring as it did in an atmosphere of personal soul-searching and troubled allegiance. In Accra, the danger of silent expiration gave place to actual or threatened confrontation. Neogy found there new controversies, which he was not now entirely up to facing; the resurrection of an old controversy that he had every right to have put behind him four years before; and then a sudden and unpropitious change in government that brought with it adjustment, intransigence, and delay. Ghana, in a sense, though to Neogy "essentially the friendliest country" in Africa,[123] nevertheless became the last straw. Boahen summed up Neogy's feelings in *Transition* no. 44:

> He [had] resurrected *Transition* in a new environment . . . [in] a country that at the time in 1969, held out the best hope for the rule of law and human dignity in Africa. Probably it is to the failure of Ghana to live up to his expectations that may be attributed his disillusionment and eventual resignation as editor of *Transition*.   (p. 4)

Abdication and Interregnum

Although Neogy began thinking about leaving *Transition* almost immediately after the Acheampong coup of January 1972, it took him a full two years to complete arrangements for the installation of a new editor. Part of the problem—delay in securing a new publishing license—has been mentioned. There remained the further problem of settling on a new editor. Neogy himself wanted the new editor to be Kofi Awoonor, who had been contributing editor for Ghana since 1962, and who, though he had left Ghana following Nkrumah's overthrow to teach in the United States at the State University of New York at Stony Brook, would be both comfortable with the magazine's editorial philosophy and familiar with its new Ghanaian surroundings. Shepard Stone, however, urged Neogy to favor another candidate, Wole Soyinka, whose recent incarceration during the Nigerian War had made his voluminous and exceptional writings better known in Europe. "It was thought in Paris," Neogy writes, that "his was a more fund-raising name." [124]

Meanwhile, the arrangements for the transfer of the editorship hung fire. No doubt neither Awoonor nor Soyinka were in any hurry to press forward with discussions about the job: both were then much occupied elsewhere (Awoonor in New York, Soyinka in Paris and at Cambridge University). Both, moreover, may have felt, as Neogy did, less than sanguine about the new Ghanaian regime. Awoonor, a one-time Nkrumah appointee (he had been president of the Ghana Film Corporation), was hesitant to return to Ghana at all. [125] And so *Transition* continued for almost another two years under Neogy's increasingly restive leadership. It is, in fact, a measure of his staunchness that, though *Transition*'s tone remained one of recapitulation and restatement during this interval, the magazine did not entirely draw in its claws.

There was a long delay before the appearance of *Transition* no.

42, the first issue to be affected by the new licensing procedure, and when it appeared it was dominated by two subjects—Wole Soyinka and repression in Amin's Uganda (including especially the expulsion of the Asians). The interest in Soyinka, of course, may have had to do with the fact that he was being considered for the editorship of *Transition* (Awoonor had been interviewed in *Transition* no. 41), and it certainly had to do with Neogy's continued fixation on the trend in Africa toward the suppression of dissent. In addition to the Soyinka interview (by Biodun Jeyifous, a Nigerian pursuing a doctorate in drama at New York University), there was also the previously mentioned excerpt from Soyinka's newly published prison journals (entitled "The Man Died" in the magazine, as in the full version).

Its rumored appearance in *Transition*, Neogy recalls, caused no rejoicing at the Castle, Ghana's government house.[126] Word somehow reached the information minister via contacts in Lagos, and Neogy was summoned to a meeting on the very day when, coincidentally, he had himself made an appointment for a courtesy call. He was, he recalls, "politely asked to withdraw [*The Man Died*] . . . in view of delicate relations between Accra and Lagos, under some repair work by the new regime." He would only do so, he replied, if Lagos denied the facts of the case—denied, that is, that Soyinka had ever been jailed. To Neogy's surprise, the minister of information good-humoredly conceded him the point and let the matter drop there.

The Soyinka interview, however, emphasized differences between Neogy and Soyinka. Though Soyinka felt as keenly as Neogy the danger, in Africa as elsewhere, of established institutions degenerating into tyranny and exploitation, he saw one major source of that decay as internal to the institutions themselves. Africans, he told Jeyifous, had a responsibility to take a hard look at inherited political systems and to reject those that were built on false models, bastardized, or corrupted. Honest intellectuals had the special role of revealing the truth of what was going on: "Then let us see which systems will collapse—the corrupt elitist structures or the virile mass movements" (p. 64).

Like Neogy, Soyinka denounced ideological justifications of totalitarian repression. Like Neogy, he espoused a passionate, personal commitment to human rights:

> Ideology, once it departs from humanistic ends, is no longer worthy of the name. The ultimate purpose of human striving is humanity. The moment we deny this, we grant equal seriousness and acceptability to *any* and *all* ideology. We become victims of dogma and verbalisation for their own sake. . . . One of my definitions of humanity is a state of being within which the diminution of any other beings is a diminution of and an assault on one's own being. (p. 62)

Soyinka, however, was committed to a revolutionary mass movement in Africa, Neogy to "the rule of law." Though he was, Soyinka said, pessimistic about results, and though he constantly saw in the background "the mocking grin of history" (p. 63), he remained determined, unless and until the path to results became completely blocked, on creative mass action: "I do not believe in futile, token twitches," he commented, "nor in that fabricated lather of sweat in which so many of our 'radicals' are lavishly coated" (ibid.). Though both disliked the status quo, Soyinka, unlike Neogy, was willing to espouse a violent overthrow of existing political structures through mass agitation. Like Neogy's, Soyinka's ideological commitment was intensely personal; he made no bones about the alienation he had felt from his colleagues at the University of Ibadan. In response to Jeyifous's question about his resignation from the chair of the Department of Theater Arts, Soyinka answered:

> The factors on both sides accumulated to a point where continuation within such a situation would have been demeaning beyond any justification. I remain faithful to the university idea. To preserve it, something akin to the Chinese cultural revolution will have to be launched against the present rotted structures. (p. 64)

In his *Transition* no. 41 interview, in contrast, Kofi Awoonor had focused not on politics but on two postulates to his own writing—the universality of the creative impulse and the profundity of the African cultural tradition. Indeed, the choice of Awoonor to succeed Neogy as editor of *Transition* might have signaled a very different future for the magazine.[127] Wedded to the idea of the suprapolitical integrity of the artist, committed to finding imaginative routes of commerce across the world's severe cultural barriers, Awoonor might have made *Transition* resemble the magazine Neogy had originally said he intended to emulate, *Black Orpheus*.

At one point in the interview, in response to a question about his new novel, *This Earth My Brother*, Awoonor commented: "We are all humans, and in my fury of conception I wrote me, my spirit, into this book." His spirit, Awoonor reflected, bore as much relationship, however, to the European as to the African tradition, since even the artistic language he used was a "synthesis of two cultural experiences." He added, "Though our oral tradition is the warp, we need the weft of our education to complete the weaving of the tapestry. But though we may speak with clearer voices to the world, our roots are deep within us, within our Africa" (p. 44).

Awoonor, like Soyinka, nevertheless saw and felt "the mocking grin of history," particularly in reference to the attempts of the first generation of African writers to "repudiate what the 'colonial' novelists wrote about Africa," and his comments about his literary generation to the *Transition* interviewer gave every indication that, for all his different lights, he would have made every bit as tough and independent an editor as Neogy had been, and Soyinka would be:

> That old kind of writing, the setting up of a false myth in response to another false myth, was of course . . . false. Our ancestors were as barbarous and as cruel and as devious as anybody else's ancestors. And there was no Golden Age in Africa any more than there was one anywhere else. The corruption of Africa is an aspect of its humanity. To deny that corruption—that we sold people into slavery and did all the usual horrible human things—is to suggest in a way that we are not human. It's a lot of bullshit, the way that some Europeans have lionised Africans as saints, as black faces with hearts of gold.   (p. 43)

That Awoonor's aesthetic might have placed *Transition* back on its original track was further emphasized by his ending the interview with an otherworldly quotation from *Transition*'s first West African contributing editor, Christopher Okigbo, killed nearly five years earlier in the Nigerian Civil War: "I don't write the poems, I only hear the voices. I am the medium that the spiritual forces use" (p. 44). Like Awoonor, Okigbo had often spoken for literary universalism.[128] There was thus, in the Awoonor and Soyinka interviews, a continuity with *Transition*'s two earlier distinct editorial philosophies—one emphasizing literary internationalism and artistic universalism (as had Beier's *Black Orpheus*, although its internationalism, as Okigbo had pointed out, sought links first with the black diaspora); and the other emphasizing political idealism, social transition, dissent, and free speech. Awoonor and Soyinka had picked out different strands from *Transition*'s original editorial fabric. On that ground alone, even leaving aside Soyinka's commitment to popular revolution, the two proposed editors seemed likely to portend very different futures for the magazine.

Transition's three remaining issues under Neogy's editorship were also recapitulative in another way. They continued, that is, to keep one eye firmly fixed on Uganda. *Transition* no. 42, for instance (along with the emphasis on Wole Soyinka), featured two key articles and an editorial about Uganda, and also reprinted the report of a special Ugandan commission of inquiry. In fact, exclusive of letters and publisher's notes, the first thirty-six pages of the magazine were devoted entirely to Uganda.

Neogy's fixation with Uganda had changed materially in one way, however. After the summary expulsion of the Ugandan Asians, Neogy's disillusionment with Idi Amin, the man for whom he had once reserved such high hopes, was absolute, and he now wrote without temporization of tyranny. In his editorial, Neogy gave a grim assessment of the changes in Uganda:

> Like Obote, who dismembered the army of its trained officer corps, Amin over-rides the chain of command exhorting the rank and file to report on their officers or refuse to obey "bad orders." The result is anarchy and a reign of terror the likes of which Uganda has never experienced in her history. A return to civilian rule seems doomed for at least a decade.

Neogy cited frequent reports of resignations, disappearances, and outright executions,[129] culminating in the mass expulsions not only of Asians but also of expatriate Africans—a move, he noted sadly, that had been met with misguided applause from some quarters:

> To many Amin symbolises a super-nationalist who has truly African-ized Uganda. He has certainly changed one of the most out-going and liberal countries in Africa into a closed society—with its contacts and free-flow of ideas with the outside world diminishing daily. . . . In the meantime, the country whose dynamic intellectual atmosphere made possible the birth and sustenance of this magazine is shrouded in silence. . . .
>
> Amin may have "saved" Uganda by destroying it. Might this be a lesson for all African countries? (p. 4)

It undoubtedly had at least been a lesson for Neogy himself.

Neogy's editorial was followed by a substantial anonymous first-person report from Kampala ("A Ugandan Diary," pp. 13–19), in a crude approximation of the old *Transition* style—a mix of cynical sniping at the petty absurdities of tyranny and of a sometimes incontinent pathos at its deliberate cruelties. Whoever the author was, he did not possess the adroitness of Mazrui, Soyinka, Neogy, or Theroux. There was a romantic opening description—a last Kampalan sunset from Kololo hill; there were rambling, often ill-expressed observations, impressions of daily life, mixed promiscuously with descriptions of public events; there were indiscriminate handfuls of fact, supposition, rumor—a stray quotation or two—all touching somehow on Amin's unrelenting campaign to bully and discredit the Ugandan Asians.

Nevertheless, in spite of, perhaps even because of, its queer incoherence, the article was somehow telling. There were exceptional photographs, a *Transition* trademark, by old hand Marion Kaplan, documenting the forced journey of the refugees by "special train" to Mombasa. And there were also stray quotations, somehow tying together and giving ironic point to the other material. One from the *People* of September 9, 1972, for instance, spoke volumes about the inveteracy of the anti-Indian prejudices:

It is being a buffoon to ascertain [*sic*] that President Amin is the only solo [*sic*] Ugandan who hates the Asians. . . . Ask any man in the village and he says with a snarl spread across his tired face, "If I were Amin, Asians would quit at gun point at a speed faster than the wink of an eye." Ugandans hate Asians that much. They must go.   (p. 18)

Mazrui's own contribution to *Transition* no. 42 was immeasurably more deft and subtle than the anonymous diarist's, and, in its own way, equally elliptical. So subtle was the connection between the Ugandan events for which it sought to provide an ironic context and Mazrui's "When Spain Expelled the Jews and the Moors" that Neogy saw fit to append an editorial subtitle, "Professor Mazrui on President Amin's Expulsion Order." Mazrui was led to compare contemporary East Africa to fifteenth-century Spain because of the very harshness of the correspondences, bringing together unexpected similarities and contrasts in far-flung and seemingly disparate events. In Spain it had been the Jews and Moors who had been the educated, privileged elite detested by a backward majority; now black Africans were on the other side of the same fence, detesting a minority of educated Jews and Asians in their midst. The comparison between Spain's expulsion of the Moors and Amin's of the Asians, though unmistakable, was teasingly left half-explicit. Mazrui wrote:

Upon being expelled from Christian Europe, where did these Jews and Africans find a home? The bulk of them found their next home in the Muslim world on the African continent. What Europe and Christianity had rejected, Islam and Africa had attempted to absorb. The question which arose was whether a reversal of the process would ever come to pass—as expelled minorities from Africa sought hospitality in a more tolerant Europe.   (p. 21–22)

The unstated answer suggested a further parallel between the consequences of the two expulsions. Citing historians Parkes Galton, C. D. Darlington, and R. H. Tawney, Mazrui ascribed Spain's centuries of fanaticism, economic incapacity, and general backwardness to its racial intolerance, concluding with an insinuating (and somewhat heavy-handed) refrain:

Yes, we study history in order to understand ourselves.

Yes, let me once again repeat myself—we study history in order to understand ourselves. But we should also study it to be wiser, more humane, less rash, certainly less brutal, and often with an eye on the future. (p. 22)

Most telling of all the Ugandan material in *Transition* no. 42, however, was neither Mazrui's small dagger of irony nor the anonymous diarist's awkward bludgeon, but a reprint of the official report of David Jeffreys Jones, C.M.G., an Englishman serving as Puisne Judge of the Ugandan High Court and commissioned by Amin himself to investigate an army atrocity—one of the first in Amin's Uganda to come to international attention. Jones's report, though extensive, scrupulous in its attention to legal form, and patiently objective, was nevertheless deeply shocking. Although it commented on the deaths of only two men, an American journalist and an American lecturer on the staff at Makerere,[130] among the many hundreds Amin's regime had already killed (and the many thousands it would eventually kill), the report's revelation of the cynical complicity of the Amin government in sanctioned murder was shocking in the extreme.

Jones also detailed the government's subsequent obstruction of his investigation, including Amin's own efforts to manipulate it via the official Ugandan press. He would have had the truth about the murders within his grasp, Jones implied, if only army authorities had cooperated. Although Jones strongly suggested that government authorities, including Amin himself, must bear ultimate authority for both the murder and its cover-up, the ensuing government white paper merely accepted Jones's statement that the two men had been murdered, twisting Jones's other findings so as to make them appear to cast suspicion primarily not on Jones's chief suspect, Major Juma Aiga, but on his chief witness! Jones's report had actually come as close as the circumstances of his impeded investigation allowed to fixing guilt squarely on Major Juma. With uncharacteristic warmth, Jones wrote, "In all my experience as a judge, I have never seen a more arrogant, almost insolent witness in a witness box. He was also a consummate liar. . . . Major Juma may well have had something to do with the actual killing" (p. 35).

As Neogy had observed in his editorial, many people, all over the world, continued to support Amin, in spite of disturbing reports from refugee Ugandans; and Neogy's publication of Jones's report and the other Ugandan materials now won *Transition* fresh enemies from a new quarter. Neogy would henceforth be persona non grata with both the Amin and Obote factions. Neogy's *Transition* nevertheless continued to court, and merit, fresh controversies right to the end. The Afro-American material in *Transition* no. 41, for example, struck fire in subsequent correspondence columns, as had the controversies about nonpartisanship and foreign sponsorship of the magazine. *Transition* no. 41 also contained an article ("*Bound to Violence*, a Case of Plagiarism," pp. 64–68) by Robert McDonald that accused Yambo Ouologuem of Mali, a Prix Renaudot winner, of plagiarizing his *Bound to Violence* from an early Graham Greene novel, *It's a Battlefield*.

McDonald's article precipitated an international hue and cry that eventually drew in publications of the stature of the *New York Times* and the *Times Literary Supplement* of London. McDonald had uncovered clear evidence of parallels between brief passages from the two novels. Subsequently, a *Transition* correspondent named Alec Rutimirwa, then a final-year student at Makerere, suggested in *Transition* no. 42 (1973) that Ouologuem's publishers, Editions du Seuil, might have been responsible for another egregious borrowing in Ouologuem's work (whose French title was *Le Devoir de violence*) from another novel on their list, André Schwarz-Bart's *Le Dernier des justes*. This second borrowing, Rutimirwa said, was more extensive, encompassing matters of transition and structure as well as turns of phrase and details of description. Such an unmasking, coming in a magazine already controversial for its unmasking of African political and literary demigods, might have raised cries of protest from literary idolaters of the type Awoonor had alluded to in his *Transition* no. 41 interview, were it not that Ouologuem's novel itself tended toward an unmasking of the new cultural idols, in particular of Frantz Fanon.

(Ouologuem has maintained, with support from some quarters, that these sources were not intended to be secret and were used for the sake of parody and ironic juxtaposition.)[131]

Transition no. 43, appearing a few months after *Transition* no. 42, returned to another subject of current controversy, political polarization in the United States, focusing on the Watergate affair. Mazrui made the Watergate scandal an occasion for a meditation upon the significance for Africans of the Vietnam War, Neogy an opportunity to belabor his antagonists and the African public at large for a lack of appreciation of the value of free speech and a free press. Africa's reaction to the Watergate affair, Neogy observed, seemed to be a collective yawn, and such complacency was evidence that Africans did not appreciate "how a free press can safeguard liberty." He asked:

> Is it possible to envisage anywhere in Africa a newspaper which can play a similar investigative role [to the *Washington Post*] with regard to matters of state? Yes, we all know the reasons why this is an almost ridiculous question to ask: [that] the press is almost everywhere government-controlled if not owned, that safeguards for freedom of speech are non-existent, and that official retribution is swift and deadly, and that the lot of the journalist is a humiliating and debasing one.
>
> (p. 4)

For Mazrui, African apathy about international politics revealed that most Africans had not yet read the subtle signs in international relations; his old antagonists, Nkrumah and Obote, he thought, had been more farseeing. Both had envisioned African political leaders playing an important creative role in international diplomacy. Their independence and initiative, Mazrui thought, might guarantee balance and perspective in international council rooms; and at any rate it was time Africa sought an equal place at international bargaining tables. Nkrumah, he recalled, had attempted to involve himself in the discussions about Vietnam, first with Lyndon Johnson, and then with Mao Tse-tung and Chou En-lai; Obote, following the lead of Nkrumah, had taken a deliberate stand against U.S. "imperialism," particularly distrusting American intentions in the Congo (Zaire).

Africa's lesson from Watergate and Vietnam, for Mazrui, was simply that "the weak can defeat the strong" (p. 39), in diplomacy as in journalism and warfare ("Nkrumah, Obote, and Vietnam," *Transition* no. 43, pp. 36–39).

The key article in *Transition* no. 44, Neogy's last issue, actually appearing after his departure, broached the other half of the same topic—that is, Africa's unequal position as a subject for international press reports. Adepitan Bamisaiye, a Nigerian educated in Canada and Sweden who was then a research fellow at the Institute of African Studies, Ibadan, used the reporting of the Nigerian civil war as his object lesson in bias, distortion, and shoddy research—faults characteristic, he thought, of Western reporting of the African news in general (he particularly criticized Lloyd Garrison of the *New York Times*). Biafra's "underdog status," he felt, had appealed to a foreign press corps intent upon turning the facts of the conflict to account in manufacturing cheap melodrama that would sell newspapers at home.

Mazrui's and Bamisaiye's articles thus put *Transition* back on the other side of the political fence, to a certain extent—as an advocate of diplomatic non-alignment, a critic of European hegemonists, and a skeptical observer of the probity of the European "free press." It was not a fence of Neogy's choosing. Nevertheless, *Transition* had at last begun to right itself, to regain its editorial balance. Unfortunately, however, by the time it had begun to do so, Neogy already had in hand his air reservations to depart.

As Adu Boahen wrote of him, Neogy's commitment had been personal. In a strange way, Neogy had never really been any more ideological than Ulli Beier had been at *Black Orpheus*. Neogy was committed to what he had spoken out for all along—stubborn self-reliance, dialogue, freedom to dissent—"transition" with a lower-case *t* and without the italics. That commitment had in the beginning, in the last few months of colonialism and the first few months of new nationhood, made him something of a bohemian. Later, in an atmosphere of increasing personal political confrontation and ideological polarization, it made him suddenly seem an ally of conservative forces. Partisanship was never Neogy's style, but neither was reaction.

In his reponse to his critics, in *Transition* no. 41, Neogy had written:

> In this space we wish to merely remind our more ideologically-oriented readers that the name of this magazine, ever since its inception, is *Transition*, which means, if anything, a commitment to change—perpetual change which is the nature of live bodies, be they governments, societies or people. (p. 5)

To the magazine's critics, *Transition*'s insistence on intellectual independence and freedom of speech looked like a banner of reaction. *Transition*, however, had never abrogated its allegiance to the ideal of change. Like Wole Soyinka, Neogy did not believe that such change could occur under some imported pattern of prescribed dogma, and unlike Soyinka, he distrusted the partisanship of idealistic mass movements. It remained to be seen whether the magazine would make a new, partisan commitment under Soyinka once Neogy had gone. If the new editor were to be Kofi Awoonor, it remained to be seen whether the magazine would return to the other half of its initial editorial philosophy and strive once again to attain Ulli Beier's, and Awoonor's, ideal of joining the integrity of the African artistic tradition to the international creative stream of modernism. It remained further to be seen whether the magazine would, under either new editor, somehow bring itself out from under the CIA cloud that had for so long obscured its intellectual independence and honesty.

There were even, in those last few issues, a few pregnant gestures in Awoonor's direction, the direction of cultural universality—including, appropriately enough, a final tribute to the work of Ulli and Georgina Beier, by then holding court not in Ibadan, Nigeria, but Papua New Guinea. *Transition* no. 43 featured three pages (40–42) of the work of the Beiers' latest protégé, a New Guinean named Kauge—two drawings and photographs of two beaten copper panels reminiscent of an earlier Nigerian protégé, Ashiru Olatunde. *Transition* no. 44 carried a review by one of the *Black Orpheus* stalwarts, Abiola Irele, of the new activities of its old guard, the Beiers. Irele reviewed novels, autobiography, stories, and poems from the fledgling literary movement that Beier had attracted to the pages of his new cultural review, *Kovave*. Though Irele admitted that the Beiers' continuing emphasis on creative experiment and penchant for molding very raw talent threatened to make *Kovave* something of a "storehouse of exotica" (p. 51), he nevertheless praised the *Kovave* contributors for their honesty, clarity, and imaginativeness in using indigenous myths to bridge familiar cultural barriers. He also praised their effort to ally traditional values with nationalistic self-affirmation in combating the legacies of colonialism, particularly those fostered by colonial educational systems. Neogy's *Transition*, in a sense, thus ended where it had begun, with an acknowledgment of its original Nigerian model, *Black Orpheus*, now transplanted as *Kovave* across a whole new range of cultural borders and boundaries. Under Awoonor, the editor that Neogy himself favored, *Transition* might likewise have found new cultural borders and boundaries, within Africa, while returning to its original emphasis on creating a meeting ground between indigenous culture and a universal creative impulse.

That Soyinka, rather than Awoonor, became the new *Transition* editor was partly due to circumstances—to his greater celebrity. Soyinka's plans to emphasize the magazine's political aspect seem not to have entered into the picture. By the time he arrived in Accra, Soyinka had determined on a number of changes in emphasis as well. He meant, first, to substantially alter *Transition*'s tone, its unique style; second, to maintain all the more stubbornly its independence of voice; and third, to bring a tough new dedication to the concept of change that the magazine's name implied—to make it pointedly partisan. This rededication, Soyinka hoped, would command the respect, if not the agreement, of *Transition*'s inveterate critics.

Meanwhile, however, neither Soyinka nor Awoonor was in any hurry for the talks with Neogy and Shepard Stone to come to a head; both were heavily committed elsewhere. Neogy continued to flirt with the idea of hiring Awoonor to replace him, and Stone continued to urge the merits of Soyinka. Finally, when Neogy had pretty much made up his mind to accept Soyinka as his successor, the issue was settled by default. In a telephone conversation with Neogy, Awoonor withdrew his name from consideration.[132] Soyinka was ultimately induced to take over the editorial reins, but since he was not able immediately to disentangle himself from other commitments, Neogy was left to put out a few last issues as a lame-duck editor. Even *Transition* no. 44, which appeared after Neogy's departure, had been largely a product of Neogy's hand. Soyinka did not arrive until after it had gone to press.

Perhaps the most thoughtful farewell tribute to Neogy in *Transition* no. 44 was one from Ali Mazrui (then a resident scholar at Stanford University's Hoover Institution). "It is not often realized," Mazrui wrote, "that writers can sometimes be profoundly changed by the very media they use. I as a writer have used *Transition* as a medium over the years. I may have influenced *Transition*; what is certain is that *Transition* influenced me. I regard *Transition* as an important factor in my own personal intellectual history. Was that association for better or worse? All I know is that it was for real" (p. 4).

Wole Soyinka, ironically, seems to have felt that for *Transition* the association had been for worse. In his farewell tribute to Neogy and in a separate correspondence with Soyinka, Mazrui had made the gesture of first publicly, and then formally, offering his resignation as associate editor—in order, he said, to give the new editor a fresh start. Neither of the men who had been considered for the *Transition* editorship, however, were at all admirers of Mazrui's distinctive writings. Soyinka promptly did what Awoonor also might very well have been tempted to do: though he suspected that Mazrui's resignation may have been simply pro forma, he immediately accepted it.[133]

"Anti-Men" and "Masquerades": Soyinka Takes Over

As his first signature issue, *Transition* no. 45 (no date, but probably 1974), manifested, Wole Soyinka had every intention, in fact, of accomplishing his reconstruction of *Transition* by first dismantling it. Although he had been very much an admirer of the early *Transition* and continued to believe in Neogy's integrity, Soyinka felt strongly that at some point the magazine's tone had become flippant and frivolous.[134] He seems to have largely blamed Mazrui for this. He meant to make clear from the outset that his *Transition* would be more serious, more thoughtful—while at the same time if anything *more* independent in its outlook, and more controversial.[135]

That he intended to make *Transition* thereafter an independent partisan of mass movements was indicated by the dedication of the new issue, announced on the cover, to Amilcar Cabral's PAIGC (African Party for the Independence of Guinea and Cape Verde) in Guinea-Bissau, which had then just unilaterally announced its own successful liberation from Portugal. That he meant to change *Transition*'s tone and format was announced by Soyinka's first editorial, which casually mentioned that *Transition* would, "after this initial exception," revert to "its founding tradition of issuing no editorial" (p. 4), and by a severely truncated Letters section, which included only a scribbled cartoon from a would-be contributor and a long, extravagant missive from a black American reader, complaining of "historical ignoramuses" who had forgotten the treachery and savagery of the Muslim colonizations of Africa. Soyinka's meditated de-editorialization of the magazine, of course, would have been a striking about-face for a periodical whose editorial page and Letters section had often greatly overshadowed even its feature articles. Soyinka's interest in breaking with *Transition*'s old controversies and controversialists was further attested to by a somewhat irritated attempt, in the editorial, to disengage himself once and for all from the

256

CIA-funding controversy, and by his publication of a summary ex-ecration of Ali Mazrui, contributed by James N. Karioki, a Kenyan on the faculty of the University of Pittsburgh in the United States.

Soyinka began his own editorial by tossing the departed editor-in-chief sincere, yet somewhat wilted, bouquets:

> The quality of the magazine and the liveliness of its debates inevitably attracted international admiration.[136] None of its fans, I am certain, en-dorsed *all* of *Transition*. . . . But not one of those who were acquainted with the operations of the journal has ever had the slightest doubt about Rajat Neogy's editorial integrity. [emphasis in the original]

He ended his editorial with a grudging and deliberately offhand ad-version to an unspecified controversy inherited from his editorial predecessor. The rest of the editorial, Soyinka said at this point, with deliberate vagueness, would "be printed in small print and relegated to some obscure page in this issue" (p. 4). Readers were left to grope about in the back pages of the magazine to locate the rest of Soyinka's comments (on p. 66) about, as it turned out, the controversy of *Transition*'s former CIA funding.

Soyinka made it clear that he was heartily sick of the whole sub-ject. *Transition* had, he was certain, been innocent of complicity, and, at any rate, "the burden of proof is on the accuser." That the maga-zine's detractors could advance no better evidence than accidental co-incidence of opinion and were inclined to "emotive sputterings," "smirks," and "pub-logic" was indication enough that the discussion had outlasted its usefulness. The lesson that Soyinka drew from all this did not differ materially from the one Neogy had drawn ear-lier—that the CIA seemed to have been prone to "mystifying contra-dictions." He described it as a "subversive organization whose prin-cipal rationale, when all the evidence is logically considered, appears to have been a policy of haphazard infiltration of everything and any-thing going, on the general principle that with such indiscriminate fishing some terrapins may actually be hooked" (p. 66).

As a more positive response to critics who had seen *Transition* as counterrevolutionary, Soyinka offered his tribute to the mass insurrections in Guinea-Bissau, which, he charged in his first "Between Covers" section (the editor's narrative highlight of the contents), had been obscured by a conspiracy of silent indifference among Africa's political leaders and their state-controlled presses. It was through such a mass rising, Soyinka wrote, with pointed reference to Amilcar Cabral and Frantz Fanon, that pan-African "solidarity" would ultimately come to pass, and he meant to make *Transition* a partisan of such struggles to break free from the "ideological cage" of elitism and neocolonial dependence. He wrote:

> There is only one foundation on which the unifying movement for the African continent can be based. It is the assertive emancipation of the African masses, at present ignored and despised by black masquerades in colonial feathers. (Editorial, p. 4)

In the service of the related struggle to liberate Africa from its new "black colonial governors," *Transition* pledged itself to a new task of education, to becoming a vehicle for change—now no longer a change from colonial status to independence, but from this neo-colonial "masquerade" to an honest self-definition:

> The new phase of transition, an activity of total self-retrieval which continues to make this journal's name both relevant and topical[,] is undoubtedly that from the state of petty neo-colonial independencies towards an enlarged self-sustaining African identity. The only question at issue is whether such a coming together of the African nations will indeed be that of an organic union of the peoples or a consecration of the alienated clubmanship of the leadership elite. (ibid.)

In focusing on Guinea-Bissau, Soyinka said, he meant quite simply to provide an "exemplar for an African revolutionary future" ("Between Covers," p. 3). In the introductory "Commentary" to his special section, he defined more precisely what he hoped Africans would find exemplary: that Guinea-Bissau had "effectively neutralised" the "subtle machinations by an outgoing imperial power" through its demonstration that "the interior liberation of man is a prerequisite . . . to a program of territorial and political liberation" (pp. 9 and 10). Guinea-Bissau was accomplishing, in a new and particularly effective way, what Guinea-Conakry, Tanzania, and Zambia were struggling to accomplish in other, less fundamental ways—the dislodgement of the "conservative, even feudal-based parties" and the "monopolistic ethos" of an advantaged, artificial elite, left in place by the departing colonial masters (p. 9).

Within the special section, a report by long-time PAIGC sympathizer Basil Davidson emphasized with more immediacy the same features that appealed to Soyinka in the Guinea-Bissau revolutionary movement—its populist orientation, its grassroots organization, its emphasis on local authority. Davidson described a broad-based network of self-help and self-rule committees working together to promote local autonomy in education, health care, transport, justice, and especially "defense." At the center of the movement, Davidson wrote, was a sort of motto that the permanent political workers endlessly repeated, urging the villagers to "decide for themselves, . . . take their own responsibilities": "*Que povo na manda na su cabaca*" ("Notes on a Liberation Struggle," pp. 21–22).

The centerpiece to the special section was a speech by Cabral himself, delivered on the anniversary of the assassination of another lusophone African revolutionary leader, Eduardo Mondlane of Mozambique (Mondlane had been assassinated on February 3, 1969). To the special poignancy of the situation (Cabral had, by then, himself been assassinated in suspicious circumstances) was added, for Soyinka, the personal relevance of Cabral's message of self-liberation as a necessary prerequisite to a national struggle for political liberation. If a people was not able to assert its "cultural personality," defined on a popular level, Cabral had said, then its struggle was ultimately doomed to be coopted by "non-converted" opportunists— people who, "armed with their learning, their scientific or technical knowledge, and without losing their class prejudices, could ascend to the highest ranks of the liberation movement" (p. 14). Like Soyinka, moreover, Cabral had stressed both his distrust of the African elites and his consciousness of "the mocking grin of history":

> Undoubtedly, the denigration of the cultural values of the African peoples based on racialist prejudices, and on the aim of perpetuating their exploitation by foreigners, has done much harm to Africa. But in the face of the vital necessity of progress, the following acts and prac-

tices will be just as harmful: undiscerning praise; systematic exaltation of virtues without any criticisms of faults; blind acceptance of cultural values without considering the negative, reactionary, or retrogressive aspects . . . [they have] or can have; confusion between that which is the expression of an objective and material historical reality and that which seems to be a figment of the mind, or the result of a specific nature; the absurd linkage of works of art[,] be they valuable or not, to claimed characteristics of a race; and finally the unscientific critical appreciation of the cultural phenomenon. (p. 15)

In offering *Transition*'s readers pointedly the example of Guinea-Bissau, Soyinka thus sought to find a meeting ground for several strongly held, and seemingly somewhat divergent, opinions: that the African elites had almost universally betrayed the African masses; that Africa's heritage was as much a mixture of good and bad as anyone else's; that the work of "development" would ultimately occur only if preceded by a sort of mass cultural self-examination; that some sort of rigorous mass self-mobilization from beneath must then follow, rather than a lifting up from above by the Western-oriented elites.

Soyinka, though in emotional and practical sympathy with the idea of revolutionary mass movements, was thus able to retain his skepticism about the dogmatists, idealists, and importers of ready-to-wear ideologies who had begun to dominate post-independence Africa. In signaling his unwillingness to commit *Transition* in advance to every new African "revolution" that came along, and in demanding of Africa's next generation of political leaders much more than radical slogans, Soyinka had given notice of his intention to maintain *Transition*'s stubborn independence of outlook. He did not mean, any more than Neogy had, to accept Yambo's contention that "you are either for or against the revolution of the African peoples" (see above, p. 233). It was a question of which "revolution" was at issue. Although the Guinea-Bissau revolution had been fought against one of the last of the colonial regimes, Soyinka seemed intent as well on reserving to the African masses the right to foment similar grassroots revolutions against the elitist governments of independent black African states.

Soyinka's key gesture in the direction of the other strand in what had been *Transition's* essential editorial philosophy—literary universalism—was through his publication of another of the central figures in the foundation of the modern African cultural movements at both *Black Orpheus* and *Transition*, Ezekiel Mphahlele. Soyinka commissioned Mphahlele to contribute a piece about "The Function of Literature at the Present Time." Mphahlele's essay, subtitled "The Ethnic Imperative," set for itself the task of testing and balancing two opposed concepts—the literary equivalent of Soyinka's two divergent, almost contradictory, political ideals: absolute partisan commitment and absolute integrity, objectivity, and independence. Art, that is, must serve social necessity, or, conversely, must be defined by some inner necessity whose standards are impervious to social or political imperatives. Mphahlele's metaphor for the latter, universalist case was the tortoise—mysterious, oblique, imperturbable—whose role is central in so much West African oral narrative and proverb.

Although Mphahlele's sympathies seemed to be distinctly with nonpartisan, non-nationalist, "universalist" art, he also made a gesture in the direction of artistic social militancy.[137] Black literature, he wrote, must combat the condescensions of white literature. This was its "ethnic imperative." If you could not command the tortoise to "participate in human quarrels," nevertheless, Mphahlele hoped, the tortoise's very stubbornness and integrity must inevitably induce him to become "a vehicle of revolutionary passion." This was having it both ways with a vengeance, as Mphahlele himself admitted:

> We need constant control of language, and *always* we want literature to help us do this. To the extent that it portrays human endeavor, human possibilities, and is a thrust of the imagination, it must always be revolutionary. . . . The imperative that sees ethnic goals being collectively realized out of individual sensibilities shows a tremendous if desperate act of faith.
> (p. 53)

Transition no. 45, thus, issued two "imperatives"—Soyinka's on the issue of political commitment in life, and Mphahlele's in literature. For both Soyinka and Mphahlele, the absolute necessity for a coexistence of "individual sensibilities" and firm partisanship required a "desperate act of faith." In both realms, the political and the artistic, the new *Transition* seemed determined to have its cake and eat it too. Because it now meant to be partisan did not mean that it no longer cherished its absolute independence; because it believed in "socially relevant" literature did not mean that it thought literature a sub-servient or ancillary activity to politics.

There were other mixed signals of continuity with the old *Transition* as well. Neogy's editorial hectoring of his readers about the Watergate affair was followed ingeniously in Soyinka's first *Transition* by the announcement of a contest, with a year's subscription as prize, for the best parallel African scenario of corruption and political dirty tricks. *Transition*'s emphasis on graphic design was also perpetu-ated—the same issue, for instance, contained a full-page woodcut by the well-known contemporary German graphic artist Karl Schmidt-Rottluff. A report by a trio of Ethiopeans in *Transition* no. 45 also continued the magazine's emphasis on firsthand observation meant to shock readers out of their complacency and their reliance on con-ventional explanations. As in the past, the article and the editorial lead-in "Between Covers" were notable for their barbed allusions to the political reality behind the writers' impressions and observations, and the article's tone was set by a particularly arresting and ironic graphic reproduction of the menu card from an Organization of Af-rican Unity banquet in Addis Ababa, which, at the height of a fam-ine, promised the distinguished visitors *poulet sauté au curry*, which they could wash down with a 1966 Meursault; and, several courses later, *petit gâteaux aux fraises* with Moët et Chandon champagne (p. 68).

If anything, Soyinka's *Transition* was even more feisty and trouble making than Neogy's had been. Let none suppose, Soyinka com-mented in "Between Covers," that he had chosen to focus on Ethi-opia because he wanted to let other African states off the hook. Many other African political leaders, he charged, had been equally to blame for famine in their own countries during the preceding year. He concluded with a somewhat insulting invitation:

> The pages of *Transition* are open to statements of reassurance by the af-
> fected governments backed by programs which have been set up to pre-

vent a repetition of last year's disaster. It will be an unforgivable crime if such governments resort yet again to a last-minute call for help to international bodies. (p. 3)

The Ethiopian contributors went even further, condemning their government and virtually calling for agrarian revolution:

> When millions of people suffer[ed] from the famine, the Ethiopian government was occupied in the self-serving effort of imperial pageantry and aggrandizement. Caught up in the mysticism of its own pretensions, dubbing itself Leader of Africa, Father of Africa, the Ethiopian government was wasting five million dollars in . . . scenarios of extravaganza.
> . . . It must be clear that any aid sent through the government will not reach the people. Those who nibble the aid in the government from the highest to the lowest level are many. The corrupt officials will pocket any money sent for the victims. (p. 67)

Even more searing were their conclusions:

> The famine is not a result of the drought alone. The drought plays a part, but the main reason for the famine is the basic irrationality of the socio-economic make-up of the Ethiopian polity. The irrationality of the land-tenure and holding system, the fact that the majority of the Ethiopian people are dispossessed and those who own fatten at their expense, that the government is wholly irresponsible to the people explain the poverty and famine in Ethiopia.[138] (p. 69)

Transition was again inadvertently beating a dead horse, however. The target of the trio's invective (though never alluded to by name), Emperor Haile Selassie, had, in the interval between the article's contribution and publication, been deposed by an army coup. The political radicalization called for in the article, moreover, was soon to take place, with the institution of some measure of agrarian reform under the military Dergue, and with the growing prominence of the radical Ethiopian People's Revolutionary Party. Ultimately, of course, in 1984, the survivors of Ethiopia's military regime would face an even more severe famine, and they, likewise, would be charged with obstructing the famine relief efforts and wasting money on national "pageantry."

Another first-hand report in *Transition* no. 45 recalled Neogy's long obsession with Uganda and its "Asian question." The article, "Farewell Uganda" by Ugandan Indian novelist, poet, and journalist Bahadur Tejani, seemed almost assembled from fragments of earlier nonfiction sketches of Uganda by Paul Theroux and several anonymous Ugandan Asians, except that the fragments made a completely different whole. Like Theroux's earlier sketches, Tejani's sketch told a grim, fatalistic narrative of people caught within, and debased by, the fragile context of political events (in this instance not simply Amin's expulsion order, but the whole history of distrust and alienation for East African Asians), but it seemed more deliberately to seek a balance between Mphahlele's "ethnic imperative," the hard reality of this particular inversion of racism, and the integrity of the individual perception—of art, of literature.

For both Tejani and Theroux, racism was a depressingly inevitable fact of life, in Africa as elsewhere. For Tejani, as for Theroux, the universal bond between men seemed to be nothing more or less than their capacity for defeat, for cruelty; their powerlessness. In recalling his own Kampalan childhood, he wrote:

> The rooms were perched above a motel famous for pimps, gamblers and whores, next door to the dark, mucky slums of Kisenyi where all the V.D. infested, alcoholic derelicts and petty thieves eked out their miserable lives. There were no street lights in the area. If a man was caught stealing he would be beaten to death, a drama in which I often took part.
> . . . Our Punjabi neighbor called her children "chuwe," rats; the stairs opened onto six loos for the use of taxi-drivers and tired Asian traders who came to ravage the black kids at night.   (p. 65)

Tejani, however, ended his essay with a Soyinkan gesture of defiance, a "desperate act of faith"—his refusal to apply for exemption to Amin's expulsion order ("When it comes to queuing up as an Asian to prove that I am a Ugandan," Tejani wrote [p. 66], "then I say the General can have it back—with a citizen's compliments"). Tejani's gesture was meant, to borrow Soyinka's expression, to be more than a "token twitch" or "fabricated lather of sweat," [139] of which ultimate irrelevance Soyinka seems to have deemed Theroux guilty in his Ugandan sketches.

Soyinka made it abundantly obvious in *Transition* no. 45, however, that the *Transition* insider whom he held most guilty of irrelevance—and also of irresponsible, almost flippant reaction—was Ali Mazrui. Karioki's article (given the rather bludgeoning title "African Scholars Versus Ali Mazrui," on the grounds of the author's assertion that his article expressed a disaffection shared among the majority of African scholars) closely mirrored attacks that Yambo, Kallu-Kalumiya, Mkandawire, and others had earlier leveled against Neogy and the magazine itself. Karioki, who confessed to an initial admiration for Mazrui, summed up Mazrui's influence thus:

> When he is not busy entertaining his erudite audience in the West with academic puzzles, or defending elitism in Africa, or attacking imaginative African leadership, he is content to remain a semi-detached, backward-looking polemicist in the deliberations of colonial liberation. (p. 63)

It would be a mistake to go too far in identifying Soyinka's sentiments about Mazrui with Karioki's. Soyinka was at least in partial sympathy, however, with Karioki's deploring of Mazrui's political predilections and influence, and perhaps even more in sympathy with Karioki's derogation of the identifiable features of the Mazrui style: its thriving on "iconoclasm," its "propounding of unexpected themes and unpopular theories" clothed in "scholarly jargon" (p. 56).

One hesitates, however, to believe that Soyinka could much have sympathized with the logic or extension of Karioki's argument, which charged that Mazrui's love of paradox, contradictions, and seeming historical misdirection was simply a cover for sniping against socialism, revolution, and "constructive African leaders" (p. 63). Soyinka himself was no advocate of blind loyalty of the which-side-are-you-on? variety, and he did not believe, as Karioki argued, that "for *genuine* African scholars, Western style objectivity is a luxury they can ill afford" (p. 62). If Soyinka was inclined to fault Mazrui, it was not for his loyalties, but for his style of teasing circularity, his reliance on puns and coincidences, and ultimately for what both Soyinka and Paul Theroux saw as his casual sophistry.[140] In *Transition* no. 37, Theroux had parodied what he saw as Mazrui's self-absorbed inconsequence, embellished with Mazrui's familiar rhetorical flourishes:

> What we propose to examine in this short but controversial article [Theroux had his straw man, "A. Mzuri," write] is how the pill *vis-à-vis* the shifting trends of newly-independent developing areas of the third world can provide a basis for National Unity and/or a focus for the aspirations of those with rising expectations. Or, to put it another way, do the underdeveloped like kids and if so how?
>
> ("The Politics of the Pill by A. Mzuri," pp. 39–40;
> "Mzuri" is Swahili for "good") [141]

Mazrui's reply to Karioki, as Soyinka had promised, appeared in *Transition* no. 46 (as "Africa, My Conscience, and I," pp. 67–71), and the debate about Mazrui continued also thereafter in *Transition*'s now much reduced Letters section. Although he took pains to point out logical flaws and factual errors in Karioki's denunciation of him, Mazrui's response was otherwise more bemused than aggrieved. Karioki, Mazrui said, paid him an inadvertent compliment: if Mazrui's writings really were irrelevant, it would hardly have been necessary to take issue with them at such length, so long after their first publication.

The gist of Karioki's antagonism, however, as of Soyinka's, seems really to have been directed more at style than at content; at the combination of symbol with impressionistic observation, of controversiality with independence of outlook, of topicality with irony and indirection. Soyinka meant to purge some of these eccentricities from *Transition*. His editorial revolution aimed at bringing a new urgency and asperity to its style, modifying its tone, and redefining its basic editorial philosophy. Where *Transition* had been brash under Neogy's editorship, it was to be militantly assertive under Soyinka. Where it had often been detached and sardonic under Neogy, it was to be more often severe or impassioned under Soyinka. If the magazine retained its unpredictable independence, its "questing irreverence," as Alfred Friendly, Jr., described it in the *New York Times* (see above, p. 170), was to be chastened—this in spite of the fact that Soyinka's own writing had in the past more often been brash or sardonic than severe.

In addition, *Transition*'s denial of what Christopher Okigbo had called the "black mystique"—"blackness for its own sake"[142]—was now absolutely to be rescinded and reversed. Soyinka's militancy was to be international in its scope, pan-African in its sympathies, and absolute in its racial identity. The new *Transition* was to second *Black Orpheus* in dedicating itself to "blackness for its own sake." Neogy's *Transition* had from time to time shown an interest in the black diaspora (for example, an important critical survey by Langston Hughes, "Two Hundred Years of American Negro Poetry," had appeared in *Transition* no. 24), but it remained for Soyinka to make black America a major focus of the magazine. The first few issues featured articles about Marcus Garvey and Frantz Fanon, interviews with Eldridge Cleaver and Ted Joans, and a special memorial to the Attica Prison uprising.

Soyinka also gave notice, however, that racial assertiveness would not blind the new *Transition* to "the mocking grin of history." *Transition* no. 48 began a feature series entitled "The Anti-Man Cometh," designed by Soyinka as a forum for the evenhanded and unvarnished exposure of mankind's universally shared characteristic—which was not artistic creativity but barbarity and inhumanity. The first installment (a collage of graphic illustrations, firsthand reports, and commentary) bitterly recalled the Attica incident and denounced New York State's harsh response, under orders from then Governor Nelson Rockefeller, to the inmate revolt there. The second installment, in *Transition* no. 49, Soyinka promised, would deal with Idi Amin and "Africa's sleepy conscience" (*Transition* no. 48, p. 75). More than half of number 49, in fact, would be devoted to detailing Amin's brutalities.

Although he had superficially stuck to his plan to do away with *Transition*'s opening editorial section, Soyinka more than made up for the deficiency in the "Commentary" sections that introduced special features. The "Commentary" that introduced the first "Anti-Man" feature, for instance, spelled out in plain terms the new editor's essentially equal distrust of American and African political leaders. Amin's proposed hosting of that year's OAU summit meeting, in particular, was deemed a gross and cynical betrayal of the African masses by the political elite. "No government on this continent," Soyinka wrote, "can pretend any longer that Amin is merely a victim of the foreign press, a misunderstood hero of the African peoples, a rough diamond whose unusual style has earned him the disapproval of a few bourgeois-mannered co-heads of state." He added,

> Amin is *not* a man of the people; he is a man against the people, he is not so much human as anti-man. . . . His antics are no longer amusing, and those who still consider him the finest product of the Black Man's assertiveness should, at the very least, ask themselves why so many of the black men on behalf of whom he is so heartily asserting are horribly dead and others, including his closest Ministers, fled the country.
>
> (p. 45)

In his references to Attica, Soyinka was equally harsh and un-compromising. As an ex-prisoner, as a black man, his sympathies were with the inmates, but he refused a "facile glamorisation" of the inmates as heroes. He expected to find "fascists" on both sides of the bars; nevertheless, for Soyinka, the supreme injustice was the prose-cution of the already brutalized Attica survivors, and the supreme "anti-man" of Attica was Nelson Rockefeller. "As long as the man most responsible for the murder of forty-three men has been left to enjoy the position of the second highest citizen of that society," he wrote, "as long as the criminally guilty of the officials . . . are not prosecuted, it is turning justice upside-down to persecute the survi-vors of that massacre" (p. 47). Nor did Soyinka's "Commentary" stop with Amin and Rockefeller. In a broad condemnation, there were also specific allusions to Francisco Macías Nguema of Equa-torial Guinea, to Jean-Bedel Bokassa of the Central African Republic (then styled the Central African Empire), and to the junta in Chile, as well as to Burundi, Ethiopia, and Somalia.

His choice of Ted Joans as an interview subject in *Transition* no. 48 is also particularly revealing of the elements that colored Soyinka's reversion to the "black mystique." In a way, it is also an interesting reflection of the circumstances surrounding the magazine's founding. Joans, who was interviewed in London for *Transition* no. 48 by Skip Gates, had, after all, been a central figure in the Greenwich Village jazz scene of the 1950s that had so fascinated *Transition*'s founding editor, Rajat Neogy. Joans's interview was the cover feature to *Transition* no. 48, illustrated by a black-and-white photograph showing him with "bold hand extended, nostrils flared," as the introductory blurb to the interview put it (p. 4), pointing an ambiguously accusatory finger at subscribers or potential newsstand purchasers.

The cover, the interview, the Attica memorial—all seemed to add up to a deliberate announcement of black militancy. And yet, like Soyinka, Joans had remained a kind of maverick militant in the 1970s, dedicated to a "partisan" revolution of his own defining. His own poetry had been influenced as much by the "cantor-like chant" (p. 9) of Allen Ginsberg and the surrealism of André Breton as by the racial assertiveness of Langston Hughes or the colloquial radicalism of his friend Imamu Amiri Baraka (the former Leroi Jones). Like Soyinka, moreover, Joans was a sort of inside-out internationalist (spending his summers in Europe and his winters primarily in Mali, where he hoped to found a black cultural institute), speaking up for a kind of universalism—with racial dominance reversed, however, and scores settled. Joans reflected:

> We are at a crucial moment of change. As Frantz Fanon said, Africa must be that which European man never was. We must be something much greater. We must use our black magic and our white magic. (By white magic I mean, say, a jumbo jet, or a telephone.) Our black magic is soulful, something that is withinside, something that can't be taught, something that has to come from our environment, experience, heritage, something deeper than a learned thing. (p. 11)

Asked to choose "the most significant political event" of the past five years, Joans responded, "When the first African guerrilla took the first gun and shot a European. I don't know who he was, but we should plant a giant tree in his memory" (p. 12). He even found in "Brother Amin" something to praise—his "naturalism," his lack of British affectations (pp. 6 and 12). European culture, Joans wrote, was "one big cemetery—dead, dead, and dull, dull" (p. 12).

And yet the solution to cultural stagnation for the black artist was neither in the facile appropriations of African cultural accessories so fashionable in the 1960s (a few words of Swahili, for instance) nor in what Mphahlele had called the "ethnic imperative." Joans had written his own "hand grenade" poems in the sixties, he said— poems that you "pulled the pin out of, threw and BOOM that was it" (p. 8), but those were not, he thought, "my stronger poems." Like Soyinka, he had no use for those who would limit originality for political reasons:

> You see, if we get all constipated, and declare that a brother can't wear this because it's "counter-revolutionary," or a brother can't eat that, because it's not revolutionary, or you can't read *Newsweek* magazine because it's "counter-productive," then we are in trouble. You lose a lot of people that matter, that count. (p. 10)

Joans wanted to bring something of his own, something freely creative, to Africa—or, rather, to pan-Africa. He commented:

> Like André Breton said, if there is a continuation of surrealism, it would come out of the Third World, the dues players [*sic*]. A lot of people are trying to sneak into Britain, but when Judgement Day comes, they won't have to sneak out. We must return to Africa, but not physically, as Malcolm X said. We must become Overseas Africans. (p. 12)

There was even a vision of the role that a magazine like Soyinka's might play in all this. "First of all," Joans said, "we need a mass distributed magazine, another *Black World*, but distributed on the scale of *Ebony*. In fact, it is more important for *Black World* to have that kind of distribution. We as a 'nation of people' (to use Don Lee's term) need a magazine, but a universal one. One sold in Harlem, but in Hong Kong, too" (p. 10).

In a way, Joans predicted *Transition*'s (or rather *Ch'indaba*'s) future. Soyinka continued to peg the magazine's traditional internationalism to a new interest in "blackness for its own sake," and his efforts to achieve fiscal independence eventually led him to the commercialization of its management and diversification of its distribution. With its changed character came a new name, and openhanded overseas subsidy gave way to commerical acquisition.

Transition to Ch'indaba

What is most ironic about Soyinka's radical modifications of *Transition*'s policies and style, however, is that they seem not to have had the slightest effect in deflecting the ire of the magazine's critics. If anything, *Transition*'s detractors, old and new, thrived and multiplied. Although Soyinka had abruptly reversed *Transition*'s editorial course, publicly and deliberately committing it to the ideal of black revolution, the controversies and embarrassments of the old *Transition* continued to stalk the new one. In spite of Soyinka's confident assertions in *Transition* no. 45 about the earlier CIA funding, for example ("For *Transition*, the subject is now closed" [p. 66]), that controversy did not die. In fact, its presence in the background added acrimony to each new controversy Soyinka's outspoken "Commentary" sections touched off. In the resulting atmosphere of distrust, Soyinka became convinced that in order to finally free the magazine from innuendo and suspicion, he must separate it entirely from the International Association for Cultural Freedom. He therefore began to look around for other, less suspect, sources of outside support.[143]

Even more surprising was that the revolutionary stance of Soyinka, and *Transition*, did not make them any less vulnerable than Neogy had been to charges of false liberalism and pro-Western reaction from a rising generation of African writers and intellectuals. In fact, the first skirmishes followed hard on the heels of Karioki's denunciation of Ali Mazrui and seemed almost a provocation, a deliberate challenge to Soyinka's editorial integrity—as if daring him to demonstrate his illiberality by not printing his own chastisers. One such suspicious young intellectual was Neogy's old nemesis, Thandika Mkandawire, whom Soyinka had commissioned to review Paulo Freire's *Pedagogy of the Oppressed* in *Transition* no. 48. Mkandawire promptly made use of the occasion to decry Soyinka's counterproductive "cult of despair," adding in a footnote:

> How Soyinka will transmogrify his life-denying philosophy into the revolutionary calls that he has been making lately is awaited with great

suspense. My suspicion is that in the name of consistency, he will be compelled to abandon one of his positions. You can't have your despair and eat it too! Revolutions eat up despair. (p. 73)

A more lengthy and substantial assault on Soyinka in the same issue came from a trio of young Nigerians—Chinweizu, Onwuchekwa Jemie, and Ihechukwu Madubuike—whose "Towards the Decolonization of African Literature" charged Soyinka with literary neocolonialism and cultural subservience.[144] Reminiscent of Obi Wali's "The Dead End of African Literature" (*Transition* no. 10) in its brashness and venom, this new rebuke charged the first generation of African writers in general, and Soyinka in particular, with copying Western literary styles and parroting Western literary themes in a transparent effort to pander to overseas publishers and critics. The trio's style is perhaps best exemplified by a comment on four lines from Christopher Okigbo's "Distances" ("the only way to go / through the marble archway / to the catatonic pingpong / of the evanescent halo"). "What does this mean?" the three critics asked. "Is this a joke? *Or* is he seriously trying to communicate something, and if so, what?" (p. 30).

The absolute predominance of this school of literary obscurantists, addicted to complexity for its own sake, the trio added, boded ill for African writing. And Soyinka was one of the worst of the lot. Of his best-known and most ambitious poem, they wrote:

> "Idanre" is a failure. At best it is a private cipher meaningful to no one but the poet himself—perhaps. It may be that mystical experience is, in the final analysis, verbally incommunicable. If so, why try? If Soyinka's educated countrymen, who have access to the mythology and local custom that inform the poem, cannot figure out what he is saying, even after several careful readings, then who on earth can? This kind of exercise in senseless narcissism, this publicly enacted retreat into private language must stop. (p. 32)

In an exercise in facetious criticism, the trio even went so far as to "translate" another well-known Soyinka poem, "Malediction," into plain English—after which transformation it became a brief, and rather simple, curse. Why, Chinweizu, Madubuike, and Jemie rhetorically asked, had Soyinka chosen to confuse the issue in the first place?

> The answer is simple: (1) It is voluntary cultural servitude—and worse, servitude to somebody else's dead past. It is a denial of the validity of our own culture. . . . (2) It blocks the channel of cultural transmission. Two hundred years from now, when perhaps everyone has gone to school and our oral literature may have died out, people will go to books to find out how we cursed. (p. 31)

Nor was Soyinka (whose *Dance of the Forests*, alone among his writings, was begrudgingly praised) the only African writer thus excoriated. Okigbo's "Heavensgate," for example, was decried for its "dressed up Christian ritual." Its invocation of an indigenous deity (Idoma) was called "insincere" (p. 33; Okigbo's later poem "Path of Thunder" did, however, draw strong praise). In contrast, Chinweizu, Madubuike, and Jemie praised writers such as Okot p'Bitek, Matei Markwei, and Amos Tutuola whose writing was simple and direct, they said, while bridging the gap between modern realities and traditional imagery. As examples of poems that were deceptively simple, yet capable of yielding "metaphysical profundities" to readers either sensitive or industrious, they cited Blake's "Tyger" and Langston Hughes's "Harlem," along with traditional poems like the Yoruba song "New Yam" and the English nursery rhyme "Humpty Dumpty" (pp. 37 and 54). Of J. P. Clark, however, they wrote, "On the whole his poetry suffers from a blameless blandness" (p. 34).

These young lions were no more gentle with the indigenous critics of the Africa writers:

> The Nigerian critics' preference for textual explication is the scholars' counterpart of the poets' cult of obscurity. Since this type of criticism feeds on poetic obscurity, our insistence on clarity may be taking the yam out of the mouths of a certain breed of critics, but these critics should be able to reinvest their energies in more valuable critical activities. (ibid.)

Chinweizu and company particularly called on African writers to ground their work in the "uncontaminated reservoir of African sensibility," the African oral tradition (p. 36), and to dedicate themselves to writing literature accessible to a wide public of literate Africans, rather than writing "exotic marginalia to the literatures of Europe" (p. 37).

African writers should, in making their idiom coherent, also broaden their range of subjects. Though protest poetry had its value, the trio allowed, it should not be all-pervasive, and "privatist or mystical poetry" (such as Okigbo's and Soyinka's) should give place to poetry at once traditional and dedicated to the realities of everyday life in contemporary Africa:

> A general survey compels us to ask: where is the narrative tale? Where are the parables, fables, paradoxes, myths, legends and proverbs? Our forebears were minters of proverbs; we are their heirs, are we not? Where is the poetry of tenderness that conveys the tenderness and does not merely refer to it? Where are the celebrations of laughter and joy? . . . Where is the choral poetry . . . ? Where are the love songs, the songs of courtship, wedding songs, farm songs, . . . funeral dirges, hunting songs, drinking songs, the songs that celebrate absences, deaths . . . ? Our forebears were entertainers; we are their heirs, are we not?

"We ask," the trio added, "that privatist poetry be made lucid and accessible, and that our protest voices should not be turned exclusively outward to Europe, to America, to audiences of white faces." They concluded, "Our poets should stop regarding themselves as primarily orphic messengers to the West" (p. 37).

Though Soyinka's moratorium on the subject of *Transition* and the CIA and his truncation of the *Transition* Letters section made clear that he did not feel duty bound to chastise himself with every new rebuke that came in over the transom, he printed "Towards the Decolonization of African Literature" side by side with a pointed and detailed rebuttal under the title "Neo-Tarzanism: The Poetics of Pseudo-Tradition" (*Transition* no. 48, pp. 38–44), echoing an earlier *Transition* controversy. Soyinka's grounds for accusing Chinweizu, Madubuike, and Jemie of "Tarzanism" was what he saw as their facile reduction of the African tradition to fit their own one-dimensional prejudices. Like the colonial ethnomusicologists for whom African polyrhythms amounted to no more than childlike cacophony, the critical "troika" was blind to the deliberate complexity, syntactic disjunction, and subtle rhythmic texture of traditional indigenous poetry. There was as much "sprung rhythm" in traditional Yoruba poetry, Soyinka argued, as in the poetry of Gerard Manley Hopkins that he was alleged to have copied.

Although Soyinka was complimentary in his assessment of Chinweizu's and Jemie's own poetry and was willing to admit, in response to charges of deliberate obscurity, that "some of the examples they provide are justified" (p. 43), he was unwilling to back down on the essential issue:

> Just as critics like [Sunday] Anozie [in his study of Christopher Okigbo] do not help by clogging up understanding further by undue fascination with structuralist faddism, nor a Paul Theroux [in *Black Orpheus* no. 20] by abdicating critical judgment as premature, the Simple Simons of criticism, as represented by Chinweizu and Company, subvert the principle of imaginative challenge which is one of the functions of poetry. And the denigration and misunderstanding of traditional forms of African art should now stop. (ibid.)

Even Christian symbolism, he added, could not be banned from African poetry, since modern Africa was naturally full of Christian religious symbolism, just as it was full of enthusiastic Christians (pp. 41–42).

Nor did Soyinka hesitate to match his antagonists' venom with some of his own. Chinweizu, Madubuike, and Jemie, he suggested, in light of the deficiencies of their critical understanding of traditional African literature, would be best advised to confine themselves "to extolling the virtues of European nursery rhymes—a field which appears more suited to the analytical capacity of our critical troika" (p. 38). He then proceeded to lacerate them for their misunderstanding, among other things, of the historical context that had given rise to "Humpty Dumpty" and on which it was a commentary. Of their comparison of the nursery rhyme to Blake's and Hughes's poems, Soyinka sarcastically commented, "Is this a joke? Or are our critical troika indulging in that mystification of which they accuse other critics and poets?" (p. 39).

He was, moreover, particularly offended by Chinweizu, Madubuike, and Jemie's all-out attack on Okigbo's early poetry (even though he admitted his own occasional "irritation" with it). Their grounds of an insufficient "social commitment" he found contradictory and inadequate: Okigbo had been "damned because he has larded his poems with christian and private mythology, though, 'luckily for him, just before his death,' he was saved by events which gave him a public voice." "We hope," Soyinka commented, "that our three-headed Pontifex Maximus Simplicissimus will not keep poor Christopher Okigbo burning too long in Purgatory" (p. 43). As much as anyone else—"the carpenter, the mason, the banker, the farmer, the customs officer *etc.*"—a poet ought to have the right, Soyinka concluded, to devote only a part of himself to social commitment; yet he was expected to work at commitment twenty-four hours a day. "That non-stop mandate is miraculously reserved for the artist alone" (p. 43).

Although Chinweizu, Madubuike, and Jemie showed no inclination to let the controversy die with this one exchange, Soyinka eventually decided that what he considered irresponsible extravagance had gone far enough. He did not print further denunications by the "critic-trio" or respond when these appeared elsewhere. Originally, he writes, he had "expected not only their response but the response of readers—some of which I certainly intended to publish in one single issue, with their own response being just one of others." When it came, however, the response of the "critic-trio" seemed to Soyinka to be evidence that its authors had taken leave at least of their equanimity and sense of fair play, if not of their senses. And at any rate, what had started as simple charge and countercharge had certainly by now hardened into indiscriminate invective. "So the question was," Soyinka writes, "did this . . . belong on the pages of *Ch'indaba*? My answer was no. There was no moral dilemma involved. I merely asked myself the question: would I publish such material on any subject under the sun? Answer—No."[145] To participate further would be to encourage the irresponsible sensationalism that he had seen as a chief flaw of Neogy's *Transition*. For Soyinka, integrity did not require an editor to print contributions whose absolute quality, or even relevance, he questioned.

Neogy and Mazrui had, moreover, been inclined to open *Transition* to a wide variety of antagonists as long as an objective standard in the logic and evidence of debate was approximated. Soyinka, on the other hand, was sometimes inclined to cut off debate when he saw its ends or purposes as idle or counterproductive. Ugandan writer and critic Erisa Kironde, for instance, who had been one of *Transition*'s first contributors and whose family had suffered greatly at the hands of Amin, submitted to Soyinka an article that, though critical overall, gave the devil his due in pointing out certain positive offshoots of Amin's presidency. Heatedly engaged in an editorial campaign to publicize Amin's reign of terror, however, Soyinka saw such broad-minded allusions as politically misguided and declined to provide Amin with ammunition for propaganda by printing them.[146]

One must not overemphasize this point. In spite of the magazine's newly defined "partisanship," and its impatience with forensic "lather[s] of sweat," Soyinka also worked hard in his first few issues to promote an even tone of scholarly detachment on nonpolitical topics. A series of such articles seemed meant in their "seriousness" to stand as an antidote to what Soyinka saw as the flippancy of the old *Transition*. In addition to Mphahlele's "The Function of Literature at the Present Time," for instance, there were several articles that sought to define the African aesthetic idiom in the arts, including one, "The Artist and the Issue of Relevance" by Moyibi Amoda (*Transition* no. 45, pp. 38–45), that seemed remarkably close to Soyinka's own critical perspective and political commitment.[147] Another on the plastic arts by Dennis Duerden ("Art and Technical Progress," *Transition* no. 45, pp. 27–37) advanced with scrupulous scholarly detail the thesis that contemporary Western art and traditional African art shared a fundamental aversion to the notion of art as a permanent memorial or capital investment, emphasizing instead its functional value, its temporariness, and its value as "performance."[148]

Nevertheless, "seriousness" seemed sometimes to override detachment. The last word on the "Decolonization"/"Neo-Tarzanism" debate came not from Chinweizu, Madubuike, and Jemie, nor from Soyinka, but from another Nigerian, Stanley Macebuh. Macebuh devoted an extensive, precise article in *Transition* no. 50/*Ch'indaba* no. 1 ("Poetics and the Mythic Imagination," pp. 79–84) to a close analysis of Soyinka's aesthetic as deriving from, and fruitfully reflecting in a contemporary mode, traditional Yoruba myths, "cultic diction," and aesthetic attitudes. Fair enough so far—except that Macebuh also proceeded to echo Soyinka's argument that the authors of "Decolonization" had grossly misunderstood traditional African literature. It was hardly fair to print Macebuh's criticisms of them, but not Chinweizu, Madubuike, and Jemie's response to Soyinka's initial criticism. Macebuh's was an impressive critical performance, and it did succeed in bringing to the debate fresh and substantial critical perspectives. Nevertheless, it left Chinweizu and his collaborators out in the cold with the conviction, as they later charged in Chinua Achebe's literary review, *Okike*, that their access to free debate had been stifled in Wole Soyinka's *Transition*.[149]

An Anniversary, and a Quiet Death

Ultimately, Wole Soyinka's discomfort with the legacy of the old *Transition*—its quarrels, its patronage, the very lingering vestiges of its personality—determined him upon a course of action that was eventually to end both his editorship and the magazine's publication. First, he decided to make explicit the magazine's changed personality and commitment by changing its name, thereby instituting a new editorial series. Second, he decided to take the risky step of blindly and unilaterally renouncing the magazine's long-time sponsor, the International Association for Cultural Freedom (which ironically had a few years before been so eager for his appointment as editor). Henceforth, there would be no sly innuendos about the sources of *Transition*'s funding,[150] since the magazine would, it announced, thereafter be published "solely and independently by Transition, Ltd." (*Transition* no. 49, inside front cover). Soyinka had not yet found a substitute source of subsidy. He was simply taking up his own dare—hoisting responsibility for the magazine's economic fate squarely onto his (and its) own shoulders.

Fittingly, the issue with which the change of name was to be initiated was also to be an anniversary number, *Transition*'s fiftieth, in which a special center section of reprints from early numbers was to appear. The new name—a bilingual coinage of Soyinka's from *cha*, Swahili for "to dawn," and *indaba*, Ndebele (or Zulu) for a great assembly—meant, he said, let the great "Colloquium" of the people begin (*Transition* no. 50/*Ch'indaba* no. 1, p. 6), and it was intended to signify a dedication to new ideals, both for the magazine and for Africa. The old name, *Transition*, connoted some halfway state between servitude and independence; the new name, *Ch'indaba*, would connote completion, initiation, and celebration of a pan-African unity and selfhood based on Soyinka's brand of cultural and political idealism.

The simultaneously ironic and hopeful allusion in the magazine's new title was intended to have been to the second international black arts festival (FESTAC), which, as originally scheduled, would have coincided with *Transition*'s death and resurrection as *Ch'indaba*. The festival had, however, been "indefinitely postponed"[151] by its Nigerian sponsors—through political and commercial chicanery, Soyinka hinted. Nevertheless, if there was no actual festival for the new magazine to celebrate, there was what he hoped would be a symbolic one: the coincidence of a new African cultural awareness with a new magazine dedicated to promoting that awareness.

One fragment of the special festival supplement was retained, a facetious prayer of libation:

> May the actual festival in Africa be protected from such a preponderance of all that is gaudy, cheap, commercial, and dispiriting in the pop-cult of the Euramerican world.[152] May we never again be assaulted and misrepresented by this confusion of a hysterical, eye-on-the-buck culture with the authentic sounds of African musicality. . . . May all such negations of the human sensibility meet unnatural ends on the earth of OBATALA, SANGO, ALA, OYA, OGUN, be shamed by the revolutionary art of the Black World of Cuba, Bahia, Guinea, Mozambique among others, crushed by the genuine explorations of the limitless idioms of human expression, traditional, contemporary or futuristic. . . .
>
> In short, may the millions of petro-naira [i.e., Nigerian oil revenues] which have been poured into bottomless holes, raise, at least, the authentic consciousness of the African peoples and especially of their Nigerian hosts, the masses of whom will derive no benefit whatever from this Roman circus, while they patiently await the day when there will be something truly lasting to celebrate, something that will be self-manifested as a genuine Fiesta of the People, not the self-glorification and prestige-hunting distraction from realities, by a handful.
>
> (*Transition* no. 50/*Ch'indaba* no. 1, p. 84)

In spite of himself, it seems, Soyinka could not resist a little "questing irreverence" of his own.

The cover to this last *Transition* and first *Ch'indaba* was a reversible and invertible pairing of the two names, unified graphically with an adaptation of the bar design from the covers of the first few *Transition*s and with the figures "50 + 1." The front cover was repeated on the inside back cover, and on the back cover and inside front cover were reproductions of a painting by Ato Delaquis, a Ghanaian artist and illustrator whose feature series about "The Dilemma of the Contemporary African Artist" would run in *Transition* no. 50/*Ch'indaba* no. 1 and *Ch'indaba* no. 2. The anniversary center section, forty-four pages on light green onionskin paper, was meant, Soyinka said, "to catch the flavour of the intellectual atmosphere in Africa, but most especially in East Africa and Uganda, that gave birth to this magazine" (p. 4).

It was an odd performance, however. Here were not, for the most part, the early pieces for which Neogy's *Transition* was most often remembered, but sidelights, oddities, and academic and political ironies. Letters were included that referred to some of *Transition*'s better-known pieces, but the articles to which they referred were not themselves included. Ali Mazrui, as has been noted, was represented by what must certainly have been his least well remembered contribution. One of the longest extracts, in fact, was a reprint of a reprint from a 1964 United Nations Special Committee report on torture in South Africa. There were, to be sure, Langston Hughes's "Two Hundred Years of American Negro Poetry," and Rajat Neogy's thoughtful essay from *Transition* no. 24, "Do Magazines Culture?" There were Abiola Irele's "A Defence of Négritude," Tom Mboya's "African Socialism," and Wole Soyinka's own "Towards a True Theatre"—important, substantial articles all. But they were not broadly representative of Neogy's *Transition*, and the "flavour" that Soyinka captured was more what he *wished* had predominated in Neogy's *Transition*, rather than what more commonly *had* predominated.

The remainder of *Transition* no. 50/*Ch'indaba* no. 1, which after all was to be *Transition*'s last issue, was otherwise remarkable for its continuity, not with Neogy's *Transition*, but with Soyinka's. The "Anti-Man" series, for example, far from being a passing irony, had become a central feature in the magazine, and, not surprisingly, a controversial one. *Transition* no. 49, for instance, had featured a cover illustration every bit as provocative and memorable as the "Tarzan" and "Leninist Czar" covers (of *Transition* nos. 32 and 26, respectively). Keyed to a pointed continuation of the reports on atrocities in Amin's Uganda, *Transition* no. 49's cover superimposed over a portrait of the General the word *Karasi*, meaning "Finish him" in Nubian. To the outraged complaints of some readers that this was after all incitement to political assassination, Soyinka denied intending any such suggestion. "We disclaim all credit," he wrote.

> The credit for the word . . . belongs entirely to Field Marshal Idi Amin Dada, D.S.O. *etc.*, *etc.* . . . Whenever his next victim has been snatched and locked up in the car boot . . . the merry Marshal is informed by telephone, upon which glad tidings he barks the word "KARASI." We have this on the authority of his ex-Foreign Minister and brother-in-law, Wanume Kibedi, and others. (p. 2)

That installment of the "Anti-Man" series had featured a long open letter from Kibedi, who had been Uganda's foreign minister from 1971 to 1973, to Amin, denouncing him for a list of specific atrocities. *Transition* no. 50/*Ch'indaba* no. 1 featured another lengthy installment in the series, this one by the English journalist Colin Legum, again focusing attention on a detailed description of Amin's brutalities, in a straightforward effort to break through the curtain of indifference and silence that Legum (and Soyinka) felt African political leaders and their government journalists had erected around Uganda ("Behind the Clown's Mask," pp. 86–96).

Transition no. 50/*Ch'indaba* no. 1 also demonstrated once again, if it needed demonstrating, that Wole Soyinka was not one who hesitated to take absolute political positions—as he did for instance in backing Julius Nyerere's refusal to take part in that year's OAU summit, which Amin was to host. The full text of Nyerere's press declaration on the subject was printed in *Transition* no. 50/*Ch'indaba* no. 1 alongside Colin Legum's "Behind the Clown's Mask." Soyinka's determination to commit himself, and therefore the magazine, to active involvement, not "futile token twitches," was further exemplified in *Transition* no. 50/*Ch'indaba* no. 1 by his announcement of the formation of an organization that was to have important influence in cases of political detention—the Union of Writers of the African Peoples. Founded, among others, by Soyinka, Ayi Kwei Armah, Dennis Brutus, and Ngugi wa Thiong'o, the union was soon thereafter to demonstrate its effectiveness as a vehicle for humanitarian indignation through its protest to Ghanaian authorities against the detention of Kofi Awoonor.[153]

The union's initial declaration bore the sure marks of Soyinka's own characteristically unequivocal hand:

> The Union of African Writers, aware of nameless atrocities perpetrated on Africans in Africa by external forces as well as by African authorities[,] hereby expresses its vigorous condemnation of such atrocities wherever they do occur. This Union wishes to stress its profound indignation against all attempts at the denial of human dignity, freedom and security as is currently the situation in Uganda and South Africa, not to mention the other concentration camps on the continent.

It closed with yet another strong statement of opposition to the venue of the forthcoming OAU meeting and to the fact that the honorary chairmanship of that organization would consequently pass to Amin (pp. 14–15).

Soyinka had thus systematically and deliberately completed the transformation and redefinition that he had envisioned for *Transition*. Soyinka's magazine was at once partisan and controversial, independent and iconoclastic. Soyinka had determined also to commit his *Transition* to a new "seriousness" of purpose and style that would convince readers that *Transition* had outgrown its troubled adolescence at last.

He certainly did succeed in publishing first-rate scholarly and intellectual articles. How "new" this was for the magazine was another question. Nevertheless, one should not fail to credit the exceptional depth and variety of perspectives Soyinka's scholarly and academic contributors brought to what remained, after all, essentially a popular magazine, although one aimed at an intelligent, educated audience. For example, in the special series on the contemporary African artistic milieu that Soyinka had initiated in *Transition* no. 45 and continued through *Transition* no. 50/*Ch'indaba* no. 1, there were extensive treatments, thoroughly researched, yet pointed in their conclusions, of everything from "Art and Technical Progress" to social commitment in art and the validity of cultural ethnocentrism. *Ch'indaba* nos. 2 and 3, Soyinka announced in *Transition* no. 50/*Ch'indaba* no. 1, were to be dedicated to an inquiry into African philosophy. Of course, Neogy's *Transition* had had its own fair share of careful, scholarly contributors, and Soyinka's *Transition/Ch'indaba*, moreover, could on occasion be as partisan, as metaphoric, and as ironical as writers such as Theroux or Mazrui had been in the old *Transition*.

At this point in the magazine's history (if indeed *Transition* and *Ch'indaba* can be spoken of as sharing one editorial history), with money becoming scarce (the IACF subsidy having been relinquished), and economic and political conditions in Ghana becoming difficult as the result of government mismanagement and an unsuccessful coup attempt against Colonel Acheampong, Soyinka faced the task of modifying the magazine's managerial and editorial arrangements if he was to save *Ch'indaba* from creeping inanition.[154] Having found no politically acceptable source of subsidy, he tried to find a way to put *Ch'indaba* on a commercial footing. He decided, first, to renounce the editorship and return to Nigeria, and second, to put *Ch'indaba* in the hands of outside publishers, who would also take over ownership.

One of Neogy's outspoken critics, following in the track of Yambo, Kallu-Kalumiya, and Mkandawire, had been a young Kenyan named E. B. Z. Kitaka, who had crudely, and somewhat coyly, abused Neogy for becoming "obsessed," "peevish," and "effeminately fretful" in the aftermath of his detention. Kitaka also charged Neogy with "escapism and intellectual cowardice" (*Transition* no. 42, p. 6). Though it had once been "well known as the best forum for divergent views in Africa," *Transition*, Kitaka charged, now stood in danger of being overshadowed by "that nascent magazine they call *Africa*." Ironically, it was to be to this periodical, *Africa Magazine*, that Soyinka ultimately transferred the management of *Ch'indaba*.

Ch'indaba nos. 2 and 3 appeared behind schedule, Soyinka concentrating on editorial matters and hunting new support while the long-distance managerial arrangement worked itself out. Soyinka's growing desperation is evidenced by the cover to *Ch'indaba* no. 2, in which red block letters on a flat pea-green field asked, "Should *Ch'indaba* Survive?"—answering with a parenthetic reference, "see pages 1–72" (the entire contents of that issue). A more direct plea for support appeared in the publisher's announcement—and on the second last page of the issue, p. 71, in the form of the single word "Help!!" Material for a fourth number of *Ch'indaba* was assembled as well. Soon thereafter, however, Soyinka again had begun to concentrate on his own affairs, while *Africa Magazine* began the process of arranging for his replacement as editor-in-chief.[155] Eventually, in 1977, Soyinka having accepted a professorship in comparative literature at the University of Ife, a Ugandan was chosen to succeed him as editor of *Ch'indaba*. Arrangements were still incomplete, however, and *Ch'indaba* no. 4 was not yet ready for press more than a year later in January 1979, when Amin's overthrow by invading Tanzanian forces induced the sudden departure of the new editor-designate and upset all the arrangements. Unfortunately, by then there had been so many costly delays and difficulties that *Africa Magazine* decided to abandon its plans to resurrect *Ch'indaba*.

In a curious way, the CIA controversy had finally killed *Transition* after all. Although the magazine had not succumbed to the original uproar over the CIA disclosures, it was in the end Soyinka's frustration over his inability to put them completely behind him, nearly ten years later, that made him decide to renounce the IACF sponsorship that had for so long kept the magazine afloat. Cut loose from dependable sponsorship, *Ch'indaba* did not stay afloat for long. A more moderate editor might certainly have succeeded in preserving the magazine, but Soyinka felt strongly that guaranteeing *Ch'indaba*'s solvency was an empty exercise unless he could also credibly certify its integrity. Moreover, though Soyinka very much regretted its passing, the magazine's fate, once he had returned to Nigeria, was practically out of his hands. He had had every assurance that it would be continued.

Though much shorter-lived than Neogy's, Soyinka's editorship had, in its different ways, brought to *Transition* its own accomplishments—as a vehicle for leading, challenging, and redefining cultural, social, and political change. Though Soyinka's maverick political eclecticism placed the magazine at greater risk than had Neogy's democratic pluralism, and put greater strains on its editorial consistency, both editorial regimes were successful, and both in the end fell victim to the mounting factionalization of African politics. Under both sets of editors and editorial associates, *Transition* was remarkable for its iconoclasm and idealism, its independence and originality. Although *Transition* in the end succumbed quietly, with no government police pounding at its door, the climate of acrimony, intolerance, and repression that Neogy had first faced in Uganda and had tried to escape by emigrating in the end returned to plague the magazine all the more in newer and subtler forms. Although Ghana had remained friendly enough even after the ascension to power of its military dictatorship, the political factionalism of Africa as a whole had brought a new bitterness to debate and an intractability to disagreements. Soyinka's *Transition* (and *Ch'indaba*), in its eccentric originality and self-driven "partisanship," might have had an uphill pull even in a more tolerant intellectual climate. In Africa in the seventies, even the will and force of personality of a Wole Soyinka barely sustained it in the face of antagonism from all sides.

It was not at all remarkable that *Transition* ultimately made itself bitter enemies. The magazine had been having it both ways for eighteen years: stubbornly steaming along a path that defined it as both politically controversial and editorially balanced, a vehicle for both debate and dispassionate reflection. Its editors had carried off an impossible editorial philosophy for years by sheer determination, conviction, and persistence. The crowning irony, indeed, may be that in the end *Transition* survived most of its antagonists and lived through its most famous pitched battles only to die quietly in temporary retirement under an assumed name. Managerial and economic uncertainty had made the appearance of *Ch'indaba* so problematic and irregular that many former contributors, readers, and supporters were unaware or uncertain of its passing.

Hardly mourned, that passing has not been made good. There

are new literary, artistic, and cultural magazines published in anglophone Africa: in Nigeria, for example, Chinua Achebe's *Okike* provides both educational materials for the Nigerian colleges and a forum for new writing and criticism; *Black Orpheus*, revived at last under its fourth editorial regime, with Theo Vincent as editor-in-chief, seeks to build upon the impetus left over from J. P. Clark's editorial tenure; and Demas Nwoko's brash, privately produced artistic review, *New Culture*, seeks to challenge a newborn cultural avant-garde.[156] Nevertheless, there is no new *Transition*—no one widely distributed, high-quality intellectual magazine covering the broad canvas of the arts, society, politics, and economics, daring in its opinions and experiments yet of independent probity.

One hardly feels inclined to fault Soyinka or Neogy for not finding some way to continue with their journal. After all, Neogy's editorship lasted more than a dozen years, and Soyinka has always been intensely active as a writer, scholar, critic, and teacher. For an intellectual magazine, *Transition* was actually rather long-lived. However much one feels its absence, the tragedy is not that it died but that it left no progeny.

Appendix: Chronology

The publishing schedules of both magazines were irregular, sometimes extremely so, but *Black Orpheus* was meant to appear three times a year and *Transition* six times a year.

Ulli Beier's issues of *Black Orpheus* were designated volume 1 by later editors J. P. Clark and Abiola Irele, whose own issues became volumes 2 and 3. Theo Vincent's revival of the magazine was volume 4. The volume number is omitted in citation of Beier's issues, but is given for volumes 2, 3, and 4 to distinguish them.

Rajat Neogy's schemes for dividing *Transition* into volumes and issues were contradictory and confusing. Later issues sometimes appeared with two different volume numbers, as well as a second issue number. Number 26, for instance, was elaborately styled "Number 26, 3–1966, Volume 6 (i)." Some issues were dated by month and year, others just by year. Since issues were simply numbered consecutively, without repetition, however, they were commonly identified by issue number alone, and that procedure is followed in this book.

Issues were dated as in the following chronologies:

Black Orpheus

No. 1	September 1957
No. 2	January 1958
No. 3	May 1958
No. 4	October 1958
No. 5	May 1959

No. 6	November 1959
No. 7	June 1960
No. 8	n.d. [1960–61]
No. 9	June 1961
No. 10	n.d. [1961–62]
No. 11	n.d. [1962?]
No. 12	n.d. [1963?]
No. 13	November 1963
No. 14	February 1964
No. 15	August 1964
No. 16	October 1964
No. 17	June 1965
No. 18	October 1965
No. 19	March 1966
No. 20	August 1966
No. 21	April 1967
No. 22	August 1967
VOLUME 2, No. 1	February 1968
No. 2	June/September 1968
No. 3	n.d. [1969]
No. 4	n.d. [1969]
Nos. 5/6	n.d. [late 1970]
No. 7	n.d. [1972]
VOLUME 3, No. 1	January/June 1974
Nos. 2/3	October/December 1974– January/June 1975
VOLUME 4, No. 1	[1982]
No. 2	[1982]

Transition

No. 1	November 1961
No. 2	December 1961

No. 3	January 1962
No. 4	June 1962
No. 5	30 July to 29 August 1962
No. 6/7	October 1962
No. 8	March 1963
No. 9	April/May 1963
No. 10	September 1963
No. 11	November 1963
No. 12	January/February 1964
No. 13	March/April 1964
No. 14	May/June 1964
No. 15	July/August 1964
No. 16	September/October 1964
No. 17	November/December 1964
No. 18	1965
No. 19	1965
No. 20	1965
No. 21	1965
No. 22	1965
No. 23	1965
No. 24	1966
No. 25	1966
No. 26	1966
No. 27	1966
No. 28	1967
No. 29	February/March 1967
No. 30	April/May 1967
No. 31	June/July 1967
No. 32	August/September 1967
No. 33	October/November 1967
No. 34	December 1967/January 1968
No. 35	February/March 1968
No. 36	1968
No. 37	1968
No. 38	1971
No. 39	1971

No. 40	1971
No. 41	1972
No. 42	1973
No. 43	1973
No. 44	1974
No. 45	n.d. [1974]
No. 46	October/December 1974
No. 47	January/March 1975
No. 48	April/June 1975
No. 49	July/September 1975

Transition/Ch'indaba

Transition no. 50/*Ch'indaba* no. 1	October 1975/March 1976
Ch'indaba no. 2	July/December 1976
Ch'indaba no. 3	1977[?]

Notes

Introduction

1. For a chronology of the magazines, see Appendix.
2. John Hanning Speke, *Journal of the Discovery of the Source of the Nile* (New York: E. P. Dutton, 1906), pp. 231, 220–21.
3. John Gunther, *Inside Africa* (New York: Harper and Bros., 1955), p. 424.
4. See Henry Kyemba, *A State of Blood* (New York: Grosset and Dunlap, 1978), p. 22.
5. Rajat Neogy, telephone interview with the author, August 8, 1984.
6. *Time*, February 9, 1953, quoted in Gunther, *Inside Africa*, pp. 771–72.
7. Chinweizu, Onwuchekwa Jemie, and Ihechukwu Madubuike, "The Leeds-Ibadan Connection: The Scandal of Modern African Literature," *Okike* 13 (1979): 37–46; rpt. in *Towards the Decolonization of African Literature* (Enugu, Nigeria: Fourth Dimension, 1980), pp. 196–208.
8. Tutuola's *The Palm-Wine Drinkard* appeared in 1952; Achebe's *Things Fall Apart* in 1958.

I. "Border Operators": *Black Orpheus* and Artistic Genesis

1. Ulli Beier's issues of *Black Orpheus* will be cited here by issue number alone. For a detailed chronology, see Appendix. Ezekiel Mphahlele's "Writers and Commitment" appeared in *Black Orpheus* 2, no. 3; the quotation used as the first epigraph to Part I of this book is from p. 39. John Thompson's remarks excerpted as the second epigraph were made in the course of an interview with the author at the Rockefeller Foundation, New York, on July 29, 1980.
2. Beier functioned as a catalyst for some artists, introducing them to new techniques and encouraging their earliest creative efforts. Others, such as Nwoko, were already sophisticated artists, but Beier helped give their work wider currency.

3. Abiola Irele, interview with the author at the Rockefeller Foundation, April 2, 1980.

4. Sources for this biographical information are a 1977 *curriculum vitae*; Beier's entry in *The International Authors and Writers Who's Who*, 8th ed. (Cambridge, 1977); a letter from Beier to the author dated August 21, 1981; and the Thompson interview cited in note 1 above.

5. Before founding *Black Orpheus*, Beier was co-editor of *Odu*, a scholarly journal of Yoruba studies.

6. Transcription Centre audiotape of a discussion with Beier and Gerald Moore of the aims of the magazine, moderated by Andrew Salkey (1966). I have used copies of the Transcription Centre audiotapes housed in the New York Public Library's Schomburg Center for Research in Black Culture.

7. Letter from Beier to the author, August 21, 1981.

8. Transcription Centre audiotape of Beier, Moore, and Salkey.

9. Ibid.

10. Ibid.

11. Ibid.

12. Ibid.

13. Beier, letter to the author, August 21, 1981.

14. Wole Soyinka's gibe about the tiger not needing to vaunt his "tigritude" was only one of many negative reactions among anglophone writers. See Abiola Irele, "A Defense of Negritude," *Transition* no. 13; rpt. *Transition* no. 50/*Ch'indaba* no. 1, pp. 39–41.

15. A second notice by "Akanji" (this time of a Lagos exhibition of Wenger's work sponsored by *Nigeria Magazine*) was, if anything, even more laudatory. See *Black Orpheus* no. 7, pp. 34–35.

16. Lewis Nkosi, Transcription Centre audiotape, London (?), 1963.

17. Christopher Okigbo, interviewed by Dennis Duerden, Transcription Centre audiotape, London, August 1963.

18. Though black writers continued to predominate in the magazine, there was room in numbers 16 and 17 to print a selection of poems by Paul Theroux that exhibited no obvious African affinities (pp. 16–20 and 8–10, respectively). Theroux influenced a group of key Nigerian poets and was much admired by Okigbo; Beier, who did not otherwise especially admire Theroux's poetry, published him on those grounds alone. Beier, letter to the author, August 21, 1981.

19. Beier, letter to the author, August 21, 1981.

20. Transcription Centre audiotape of Beier, Moore, and Salkey.

21. Ibid.

22. Beier, letter to Robert July, July 28, 1960. Rockefeller Foundation files.

23. Bernth Lindfors, "A Decade of *Black Orpheus*," *Books Abroad* 42 (Autumn 1968): 510.

24. Transcription Centre audiotape of Beier, Moore, and Salkey.

25. Beier, letter to the author, August 21, 1981.

26. Ibid.

27. Robert July, diary entry, February 26, 1960. Rockefeller Foundation files.

28. Beier, letters to Robert July stamped as received February 14, 1961, and June 6, 1961. Rockefeller Foundation files.

29. Beier, letter to Robert July received May 18, 1962. Rockefeller Foundation files.

30. Thompson interview cited in note 1 above.

31. Beier, proposal to the Rockefeller Foundation for a travel grant, forwarded to Robert July with a letter dated July 28, 1960.

32. Transcription Centre audiotape of Beier, Moore, and Salkey.

33. Transcription Centre audiotape of Christopher Okigbo, Dennis Duerden, and John Nagenda, London, August 1963.

34. See, for instance, Chinweizu, Onwuchekwa Jemie, and Ihechukwu Madubuike, "Towards the Decolonization of African Literature," *Transition* no. 48 (April/June 1975): 29–37, 54–57.

35. Transcription Centre audiotape of Beier, Moore, and Salkey.

36. Ibid.

37. Among the modernist poets that Beier and Moore saw as influencing the new university-educated Nigerian poets were Gerard Manley Hopkins, Dylan Thomas, and Ezra Pound. See their introduction to *Modern Poetry from Africa* (Harmondsworth, Middlesex: Penguin Books, 1963), p. 22. Chinweizu, Jemie, and Madubuike emphasize the influence of Hopkins in their criticism of this group of writers in "Towards the Decolonization of African Literature" and "The Hopkins Disease," *Okike* 6, 7, and 12; rpt. in the volume *Towards the Decolonization of African Literature*.

38. Beier, report forwarded to Robert July with a letter received September 24, 1962. Rockefeller Foundation files.

39. In *Black Orpheus* no. 2, p. 29, Beier described Wenger as having studied Jungian psychology before she came to Africa.

40. Abstract expressionists such as Mark Rothko, for instance, also extolled the undistorted artistic eye of children and "naive" adult primitives.

41. The debate about the quality of the naive artists reminds one of the debate about Tutuola, another Beier favorite. See J. P. Clark, "The Legacy of Caliban," *Black Orpheus* 2, no. 1, pp. 16–39.

42. Michael Crowder, interview with the author, Bellagio, Italy, September 20, 1980.

43. Beier, letter to the author, August 21, 1981.

44. Transcription Centre audiotape of Beier, Moore, and Salkey. Beier cited three experimental stories as worthy of note: E. A. James' "Brion and the Flames"; Adrienne Cornell's "Because of the King of France"; and Camara Laye's "The Eyes of the Statue." Of these, only Laye was an African, however, and his reputation was already established.

45. Lindfors, "A Decade of *Black Orpheus*," p. 515.

46. Beier, letter to the author, August 21, 1981. On the one occasion in which "Akanji" did appear in the contributors notes, in *Black Orpheus* no. 4, there were clues to the writer's real identity: "'Akanji' describes himself as a 'detribalized Yoruba.' Born abroad, he lived most of his life in Europe and the Near East. He has recently returned to Nigeria in order to 'rediscover his lost Yoruba self.'"

47. Even O. R. Dathorne, who contributed many reviews and served for a time as review editor, was, though black, an expatriate.

48. Erich Auerbach, *Mimesis*, trans. Willard Trask (Princeton, N.J.: Princeton University Press, 1968), p. 23.

49. As noted by Moore, Transcription Centre audiotape of Beier, Moore, and Salkey.

50. Crowder, interview with the author, September 20, 1980.

51. Beier, letter to the author, August 21, 1981.

52. Transcription Centre audiotape of Beier, Moore, and Salkey.

53. Ibid.

54. Abiola Irele, interview with the author, Rockefeller Foundation, New York, April 2, 1980.

55. Irele, Clark, and their colleagues were relatively unperturbed by the news for the simple reason that *Black Orpheus*, unlike *Transition* under Rajat Neogy and Wole Soyinka, for example, had always been so obviously nonpolitical.

56. Irele, interview with the author, April 2, 1980.

57. Even in the midst of the crisis, Irele recalled, Okigbo continued to keep in touch with Clark, Higo, and Irele by telephone from Enugu, as did Achebe and other influential Ibo intellectuals.

58. Beier, letter to the author, August 21, 1981.

59. The slight delay had been occasioned by yet another stratagem for regularizing support: the editors had talked the *Daily Times* of Lagos into handling printing and distribution. Unfortunately, the arrangement was short-lived. Irele, interview with the author, April 2, 1980.

60. Part of the hostility toward Beier was a residue of the dismantling of Mbari Ibadan; part simply related to his domination of cultural matters in Nigeria. Before leaving Nigeria in 1966, Beier also made, or was reported to have made, a statement to the effect that "all the talent had gone east" with the civil war, a remark that rankled among non-Ibos.

61. Theo Vincent, interview with the author, Gainesville, Florida, April 1980.

62. Vincent's long-delayed revival of the magazine in 1982 quickly produced two new issues of *Black Orpheus*, predated to 1978 and 1980 respectively and styled volume 4.

63. Abdul R. Yesufu, *Research in African Literatures* 14, no. 4 (Winter 1983): 545.

64. Achebe and Soyinka, for example, have been touted as candidates for Nobel laurels.

65. Auerbach, *Mimesis*, trans. Trask, pp. 552–53.
66. Beier, letter to the author, August 21, 1981.

II. "My Contribution in Iron and Steel": *Transition* and Intellectual Controversy

1. Obote began to suggest to the East African press corps as early as November 1968 that Neogy had been arrested for alleged CIA connections. Ali Mazrui's letter to the editor, reproduced here as the epigraph to Part II, was published in *Encounter* 32 (January 1969): 92–93.
2. "Neogy Out: Future Uncertain," *East African Reporter*, April 4, 1969, pp. 9–10. Obote's remarks were also quoted in the *Uganda Argus*, January 18, 1969, and in "A Matter of Transition," *Transition* no. 38, p. 45. See also "Asians under Notice in Uganda," *The Times* (London), January 6, 1969, p. 1.
3. Rajat Neogy, "How It Feels to Be a Political Prisoner," *New York Times*, October 25, 1969, p. 32.
4. Valeria Hume, "How It All Began," *Transition* no. 34, p. 35. Neogy's schemes for dividing the magazine into volumes and issues were contradictory and confusing. Since the issues were simply numbered consecutively, without repetition, however, they were most commonly identified by issue number alone.
5. Daniel Dereszynsky, "*Transition* to the Mission: Rajat Neogy," *North Mission News* (San Francisco) 3, no. 9 (November 27, 1982): 10.
6. Neogy, telephone interview with the author, August 8, 1984, and letter to the author, August 30, 1984.
7. Hume, "How It All Began," p. 35.
8. Neogy gave this figure to *New York Times* correspondent Alfred Friendly, Jr. (see "Slick African Magazine Gains Wide Following," *New York Times*, August 11, 1968, p. 3). More recently, in a letter to the author dated March 31, 1981, he has said that only 1,200 copies of *Transition* no. 1 were sold and that *Transition* no. 2 fell to a discouraging 800.
9. Hume, "How It All Began," p. 36.
10. Neogy was interviewed by Nkosi on a December 1962 Transcription Centre audiotape. Alan Ogot's comment was made on Transcription Centre audiotape (at Kampala?) in 1964, during a panel discussion with John Nagenda, Ali Mazrui, and Erisa Kironde.
11. Alan Ogot and John Nagenda, Transcription Centre interview with Ali Mazrui and Erisa Kironde, loc. cit.
12. Abiola Irele, review of *Transition* nos. 1–32, *Journal of African Studies* 5, no. 3 (Spring 1967): 444.
13. "He put out three issues and went broke" (Dereszynsky, "*Transition* to the Mission," p. 11). *Transition* no. 1 sold for U.S. $.50 per copy, which

was insufficient to cover printing and distribution costs, and the thirteen or so pages of advertising that Hume succeeded in soliciting for that issue, some of it unremunerative, fell far short of making up the deficit.

14. It didn't, and practical difficulties ultimately forced Neogy to scrap plans for Okigbo's projected West African edition. "Our West African circulation was hampered by high air freight costs," Neogy recalls (letter to the author, March 31, 1981). Plans for a special edition from Ghana produced in editorial association with Kofi Awoonor were first delayed by Neogy's arrest and then made moot when *Transition* moved to Accra.

15. Christopher Okigbo, Transcription Centre interview with Dennis Duerden, London, August 1963.

16. Lewis Nkosi, Transcription Centre audiotape, London, 1963.

17. Though his "Song of a Goat" was excerpted in *Transition* no. 9, for instance, J. P. Clark's poetry had already begun appearing in *Black Orpheus* a year earlier. Beier had been one of the first readers of the play, and it was both staged and published in full through the Mbari Club.

18. Dereszynsky, "*Transition* to the Mission," p. 11.

19. Okigbo, Transcription Centre interview, August 1963.

20. Ibid.

21. In "The Rise and Fall of *Transition* Magazine" (Master's thesis, University of Wisconsin, 1970), Emmanuel Onuora Nwuneli tries to make the case that this shift in the focus of the magazine was a function of its sponsorship by the Congress for Cultural Freedom, and that the editors had been somehow mesmerized or coerced by the CIA. Nwuneli's statistical analysis of the magazine's contents, however, at best demonstrates only an approximate correlation between the magazine's shift to an interest in politics and the CIA's silent sponsorship. Nwuneli himself observes, moreover, that "the extent to which *Transition* gave up its pages to anyone who had anything worthwhile to say without fear or reproach is rather unusual" (p. 4). Nwuneli's analysis of its contents places the major shift in 1963, a year after the initial funding by the CCF, and a less academic reading of the magazine shows that a strong interest in politics had been evident even in the first five issues, merely arithmetical considerations notwithstanding. Neogy's perfectly reasonable explanation for the change—that he had not been entirely successful in stimulating literary creativity—also seems quite credible.

22. Ali Mazrui, letter to the author, June 1, 1981.

23. *Transition* no. 8, p. 9; reprinted in *Transition* no. 50/*Ch'indaba* no. 1, p. 65.

24. In his review of the first thirty-two issues of *Transition* (see above, note 12), Abiola Irele singled out Wali's second article for praise. In Africa the Western-style liberated individualist, with his role as self-interested questioner of social institutions, was at odds with the dominant traditional society, Irele pointed out, and Wali's had been one of the first critical articles to identify this discrepancy as a key issue in both politics and literature (p. 445).

25. One thinks particularly of J. P. Clark's "The Legacy of Caliban," *Black Orpheus* 2, no. 1, pp. 16–39.

26. Father Placied Tempels's *Bantoe-filosofie* (1946) has been translated by Colin King, *Bantu Philosophy* (Paris: Présence Africaine, 1959).

27. Nkosi, *Transition* no. 12, pp. 28–29; Cook, no. 13, pp. 38–40; Nwoga, no. 16, pp. 51–52; Carlin, no. 18, pp. 53–54; Clark, no. 18, pp. 20–26.

28. Irele, p. 46 (see note 12, above).

29. Neogy, "Do Magazines Culture?" *Transition* no. 24, p. 32; reprinted in *Transition* no. 50/*Ch'indaba* no. 1, p. 74.

30. The delay between compilation and publication of issues was not as difficult to cope with as one might imagine, inasmuch as *Transition* was more often reflective than topical. The only other occasion when events transpired between compilation and publication of an article that gave it an unexpected political context was when Milton Obote's overthrow muted the impact of Mazrui's "The King, the King's English, and I" in *Transition* no. 38. See above, pp. 211–15.

31. Nkrumah himself, in exile in Conakry, had been heard from in *Transition* no. 27. His secretary wrote to say that the Osagyefo admired *Transition* and appreciated Mazrui's "literary effort"; he was not, however, inclined to respond to it (p. 5).

32. Though somewhat more critical of Mazrui than Tandon had been, Ghanaian writer Ama Ata Aidoo was especially savage in her ironic disdain for Howe. "We . . . promise that any time we want to publish the names of our 'great Africans,' we shall submit the lists to him for approval," she wrote ("Thank You, Mr. Howe," *Transition* no. 29, p. 5). What rankled with Aidoo and others was Howe's charge that Nkrumah had been more fascist than Marxist and was destined to be forgotten by history except as a "colourful scoundrel."

33. See, for instance, Munhamu B. Utete, "The Greatness of Kwame Nkrumah," *Transition* no. 29, pp. 6–8.

34. Number 32 was, in fact, *Transition*'s benchmark issue, bringing together four of its most celebrated controversies and three of its best-known controversialists. It launched the debate on the CIA and Uganda constitutional controversies that dominated the magazine's fortunes for a number of years and ultimately played a role, ten years later and 2,300 miles away, in its final demise.

35. Controversial though *Transition*'s 1966 issues had been, Neogy had not yet felt sufficiently emboldened to focus on the Buganda emergency. The articles about the Ugandan constitutional proposals were thus a significant new test of the waters of controversy in the magazine's home country.

36. Thomas Powers, *The Man Who Kept the Secrets: Richard Helms and the C. I. A.* (New York: Alfred A. Knopf, 1979), p. 365.

37. John Thompson, interview with the author, Rockefeller Foundation, New York, July 29, 1980.

38. Ibid.

39. Ibid.

40. Neogy, Transcription Centre interview with Lewis Nkosi, December 1962.

41. "Rajat Neogy on the C. I. A.," *Transition* no. 32, pp. 45–46; interview reprinted from Tony Hall's "On the Carpet" column in the Nairobi *Sunday Nation*.

42. Friendly, "Slick African Magazine," p. 3.

43. Pierre L. van den Berghe, "The C.I.A. and the Warfare State," *Transition* no. 33, p. 5.

44. That the stigma persisted for *Transition* long after the controversy had ceased to be news (as it did not for other CCF-funded projects in Africa such as *Black Orpheus, Africa South, The New African*, the Mbari Clubs, and the Chemchemi Centre) was because of the magazine's political and social content, its conspicuousness, and its relative success. Emmanuel Onuora Nwuneli's contention in "The Rise and Fall of *Transition* Magazine" (see note 23, above) that *Transition* favored "non-African" contributors on "sensitive" (i.e., political) subjects does not hold water. Nwuneli's own statistics seem to defeat his case. Roughly 55 percent of contributors, by his definition, were "non-African" (was Neogy himself "African" or "non-African"? one wonders), and they contributed *less* than 55 percent of the material on "sensitive areas." Assuming absolutely random, non-political distribution, one would expect the "non-Africans," since they contributed 55 percent of *Transition*'s contents overall, also to have contributed 55 percent of politically sensitive material. Nor was this an unreasonably high percentage of overall contributions from non-Africans. Africa's intellectual elites were still quite small in the early 1960s, and even African universities still maintained high percentages of expatriates on their faculties. On the whole, Nwuneli's statistics seem to demonstrate that Neogy was *not* favoring "non-Africans" as contributors.

45. Friendly, "Slick African Magazine," p. 3; *The Observer* was quoted in *Transition* no. 37, p. 41.

46. *Transition* no. 37, pp. 41–42. Despite Theroux's implication to the contrary, the magazine had by 1968 alienated as many Africans as expatriate Europeans or Americans—judging from its Letters column.

47. This in spite of the fact that the amount of advertising space in *Transition* no. 37—about 13¼ pages—was almost precisely the same as it had been in *Transition* no. 1.

48. Okigbo, Transcription Centre interview, August 1963.

49. In the early *Transitions*, "blackness" seemed the least of Neogy's considerations. He seemed concerned, rather, to make the magazine completely international and scrupulously highbrow. A special column in *Transition* no. 1, for instance, featured notices of cultural events in London and New York.

50. Neogy, letter to the author, June 16, 1981.

51. Neogy, Transcription Centre audiotape, London, 1965 (?).

52. Irele, pp. 442–47 (see note 12 above).

53. Kofi Awoonor, interview with the author, Rockefeller Foundation, New York, July 19, 1980.

54. Neogy, interview with the author, August 8, 1984.

55. Neogy, letter to the author, March 31, 1981. Since he felt strongly that English and American publishers were not adequately compensating African contributors, Neogy paid what for him were very generous rates: "approximately between $10 for a poem and $150 or more for an article" (letter to the author, June 16, 1981).

56. Ali Mazrui, letter to the author, June 1, 1981.

57. Barbara Neogy, "A Matter of Transition," *Transition* no. 38, p. 44.

58. Neogy would seem to have been commenting on Ali's credentials, at least indirectly, when he later wrote: "For a while, the President's Office became a haven for unemployable young men, a few of whose qualifications were not recognized either at the university or in the state bodies in the country, who began producing a number of position papers on different subjects in the new [Marxist] vocabulary" ("On Being an African Intellectual," *Survey: A Journal of Soviet and East European Studies* 77 [Autumn 1970]: 25).

59. Barbara Neogy, "A Matter of Transition," p. 43.

60. Mazrui, letter to the author, June 30, 1981. Neogy's conscientious practice was to give the government notice in advance of criticisms in *Transition* so that it might have an opportunity for immediate rebuttal. See *Transition* no. 38, p. 43.

61. Neogy often coupled features that looked at related ideas from different angles, a corollary to his concept of the cross-relevance, universality, and interdisciplinary nature of intellectual activity.

62. As Barbara Neogy pointed out in *Transition* no. 38, however, Akena Adoko was "the second most powerful man in the country, . . . head of the ominous Security Council, Secretary of the Cabinet, and chief advisor" (p. 43).

63. Hostility from readers seems to have delighted Neogy. His response to the large volume of aggrieved mail he received on the subject of Theroux's "Tarzan" article was typical. In the next issue (*Transition* no. 33), he printed both a special section of letters denouncing Theroux, under the heading "Letters from the Tarzans," and Theroux's article "Hating the Asians," which blamed East African racial antagonisms on the British colonial legacy.

64. Perhaps this was done on the theory that it would be undignified for Akena Adoko to reply on his own behalf.

65. Neogy, "On Being an African Intellectual," p. 24.

66. Mazrui, letter to the author, June 30, 1981.

67. Davis Sebukima, interview with the author, Nairobi, Kenya, March 15, 1985.

68. Even more ironic, perhaps, is the fact that *Transition* no. 37 con-

tained an article by one of the magazine's associate editors, Raymond Apthorpe, then visiting professor at the University of Sussex, England, entitled "Does Tribalism Really Matter?" (pp. 18–22), which belied what was to be a prime irritant in the controversy responsible for the arrest of Mayanja and Neogy.

69. Mazrui, letter to the author, June 30, 1981.

70. Ibid. Although Mazrui was not named, he was then the only professor of political science at Uganda's only university college.

71. Ibid.

72. At the Commonwealth Conference in London a few months later, Obote admitted to reporters that he had always been a faithful reader of *Transition*. See above, p. 101.

73. Mazrui, letter to the author, June 30, 1981.

74. Abu Mayanja, interview with the author, Nairobi, Kenya, March 26, 1985.

75. Neogy, letter to subscribers, *Transition* no. 38, p. 6.

76. Henry Beinen, "Kenya and Uganda: When Does Dissent Become Sedition?" *Africa Report* 14, nos. 3–4 (March/April 1969): 10–14.

77. *Uganda Argus*, November 21, 1968, quoted in *Transition* no. 38, p. 45.

78. See *Transition* no. 38, p. 45, and also the brief report in *The Times* (London), November 23, 1968, p. 5.

79. Just before the first trial date, on January 10, three more counts were added with reference to Mayanja's implication in his letter in *Transition* no. 37 that Obote's government was slyly perpetuating colonial instruments of repression for its own purposes (Beinen, "Kenya and Uganda," p. 14).

80. Neogy, "How It Feels to Be a Political Prisoner."

81. Mazrui, letter to the author, June 30, 1981.

82. *The Times* (London), January 6, 1969, p. 1.

83. Beinen, "Kenya and Uganda," p. 14.

84. Obote had personally promised Nelson some sort of financial restitution for the mistake made by the newly formed military police, but Nelson's claim to £1,000, made from London, was never honored. See "Times Diary," *The Times* (London), March 24, 1969, p. 8.

85. Under the emergency regulations, the government had to inform Neogy of the grounds for his detention within ninety days, but there was no requirement that he *ever* be *tried* on those charges. Neogy was handed a formal written statement of grounds on January 14, the last possible day under the law, and was brought before the tribunal a few days later. See Beinen, "Kenya and Uganda," pp. 13–14.

86. Quoted in Beinen, "Kenya and Uganda," p. 14.

87. Later the government countered that the 2-point difference between the typefaces used for Mayanja's criticism of the constitutional proposals in *Transition* no. 32 and Akena Adoko's response in *Transition* no. 33 was evidence of Neogy's "disaffection from Uganda." See *Transition* no. 38, pp. 43, 45.

88. Lawrence Fellows, "Uganda Sedition Trial May Affect Future of a Free Press in Africa," *New York Times*, January 10, 1969, p. 6.

89. Fellows, "Uganda Sedition Trial," p. 6; "Uganda Tries Magazine Editor," *The Times* (London), January 10, 1969, p. 6.

90. Fellows, "Uganda Sedition Trial," p. 12.

91. Quoted by Lawrence Fellows, "Verdict Is Delayed in Trial of Editor in Uganda," *New York Times*, January 12, 1969, p. 14.

92. "Uganda Takes 'Lesson' from Colonialists," *The Guardian* (London), January 11, 1969, p. 2.

93. According to *Transition* no. 38's later account, the original press release also suggested that Syracuse University itself, formally and officially, had sent the cable, and not just a few faculty members speaking on their own behalf. *Transition* no. 38, p. 45.

94. *Uganda Argus*, January 18, 1969, quoted in *Transition* no. 38, p. 45.

95. Neogy, "On Being an African Intellectual," p. 26.

96. Lawrence Fellows, "Two Cleared of Sedition but Return to Jail," *New York Times*, February 2, 1969, p. 16.

97. Saied's judgment was reprinted in full in *Transition* no. 38; quotation is from p. 47.

98. "Acquittals in Uganda," *The Times* (London), February 3, 1969, p. 4.

99. Interviewed by a *New York Times* reporter at his home in Yonkers, New York, Neogy's father-in-law said he was "pleased," but "not too much, since he [Neogy] was immediately returned to detention" (Fellows, "Two Cleared of Sedition," p. 16).

100. "Acquittals in Uganda," p. 4.

101. Barbara Neogy, "A Matter of Transition," p. 46.

102. Neogy, letter to the author, August 30, 1984.

103. "Times Diary," *The Times* (London), May 2, 1969, p. 10.

104. "Freed Poet Here for Lecturing," *New York Times*, May 14, 1969, p. 94.

105. Neogy, "On Being an African Intellectual," pp. 18, 27.

106. "Times Diary," *The Times* (London), January 28, 1970, p. 10.

107. This despite the fact that before his arrest Neogy seems neither to have considered himself a dissident nor Obote entirely a tyrant.

108. "Times Diary," *The Times* (London), August 26, 1971, p. 10.

109. Mazrui, letter to the author, June 1, 1981.

110. Ibid.

111. Neogy, 1984 *curriculum vitae*.

112. Neogy, letter to the author, March 31, 1981.

113. John Thompson, interview with the author, Rockefeller Foundation, New York, July 29, 1980.

114. Quoted in the Kumasi *Pioneer*; reprinted in *Transition* no. 39, p. 36.

115. Neogy, letter to the author, June 16, 1981.

116. Mutesa's role, that is, in consistently opposing Ugandan centralization—and therefore, to some, Ugandan nationhood—in favor of the traditional autonomy of Buganda.

117. For a summary of this trend, see Robert July, *A History of the African people*, (New York: Scribners, 1980), pp. 682–96.

118. *Transition* no. 39, p. 33; reprinted from the University of Legon student magazine, *The Forum*.

119. C. Kallu-Kalumiya, "*Transition* is an Illegitimate Child of Uganda," *Transition* no. 41, p. 8.

120. A few years later, the charges of CIA collusion having gradually become more explicit, Mazrui finally initiated a libel suit against one of the most outspoken of his calumniators, a South African ex-academic on the editorial staff of Zed Press named Robert Molteno. Ultimately, Mazrui dropped his suit in return for Molteno's assumption of all his court costs and issuance of a full retraction and apology (subsequently published in *Africa Now*, December 1983, p. 11).

121. Neogy, letter to the author, March 31, 1981; interview with the author, August 8, 1984.

122. Neogy, letter to the author, March 31, 1981.

123. Neogy, letter to the author, June 16, 1981.

124. Neogy, letter to the author, March 31, 1981.

125. Awoonor's subsequent arrest by the Acheampong regime in 1976 in connection with an attempted coup proved his doubts to be well founded.

126. Neogy, letter to the author, August 30, 1984.

127. Awoonor's views of the political role of the African writer changed radically after his own arrest and detention, however. See his essay "The Writer and Politics in Africa," in *African Cultural and Intellectual Leaders and the Development of the New African Nations*, ed. P. Benson and R. July (New York and Ibadan: Rockefeller Foundation and Ibadan University Press, 1982), pp. 184–95.

128. For instance, in his Transcription Centre interview with Dennis Duerden in London in August 1963.

129. During this period, late 1972 and early 1973, Amin instituted a particularly grisly reign of terror. Following an ill-starred guerrilla invasion by Obote partisans from neighboring Tanzania, there were wholesale mass executions of captured rebels, including most notably Abu Mayanja's old adversary Picho Ali, who as a leader of the guerrillas was beaten to death immediately following a private (and cordial) face-to-face chat with Amin in September 1972. Other prominent victims were Benedicto Kiwanuka, chief justice and former prime minister, who was murdered the same month; Frank Kalimuzo, vice-chancellor of Makerere, who was murdered the following month; and Shabani Nkutu, Obote's former minister of works, who was murdered in January 1973. Among those forced to flee were Amin's minister of education, Edward Rugumayo, early in 1973; Amin's foreign minister and brother-in-law, Wanume Kibedi, in April; and, at about the same time,

Ali Mazrui. See Henry Kyemba, *A State of Blood* (New York: Grosset and Dunlap, 1977).

130. The American journalist, Nicholas Stroh, was the son of a wealthy Detroit brewer. He had gone with a friend, Makerere lecturer Robert Seidle, to investigate reports of an army purge at the Mbarara barracks. Stroh and Seidle disappeared soon after Stroh had an interview with Major Juma at Mbarara.

131. Political demigods such as Kenyatta, Nkrumah, and Nyerere. A letter in *Transition* no. 19 from R. L. Wigglesworth of Makerere had similarly charged David Rubadiri with plagiarizing Ezekiel Mphahlele's *The African Image* in writing his own article "Why African Literature?" (which appeared in *Transition* no. 15); for a defense of Ouologuem, see Yusufu Maiangwa, "The Duty of Violence in Ouologuem's *Bound to Violence*," in *New West African Literature*, ed. Kolawole Ogungbesan (London: Heinemann, 1979).

132. Neogy, letter to the author, June 16, 1981; and Kofi Awoonor, conversation with the author, Bellagio, Italy, September 19, 1980.

133. Wole Soyinka, conversation with the author, July 7, 1981. *Transition* no. 1 had listed Francis Kasura, Don Mann, and Ganesh Bagchi as associate editors. By 1966, the regular editorial board consisted of Christopher Okigbo, Ali Mazrui, Raymond Apthorpe, and Denis Williams, in addition to Neogy. When the final Ugandan issue came out in 1968, Okigbo (who had died in the Nigerian civil war) and Williams had been replaced by John Goldblatt and George Awoonor-Williams (Kofi Awoonor). Along with Mazrui, the majority of Neogy's Accra staff left the magazine when Soyinka took over, including associate editors Raymond Apthorpe and Abiola Irele and contributing editors Kofi Awoonor and Paul Theroux. Soyinka brought in Eseoghene Barrett as associate editor and Kojo Bentsi-Enchill and Gladys Quarshie as staff members, among others. Associate editors Adu Boahen and Robert Serumaga were retained from Neogy's editorial board.

134. It is interesting in this regard that apart from Neogy's own "Do Magazines Culture?" from *Transition* no. 24, Soyinka's anniversary number, *Transition* no. 50/*Ch'indaba* no. 1, included nothing subsequent to *Transition* no. 19 in its center section of reprints. Theroux was not included at all, and Mazrui was represented only by his earliest contribution, "The Scholar and His Residence Permit," a brief statement about academic freedom that he had penned for *Transition* no. 14. Issues nos. 20 and 21 had, of course, begun the shift toward the largely symbolic or ironic treatment of serious political issues, of which Soyinka had disapproved. They had also initiated a shift in tone toward an emphasis on single controversial themes, keyed to provocative cover designs, and had brought into prominence a new group of contributors led by Mazrui and Theroux.

135. Soyinka, interview with the author, New York, July 7, 1981.

136. In *Transition* no. 38, Neogy had demonstrated the truth of Soyinka's contention by printing a pageful of plaudits from all over the world—

everything from the *Reporter* of Nairobi to the London *Sunday Times* and the *Toronto Globe and Mail.* "Africa's most interesting magazine," the quote from the *Economist* read; "a combination of *Ramparts* and the *New Republic,*" added the *Washington Post.* "Who could foresee that there would be a periodical from Kampala that no one can afford to miss?" asked Hamburg's *Die Zeit.* See *Transition* no. 38, p. 71.

137. As he had also done, of course, in his earlier critical exchange with Chinua Achebe in *Transition* nos. 8 and 9.

138. Getachew Haileg, Abraham Dnoz, and Alula Abate, "Famine in Ethiopia," *Transition* no. 45, pp. 67–69.

139. Seeking exemption from Amin's expulsion order proved in the end to be a futile option anyway.

140. Although Soyinka had not, oddly enough, seen Theroux's parody of Mazrui (conversation with the author, July 7, 1981).

141. Theroux also implied teasingly in his parody that Mazrui's opinions were conditioned by the source of his latest overseas grant, a charge that was manifestly untrue. It was perhaps this joking innuendo that led Obote to urge that Mazrui sue Theroux for libel in his tête-à-tête with Mazrui following Neogy's arrest. Obote himself, ironically enough, substantially repeated Theroux's tongue-in-cheek charge a few months later in all seriousness in his efforts to discredit the suspended Kampala *Transition.*

142. Okigbo, Transcription Centre interview with Dennis Duerden, London, August 1963.

143. Soyinka, conversation with the author, June 7, 1981.

144. Chinweizu, Jemie, and Madubuike stated that it was excerpted from a book that had been accepted for publication more than two years previously by Nwamife Publishers (Enugu, Nigeria) but had never appeared and was now being circulated in pirated copies among the "Ibadan-Nsukka school of writers and critics" whom it attacked. See *Transition* no. 48, p. 29.

145. Soyinka, letter to the author, August 8, 1984. Chinweizu, Jemie, and Madubuike found an outlet for their views in three articles published in issues 12, 13, and 14 of *Okike* (1978–79): "The Hopkins Disease," "The Leeds-Ibadan Connection: The Scandal of Modern African Literature," and "Soyinka's 'Neo-Tarzanism': A Reply." They subsequently incorporated them into a book, *Towards the Decolonization of African Literature* (Enugu, Nigeria: Fourth Dimension, 1980).

146. Mazrui, letter to the author, September 11, 1983. To Mazrui such a decision, based on any consideration other than objective standards of quality, reeked of censorship.

147. Amoda's identification in the notes on contributors is suspiciously vague.

148. Duerden's article was excerpted from a manuscript later published as *The Invisible Present: African Art and Literature* (New York: Harper and Row, 1975).

149. "Soyinka's 'Neo-Tarzanism': A Reply," *Okike* no. 14 (September 1978): 43.

150. "By the way . . . we would really like to know whether Wole Soyinka is suffering from cold war hangover? All this 'troika' and 'Trotsky' business? What connection is that supposed to have with a discussion of African literature? Is it possible that the notorious Congress for Cultural Freedom is still at its tricks for promoting Western cultural hegemony over us in the guise of a crusade for 'freedom'? Soyinka ought to really keep his borrowed dislike of things Russian out of this debate about liberating African literature from the cultural hegemony of the West," Chinweizu, Jemie, and Madubuike had declared in "Soyinka's 'Neo-Tarzanism,'" p. 47.

151. The Lagos FESTAC was ultimately held in 1977.

152. This reference was to an English festival of black popular music that Soyinka saw as a cheap attempt to capitalize on the enthusiasm for FESTAC.

153. Awoonor, who had returned to Ghana in 1975 to teach at the University of Cape Coast, was alleged to have harbored a subversive (Brig. Gen. Alphonse Kattah, charged with engineering an attempted coup against Acheampong). The Union of African Writers' statement was crucial in giving credibility to the international protest about Awoonor's detention. In coolly deploring the arrest, Soyinka, like Mazrui eight years before in Uganda, deliberately placed his own freedom at risk.

154. Although Soyinka would himself soon return to Nigeria, it was not then feasible to transplant the magazine once again. Among other reasons, there was the fact that Nigeria itself had just endured a coup that had toppled the government of General Gowon, followed by an assassination that eliminated his successor, Brigadier Murtala Muhammed.

155. Soyinka, conversation with the author, June 7, 1981.

156. In Ghana and Uganda, of course, hard economic necessity seems to preclude intellectual journalism on any pan-African scale for the present.

Index

Designer: Mark Ong
Compositor: G&S Typesetters, Inc.
Text: 10/13 Galliard
Display: Trump Mediaeval
Printer: Braun-Brumfield, Inc.
Binder: Braun-Brumfield, Inc.